Understanding prisons

Key issues in policy and practice

CRIME AND JUSTICE
Series editor: Mike Maguire
Cardiff University

Crime and Justice is a series of short introductory texts on central topics in criminology. The books in this series are written for students by inter-nationally renowned authors. Each book tackles a key area within crimino-logy, providing a concise and up- to- date overview of the principal concepts, theories, methods and findings relating to the area. Taken as a whole, the *Crime and Justice* series will cover all the core components of an undergraduate criminology course.

Published titles

Understanding youth and crime
Sheila Brown

Understanding crime data
Clive Coleman and Jenny Moynihan

Understanding white collar crime
Hazel Croall

Understanding justice 2nd edition
Barbara A. Hudson

Understanding crime prevention
Gordon Hughes

Understanding violent crime
Stephen Jones

Understanding risk in criminal justice
Hazel Kemshall

Understanding victims and restorative justice
Jim Dignan

Understanding community penalties
Peter Raynor and Maurice Vanstone

Understanding criminology 2nd edition
Sandra Walklate

Understanding social control
Martin Innes

Understanding psychology and crime
James McGuire

Understanding prisons

Key issues in policy and practice

Andrew Coyle

Open University Press

Open University Press
McGraw-Hill Education
McGraw-Hill House
Shoppenhangers Road
Maidenhead
Berkshire
England
SL6 2QL

email: enquiries@openup.co.uk
world wide web: www.openup.co.uk

and Two Penn Plaza, New York, NY 10121-2289, USA

First published 2005

A catalogue record of this book is available from the British Library

ISBN 0 335 21338 3 (pb)   0 335 21339 1 (hb)

Library of Congress Cataloging-in-Publication Data
CIP data has been applied for

Typeset by RefineCatch Ltd, Bungay, Suffolk
Printed in the UK by Bell & Bain Ltd, Glasgow

Contents

Series editor's foreword

This book by Andrew Coyle is the latest in the *Crime and Justice* series published by Open University Press/McGraw Hill. The series, which was launched in 1996, has become a widely used resource in universities teaching criminology or criminal justice, especially in the UK but increasingly also overseas. The aim from the outset has been to give undergraduates and graduates both a solid grounding in the relevant area and a taste to explore it further. Although aimed primarily at students new to the field, and written as far as possible in plain language, the books are not oversimplified. On the contrary, the authors set out to 'stretch' readers and to encourage them to approach criminological knowledge and theory in a critical and questioning frame of mind.

Andrew Coyle is a former prison governor with wide experience of the realities of the prisons in the UK, and as Director of the International Centre for Prison Studies at King's College London he has built up a rare combination of academic and first hand knowledge about prison systems around the world. His book not only offers a broad introduction to the main themes that are covered in most university courses on imprisonment, but adds his own valuable insights into current national and international policy issues. On the one hand, the book is firmly 'grounded', with informed accounts of the realities of prison life, including chapters on staff, prisoners, daily routines, and regimes in high security prisons. At the same time, the author raises core questions about the political and symbolic uses of imprisonment, considering how and why prisons vary in use and organization in different countries at different times. Particular examples discussed include recent changes in the former Soviet bloc and in developing countries. He tackles further major questions about prisoners' rights, national and international monitoring of prisons, and the prevention of torture. He also focuses on the current trend towards privatization of prisons, and offers his own thoughts on the future.

Other books previously published in the *Crime and Justice* series – all of whose titles begin with the word 'Understanding' – have covered criminological theory (Sandra Walklate, penal theory (Barbara Hudson), crime data and statistics (Clive Coleman and Jenny Moynihan), youth and crime (Sheila Brown), crime prevention (Gordon Hughes), violent crime (Stephen Jones), community penalties (Peter Raynor and Maurice Vanstone), white collar crime (Hazel Croall), risk and crime (Hazel Kemshall), social control (Martin Innes), psychology and crime (James McGuire), victims and restorative justice (James Dignan) and drugs, alcohol and crime (Trevor Bennett and Katy Holloway). Three are already in second editions and other second editions are planned. Other new books in the pipeline include texts on policing, social attitudes to crime, criminological research methods, race and crime, 'cybercrime' and political violence. All are topics which are either already widely taught or are growing in prominence in university degree courses on crime and criminal justice, and each book should make an ideal foundation text for a relevant module. As an aid to understanding, clear summaries are provided at regular intervals, and a glossary of key terms and concepts is a feature of every book. In addition, to help students expand their knowledge, recommendations for further reading are given at the end of each chapter.

Mike Maguire
November 2005

Preface

The title of this book begs an obvious question. Is it possible to understand prisons, at least in an objective sense? Early in the twenty-first century we have the sense that prisons have always been with us. They are a fact of life and we never question their existence. On the rare occasions that they do impinge on public consciousness the question is usually whether we need fewer of them or, more likely, more of them. In recent years in the United Kingdom they have become pawns in the political debate, with some politicians vying against each other in their promises to build more prisons and to send more people to them.

From time to time academics and others will point out that England and Wales has one of the highest rates of imprisonment in Western Europe and that the number of people in prison has increased dramatically since the beginning of the 1990s. They ask why this should be so and suggest that there should be fewer people in prison. This is not an argument which resonates with the general public. Informing people that there are around 76,000 people in prison in England and Wales conveys little. People do not know whether objectively this is a high number or a low number and are little concerned about comparisons with other countries. On being told that it costs over £35,000 of taxpayers' money to keep a person in prison for a year, the response is likely to be either that prisoners must be being mollycoddled or that this is money well spent.

The truth is that for most people the prison is a closed world, with little known about what goes on behind its high walls. This makes it very difficult to reach a considered conclusion about whether prison achieves its purpose, or indeed to be clear about what its purpose is. In some respects prisons are the same in every country. They consist of buildings in which one group of people, the staff, lock up another group of people, the prisoners. In other respects, prisons are quite cultural institutions. Arrangements for their management, the way prisoners are treated and national structures vary quite differently between regions and even between neighbouring countries. The present text focuses on one prison system, that of England and Wales, with only limited discussion about international comparative issues.

This book takes the reader on a journey of discovery about prisons in England and Wales, their history, how they come to be as they are today and who is in them. It discusses what their purposes are and how they go about achieving them. At the end of it readers will have a much better understanding of the institution which we call the prison. They may also be left with a question about whether, as one former prisoner who went on to be president of his country asked about imprisonment, there might be a better way of coming to terms with certain things.

It should also be pointed out that this book deals with key issues of policy and practice relating to imprisonment. It does not deal with the sociology of punishment nor with the relationships between incarceration and social, economic and political change. There is already a strong literature on the emergence of the prison as the central mode of penality. Readers who wish to study this issue should go to the writings of scholars such as Rusche and Kirchheimer (1939), Foucault (1975), Cohen and Scull (1983), Garland (1985, 1990, 2001) and Cavadino and Dignan (2001).

This book could not have been written without considerable help from a great number of people. First there are the prisoners and the prison staff with whom I have spent a great deal of my working life. More immediately, my colleagues in the International Centre for Prison Studies have shared their wisdom and experience with me; they include Rob Allen, Andrew Edwards, Helen Fair and Anton Shelupanov. A number of experienced people have read drafts of the manuscript and their wise comments have corrected factual inaccuracies and improved the text immensely; they include Colin Allen, Jamie Bennett, David Faulkner, Arthur de Frisching and Jim Haines. My editors, Mike Maguire and Chris Cudmore have been extremely tolerant and positive towards me. My greatest thanks go, as always, to Vivien Stern for her unstinting support and encouragement.

Introduction

The essence of imprisonment is deprivation of one of the most cherished features of human life, individual liberty. In those countries which have abolished the death penalty and corporal punishment, it is the most severe sanction which courts can impose on convicted offenders. By definition, depriving people of their liberty is a negative act and for that reason imprisonment is often described as a punishment of last resort, one which should only be imposed by a court of law when there is no other appropriate punishment.

Despite the general acceptance of this principle, the use of imprisonment has increased significantly in recent years in at least 50 major countries. It is estimated that there are now over nine million men, women and children in prison around the world, with about half of them in three countries: the United States, China, and Russia (Walmsley 2005). Rates of imprisonment are usually quoted per 100,000 of a country's total population. On that basis, in mid-2004 the rate of imprisonment in the United States was 726, while that in Western Europe as a whole was just over 100. The rate of imprisonment in England and Wales (144) is one of the highest in Western Europe. The number of people in prison in England and Wales has increased significantly in recent years, from 45,817 in 1992, to 65,298 in 1998, to over 75,000 in 2005. England and Wales has not been alone in recording these increases. For many years the Netherlands had one of the lowest rates of imprisonment in Europe. This is no longer the case. In 1992 there were 7397 people in prison in the Netherlands; by 1998 this had risen to 13,333 and by 2003 to 18,242. In Denmark, on the other hand, the number of people in prison has generally remained remarkably stable: 3406 in 1992, 3413 in 1998, with an increase to 3908 in 2003 (ICPS 2005). One of the first questions which faces any student of prisons is why there should be such discrepancies in rates of imprisonment in countries which have, in other respects, broadly comparable cultures.

The political context

In chapter one we shall discover that these discrepancies cannot be explained by purely criminal justice factors, such as crime rates and police detection rates. In England and Wales, for example, the increase of over 60 per cent in the number of prisoners in the twelve years between 1992 and 2005 was not matched by any comparable increase in rates of crime. So we have to look elsewhere for explanations.

First of all, we need to discover the purpose of prison. Why are people sent there and what is it meant to achieve? The purposes which are generally proposed are fourfold. It is a method of punishing people who have committed serious crimes. There is also a belief that as a result of being given a prison sentence offenders will be deterred from any thought of committing crime in the future. In addition, the prospect of being sent to prison will make potential offenders think twice before committing a crime. In many Western countries there is also a belief in the prison as a place of potential reform for those who are sent there. While in prison they will be taught new skills, will be given personal support and encouraged to change their behaviour. Finally, it is recognized that there are some offenders who pose a real and active threat to public safety. Sending them to prison is a matter of public protection. Academics and prison practitioners have discussed for generations the extent to which these objectives are compatible or exclusive. Is it possible to regard prison at the same time as a place of punishment and also of reform? Would it be helpful if the courts were required to indicate which one or more of these purposes it had in mind when sending an individual to prison?

Having considered the purposes of the prison in some detail, we are drawn to the conclusion that the use which a society makes of imprisonment cannot be explained totally in a rational manner. The extent to which prison is used also says something about the underlying values and culture of a society, its attitude to punishment, who should be submitted to it and what it should consist of. It is also helpful to understand that the prison is a place of great symbolism. In some respects it meets a societal need for the separation of those who are seen to be different from the majority. The symbolic function of the prison has been emphasized by the way it is depicted in the media, by the symbolism of the judge's sentence, 'Send the prisoner down', and by the clanging of the prison gate. Available research evidence indicates that levels of the use of imprisonment owe more to public attitudes and political decisions than to rates of crime (Hough and Mayhew 1985). Advocacy of increased use of prison has recently been picked up by politicians as a way of responding to modern fears about public safety and the desire to be protected from crime. This has led to policies such as 'Three strikes and you're out' in the United States of America and slogans such as 'Prison works' in the United Kingdom. These considerations have become especially relevant in the United Kingdom where senior members of all major parties have been seen to respond to the debate about imprisonment within a political context rather than on the basis of objective evidence.

The history of the modern prison

In its present form, the prison is a relatively modern invention, having been in existence for less than 300 years (Morris and Rothman 1995). It has its roots in the north-east of the United States and in Western Europe and has subsequently spread around the world, often in the wake of colonial expansion. Prisons as places of detention, where people waited to be tried, until a fine or debt was paid or until another court disposal was implemented have existed for many centuries. But the use of prison as a direct disposal of the court to any significant extent can be dated to a relatively recent period. It was not inevitable that prisons should have developed into the model which we have today. That they did so is a combination of their history and the pressure of short-term political imperatives. This evolution has been influenced by a number of key incidents, often unpredictable and sometimes relatively insignificant in themselves. Writing on this subject, one commentator noted the following:

> In the first place, rather than emphasise the 'inevitability' of the last 100 years or so of 'prison reform', it seems to me important in 1974 to recognise that they were very largely (though not entirely) a mistake, a blind alley into which the British Government wandered as much through short-sighted financial and political expediency as through any considered penal philosophy.
>
> (McLachlan 1974: 4)

A knowledge of this history is key to understanding how prisons operate today in England and Wales and particularly how the national prison system is organized. Chapter two thus sets the scene for the following one about the structure of the national prison system.

The organization of the prison system

In the United Kingdom there are three separate prison systems. The main focus in this book is on the largest of these, that in England and Wales, and chapter three describes in some detail how it is organized. The prison system stands almost alone among large public institutions in that it is wholly managed by central government. The local structures which are common in the education and health systems are completely lacking in the prison system. This has significant consequences for the way prisons are run and also for the task of helping prisoners to return to local communities as law-abiding citizens.

In general terms prisons are organized in a very hierarchical way, within a highly bureaucratized structure (Blau and Scott 1966). This affects both the way in which they operate on a daily basis and also the attitude of prison staff. It also influences the way the prison system and the Home Office, which is its 'parent' government department, respond when things go wrong or when pressures mount. This feature became increasingly important in the latter years of the twentieth century.

One aspect of modern prisons has been an increasing emphasis on what is known as managerialism, that is, a concentration on process, on how things are done, rather than on outcome, what is being achieved. It is important to understand the distinction between these two features because if the outcome which is being aimed for is wrong in the first place, then improving the process will simply mean that one achieves the wrong outcome more efficiently. For a number of years the prison system in England and Wales has been striving to clarify its objectives while at the same time creating new structures with which to implement these objectives once it is sure what they are.

A recent development in a small number of jurisdictions, including England and Wales has been the practice of contracting out prisons to commercial companies. There are various models for doing this. In England and Wales the one adopted has involved commercial consortia designing, constructing, managing and financing all new prisons since the mid-1990s. This development fits in with the philosophy of successive governments, of whatever political colour, which have sought to involve almost all public institutions in what are known either as private finance initiatives or public–private partnerships. Chapter three discusses the implications of this development and considers whether there are special considerations when the state decides to delegate control over prisoners to private contractors.

Prisons are unique institutions in that they involve locking up citizens, sometimes for lengthy periods, against their will. Severe limitations are placed on their freedoms, on what they can and cannot do. It is important that the way this is done should be subject to independent monitoring and inspection. England and Wales has some of the most highly developed mechanisms in the world for achieving this oversight and they are described and evaluated in this book.

The prisoners

If one wishes to understand prisons, one also has to understand something about those for whom they exist, the prisoners. There is a tendency to consider prisoners as a homogeneous group, defined primarily by the fact of their imprisonment. The reality is that they form quite disparate groupings. Chapter four demonstrates that the social and economic groupings in society are not equally represented in the prison populations. In most countries one can discover which are the marginalized groups of society by analyzing the prison population. Racial and ethnic minorities are invariably over-represented as, increasingly, are foreign nationals. Many prisoners have mental health problems. For example, in 1997 the Office for National Statistics found that 78 per cent of male remand prisoners, 64 per cent of male sentenced prisoners and 50 per cent of female prisoners were suffering from a personality disorder (Office for National Statistics 1998). A report published by the Social Exclusion Unit of the Cabinet Office in 2002 described in some detail the problematic social and educational profile of prisoners in England and Wales (Social Exclusion Unit 2002).

The criminal justice profile of individual prisoners is also a wide one. A significant proportion are on remand awaiting trial on a broad spectrum of charges. This means that in the eyes of the law they remain innocent and should not be treated as offenders. Of those who have been convicted, some will have committed very serious crimes, such as murder, rape or violence against another person, but this is by no means the whole story. Of the 54,000 sentenced male prisoners in June 2003, over 4000 were in prison for theft or handling stolen goods, over 900 for theft or forgery, almost 9000 for burglary, over 7000 for robbery, over 2000 for motoring offences and almost 9000 for drugs offences. Some 5.8 per cent of all convicted prisoners were women and 14.3 per cent were under 21 years old (Home Office 2003a).

Prison staff

In addition to prisoners, one other major group spends a considerable time in prison. The prison service has over 43,000 staff in all and by far the largest group are the prison officers who look after prisoners directly on a daily basis. There are approximately 25,000 of them in England and Wales, yet theirs is not a profession which attracts much public interest. Some of them will spend a professional lifetime working in prisons. Few school leavers or graduates will think of work in the prison service when considering a choice of career. So, what sort of person wishes to spend his or her life locking up other human beings?

Chapter five begins with a consideration of the historical synopsis of work in prisons and how much of the sometimes tendentious relationship between first-line staff and senior management has been coloured by this. The prison officers' trade union is sometimes described as the last dinosaur of the trade union movement. In deciding whether this is, in fact, the case, one needs to know something of the history of prison staff and why it was that some staff felt that management had more concern for prisoners than for staff.

In learning about any group of workers, one wants to learn how they are recruited and what training are they given. What are the most important features of their work and how do these relate to the purposes of imprisonment that we learned about in chapter one? Many of these staff spend more time in prison throughout their lives than the majority of prisoners. How do they respond to working for so long in this abnormal environment? To what extent do they become institutionalized? This chapter also looks at the other groups of personnel who work inside prisons.

What happens inside prison

In some respects prisons can be described as the last great secretive institutions in our society. Their mystique is enhanced by the fact that so many ordinary members of the public do not know what goes on behind their high walls. What happens to offenders once the judge has pronounced sentence, has said that they must go to prison for two months, two years or 20 years and they disappear down the stairs to the cells beneath the well of the court to be conveyed to prison? Chapter six describes the daily reality in our prisons.

Although imprisonment is in essence a negative experience, the prison authorities do what they can to help prisoners to use their time in captivity as positively as possible. In many prisons there are well-developed education and work programmes, as well as a variety of skills-training courses. There are also a number of courses aimed at helping prisoners to control their alcohol or drug abuse. The issue of health care also looms large in the prison setting. Reference has already been made to the high proportion of prisoners with some form of mental disorder. In general terms, prisoners as a group have a greater variety of health needs than comparable cohorts in the community. In recent years there has been increasing concern about the number of prisoners who have committed suicide or who have deliberately harmed themselves.

Chapter six also examines the abnormal profile of the prison population.

In the first place, it is largely male, with only 6 per cent of all prisoners being female. As a result, the overall organization of prisons is arranged to meet the needs of male prisoners; this applies to security matters, to the activities which are provided and to arrangements for family contact. Individual prisons are single sex institutions, at least as far as the prisoners are concerned. That dynamic brings a series of problems, especially since the vast majority of prisoners are young men, many of them unused to being subjected to a very disciplined lifestyle.

In a closed environment such as a prison it is important that rules and regulations are applied fairly and consistently and that due process is observed. In this environment matters of small detail, which would pass unnoticed in normal society, can assume a heightened significance. This needs to be recognized and accounted for by clear internal and external arrangements for registering complaints, with an assurance that they will be dealt with.

Order and control

Courts send people to prison to be deprived of their liberty, so one of the priorities of any prison is to ensure that the order of the court is carried out, with prisoners remaining in prison until their due date of release. This is achieved in a variety of ways, depending on the likelihood that an individual might try to escape. While no person would choose to be in prison, the majority of prisoners reluctantly accept the reality of their situation and are not determined to escape at any cost. Faced with a secure perimeter wall or fence, they will get on with serving their sentences. However, a small minority will be determined to do everything in their power to escape and for them the authorities need to make special arrangements. At the other end of the spectrum there will be some who will not attempt to escape, even if there are no barriers to prevent them. The way the prison system deals with these matters is described in chapter seven.

An issue which is linked to that of security is good order. Prisons are state-run institutions and should be places of good order and calm, rather than of chaos and violence. No one involved with them, whether prisoners, staff or visitors, should have fear for their personal safety. However, it needs to be recognized that prisons hold large numbers of people, most of whom have little in common other than their experience of the court system, in conditions of close confinement with very little private space. In such circumstances it is inevitable that from time to time there will be clashes of personality and disagreements which result, even in the best managed prison, in tension which can erupt into violence among prisoners or between prisoners and staff. In any prison system there will also be a small number of prisoners who are very violent, refusing to accept the legitimate requirements of discipline and constantly seeking to disrupt the smooth running of the prison. They have to be managed in a special manner, which combines firmness with humanity, a requirement which has been described as one of the greatest challenges to penal policy makers (Ward and Breed 1985). This chapter examines the general issues of how discipline is maintained in prisons.

Beyond the prison walls

The genesis of the prison is as a place in which offenders are exiled from their communities. Yet this exile is by no means total nor, for all but a handful, is it permanent. When people are sent to prison they leave behind families, friends and many links from their previous life. While they are in prison many will do their best to maintain and to develop these links. This is not only in the interests of the prisoner. It is important also for their partners, children and parents whose lives will be affected significantly by the imprisonment of a loved one. Chapter eight considers what efforts are made to maintain family contact for prisoners and to minimize the effect of imprisonment on other family members.

Most people spend relatively short periods in prison before returning to the communities from which they came. It makes sense for everyone that, when offenders have completed their sentences, they should leave prison with a sense of purpose and ready to contribute positively to society, rather than with a sense of bitterness and alienation which will make it likely that they will commit further offences. This sense of commitment to society will be strengthened if prisoners are given an appreciation of their worth as persons and of what they can contribute to society. There are many ways in which this can be developed, even behind the walls of the prison. The process is a two-way one, which involves the prisons and prisoners looking out and the community looking in. Chapter eight considers various models of how this can be achieved. They involve working with prisoners while they are in prison and also in preparing them for their return to society. The preparation must begin during the course of the sentence and it may also be necessary to phase the release of the prisoner, either by means of a period of temporary or conditional release or by maintaining some form of supervision immediately after release which falls short of complete deprivation of liberty.

The future of the prison

Very few human institutions last forever. Many of the methods of judicial punishment which existed when prisons first came into use have long since ceased to be used. They include the stocks, corporal punishment, transportation and capital punishment. It may be that the time has come for a radical review of the use of imprisonment as a sentence of the court and a re-thinking of whether the practice of locking up large numbers of men, women and children in very confined spaces for long periods of time is something which remains appropriate in the twenty-first century.

The final chapter of the book begins with an overview of different cultural models of imprisonment around the world before discussing the current status of the prison system in England and Wales. It concludes by presenting a different model, in which imprisonment would be used much more sparingly and in which prisons would be much smaller, with far more local accountability. The current role of the prison as a place of exile from society would be minimized and one of its main purposes would be to strengthen ties between offenders and their local communities.

The political context

The central chapters of this book will trace the development of the modern prison in England and Wales over the last two hundred years and will describe what imprisonment involves in practice at the beginning of the twenty-first century. However, before we get down to that level of detail, we need to consider some more fundamental issues about imprisonment and its use so that we are in a position to place the details which follow within a wider context.

Differences in the use of imprisonment

Individuals are sentenced to a period of imprisonment following a process which involves investigation of an offence and detection, prosecution, trial, conviction and, finally, sentence. This is intended to be a very object-ive process, based on clear presentation of evidence, dispassionately con-sidered in court, leading after due consideration to a decision that, of all the disposals available to the court, the only appropriate sentence is one of imprisonment. On that basis, one would expect sentencing to be broadly consistent, with any increase or decrease in the numbers being sent to prison being the result of proportionate increases or decreases in the number of offenders appearing before the courts or in the seriousness of the crimes of which they are convicted. Yet this does not appear to be what has happened in England and Wales since at least 1992. In that year there were just over 45,000 people in prison (Home Office 2003a), while at the beginning of 2005 there were over 75,000 in prison (Walmsley 2005), an increase of well over 60 per cent. During that same period none of the reporting from relevant agencies would suggest that there was anything approaching a comparable increase in crime rates (Hough, Jacobson and Millie 2003). Nor is there any evidence of a comparable increase in crime detection rates, nor in seriousness of the crimes being committed. This suggests that there are other influences at work in respect of use of imprisonment.

When one begins to compare international rates of imprisonment similar questions arise. It is notoriously difficult to compare crime rates across different countries because of different methods of collecting data and different definitions of crime. Notwithstanding these difficulties, we can say that there is no clear evidence to suggest that crime rates in broadly comparable Western European countries are significantly different, yet the rate of imprisonment in France is 91 per 100,000 of the total population, while that of its neighbour, Spain, is 140. In North America, the United States has an incarceration rate which is over six times higher than its northern neighbour, Canada (Walmsley 2005). The discrepancies in these figures (Table 1.1) lead one to suspect that the use of imprisonment in a country may be influenced by factors other than crime rates.

Table 1.1

	Rate of imprisonment	Place in world ranking
United States of America	714	1
Russia	533	3
South Africa	413	15
Poland	209	49
Brazil	169	72
England and Wales	144	92
Netherlands	123	103
China	118	110
Canada	116	112
Italy	100	126
Germany	96	128
France	91	136
Sweden	75	153
Denmark	72	155
Slovenia	59	171
Japan	58	174
Iceland	40	197
India	29	208

Source: World Prison Brief www.prisonstudies.org 2005.

The purposes of imprisonment

Before we go any further in discussing the use of imprisonment, we need to consider what are generally considered to be its purposes. Why are some offenders sent to prison and others are not? What does the court mean to achieve when it sends an offender to prison? This question of purpose is an important one because unless there is some clarity about this it will be difficult to discover whether or not imprisonment is effective. If we wish to know whether or not prison achieves its purposes we have to understand what they are. Traditionally, at least four purposes have been suggested. Sometimes they have different titles, but in broad terms they are punishment, deterrence, reform and protection of the public.

Punishment

The first given purpose of imprisonment is to punish persons for the crime they have committed. The argument in this case is that some crimes are so serious that the only appropriate disposal is to punish the offender by taking away their liberty. In the United Kingdom imprisonment is the most punitive sentence which a court can apply and the criminal law is quite specific in restricting the court's authority to impose a prison sentence:

> The court must not pass a custodial sentence unless it is of the opinion that the offence, or the combination of the offence and one or more offences associated with it, was so serious that neither a fine alone nor a community sentence can be justified for the offence.
>
> (Criminal Justice Act 2003, S.152)

There is general agreement that some crimes are so serious 'that neither a fine alone nor a community sentence can be justified'. They would include crimes like murder and other serious offences of violence against the person, such as rape. In most jurisdictions such crimes will be punished by a sentence of imprisonment. But these are a minority of all offences. A different picture appears when one considers property and other offences. Traditionally in England and Wales minor property and similar offences were punished in ways other than imprisonment but there has been a recent trend to imprison first-time offenders for relatively minor offences. For example, as described in chapter four, part of the large increase in the number of women being sent to prison can be explained by the fact that one-third of all women sentenced to immediate custody in 2002 were convicted of shoplifting (Home Office 2004). In previous years this might well have been seen as a draconian punishment for such an offence. In the early years of the twenty-first century it is part of the politicians' armoury for being 'tough on crime'.

The sentence of imprisonment carries great symbolism in the eyes of the public and the media. When the judge sentences someone to be 'taken down', very often they are seen to be taken directly from the dock downstairs to the cells underneath the court. In high-profile cases the press will photograph the prison van swinging out of the yard of the courthouse and later turning into the forbidding walls of the prison. The 'clang of the prison gate' carries a resonance in the mind of both the public and of the prisoner which is different from any other punishment. In terms of punishment, prison is regarded as the default option. For this reason, the media will refer to a convicted person 'getting off' with a fine or 'walking free' with probation.

Throughout most of the twentieth century in the United Kingdom there was broad acceptance of the principle that the punishment intended by the court when it passed a prison sentence was deprivation of liberty alone. Being required to stay behind the walls of a prison for the period specified by the court, not permitted to go out from the prison other than in approved circumstances, was in itself a heavy punishment. In the United Kingdom the court did not further concern itself with how the prison sentence was to be served. This was in contrast to the situation in a number of continental European countries, such as France and Spain, where the judiciary maintained an oversight of what actually happened to the offenders while in prison and continued to make decisions about how they were to be treated.

In the words of Alexander Paterson, a famous English prison commissioner in the early part of the twentieth century:

> It must, however, be clear from the outset to all concerned that it is the sentence of imprisonment, and not the treatment accorded in prison, that constitutes the punishment. Men come to prison as a punishment, not *for* punishment.
>
> (Ruck 1951: 23)

That principle does not apply in all jurisdictions. The law in the Soviet Union, for example, required the court to specify as part of the sentence the type of regime under which the prisoners were to be held and the severity with which they were to be treated and this provision remains in a number of countries in Eastern Europe and Central Asia.

A House of Lords judgement in 1982, often referred to as the Wilberforce judgement, confirmed that the punishment involved in imprisonment is not absolute but is restricted in its nature:

> Under English law a convicted prisoner, in spite of his imprisonment, retains all civil rights which are not taken away expressly or by necessary implication.
>
> (Raymond v. Honey (1983), 1 AC 1)

While this is all very well as a principle, there is room for a great deal of interpretation about which civil rights are 'expressly or by necessary implication' taken away by the fact of imprisonment. Take, for example, direct contact with family and friends. As we shall see in chapter six, in England

and Wales this is generally restricted to meeting once or twice a month in a large public room for a short period. There is no question that prisoners will be allowed any extended period of privacy with their family. In this country that is regarded as one of the civil rights which are expressly removed. But that is not the case in many other jurisdictions which allow prisoners to have extended private contact with close family members. So, the grounds for the interpretation in England and Wales are at least subject to challenge. In more general terms, the coercive nature of the prison environment means that the punitive element of imprisonment extends into many features of daily life in prison. Even within the prison walls prisoners do not have freedom to circulate at will. In most circumstances they are told what they must do and where they must be at every moment of the day. Their personal possessions are limited. They and their cells are subject to regular inspection and search. They are told how much money they may have and what they may spend it on. Their opportunities for activities such as work and education are severely limited.

The point being made by Paterson was that it was not the task of the prison system to impose punitive regimes on prisoners as part of their sentence. This principle is no longer accepted as unanimously as it once was. There has been an increasing sentiment in recent years that there should also be an explicitly punitive element within the prison; that the experience of imprisonment should be made unpleasant. This notion was first articulated in the 1990s by Michael Howard, when he was Home Secretary (Howard 1993). The phrase that prisons should be 'decent but austere' was interpreted by some as code that the regimes within them should be punitive. This was a move away from the philosophy of the mid-twentieth century which tried to make the experience of imprisonment as positive as possible in the hope that this could influence the future behaviour of the prisoner for the good. The suggestion that prison should be a place of austerity as well as deprivation of liberty was in some ways a return to the view of the prison which was prevalent at the beginning of the twentieth century.

The truth is that imprisonment is a blunt instrument of punishment and that it affects individuals in different ways. For some, the pains of deprivation of liberty and separation from family are almost unbearable. This punishment affects not only the prisoners but also other members of their families, parents, children, partners, siblings, whose contact with the imprisoned family member is severely restricted. For some prisoners, especially those who live normally at the margins of society, the prison may be a haven, a place of safety from the pressures and severity of external life. Whatever the personal reaction, there is little dispute that punishment is a major element of imprisonment.

Deterrence

The choices which most of us make in our daily lives are affected by what we foresee as the likely consequences of our actions. That means that we are sometimes deterred from doing something because we think that the adverse consequences would outweigh the benefit of what we propose to do. We may decide not to smoke because of the increased risk of cancer. We may decide to cut down alcohol consumption because of the damage being caused to our liver. Sometimes the adverse consequences are legally imposed rather than a direct consequence of our actions. For example, driving at high speed in a built-up area might well cause an accident, but the likelihood of that happening may not in itself be sufficient to deter every driver from speeding. So, there is a law which determines that everyone who is caught speeding will be fined or suffer penalty points on their licence. The possibility of that happening is enough to deter most drivers most of the time.

A similar argument is applied to the deterrent effect of imprisonment. If a person who is tempted to commit a crime knows that the result is likely to be a period of imprisonment, then that will be enough to deter that person from committing a crime. The greater the punishment, the greater the deterrent. It can be argued, for example, that the prospect of one month in prison might be enough to deter someone from stealing £100 but not from stealing £100,000. To deter someone from stealing that amount of money, the prospect might have to be several years in prison. The same principle of deterrence can be applied to other crimes, such as violence against the person.

There are two main forms of deterrence: individual and general. Individual deterrence is when the prospect of being sent to prison deters an individual from committing a specific crime, or when the fact of having been sent to prison makes one decide never to commit crime again. General deterrence exists when we see someone else being sent to prison for an offence and that makes us decide that we had better not commit a similar offence for fear that happens to us.

The principle of deterrence is based on an important premise, that of detection. If I know that no one is likely to check the speed at which I am driving then a law against speeding is not likely to be much of a deterrent. Even when speed cameras were first introduced, I might have known that a large percentage of them had no film and would not record any passing car. The likelihood of escaping detection was high and, therefore, deterrence was low. With the introduction of digital cameras, the likelihood of detection increased and with it the power of deterrence. That, at least, is the theory but there is evidence that even a high probability of detection is not sufficient to deter all speeding drivers.

The threat of prison as a means of crime control, let alone crime prevention, is even more problematic than that of cameras for the speeding driver. In terms of deterrence, the statistics speak for themselves. Of every hundred offences committed in England and Wales, only three result in a criminal conviction or police caution and one results in a custodial sentence (Home Office 1999). In the unlikely event that a potential criminal will apply actuarial considerations, these are pretty good odds and hardly an argument that the possibility of being sent to prison will act as a form of general deterrence. The value of imprisonment as an instrument of individual deterrence is equally questionable. It is true that we cannot calculate how many crimes are avoided because potential criminals are deterred by the prospect of imprisonment, but in terms of deterring those convicted from future offending the statistics do not give a great deal of cause for optimism. The Home Office (2002a) reported that 59 per cent of all prisoners discharged in 1999 were reconvicted of a standard offence within two years of their discharge. Among young offenders the reconviction rate was 74 per cent. These figures do not inspire confidence in the deterrent effect of imprisonment.

Reform

In the next chapter we will see how the concept of prison as a place of reform grew from the nineteenth century onwards, often encouraged by the claims of those who worked within the prison system. The notion that prison can be a place where individuals can be taught to change their behaviour is attractive on a number of counts. In the first place, it provides a positive justification for what would be an otherwise negative form of punishment of the criminal. The notion of prison as a place where personal reform can be engineered and encouraged is also attractive to those public spirited men and women who work in prisons and who wish to do more professionally than merely deprive prisoners of their liberty.

This idea of using the prison as a place of reform is particularly attractive if it is linked to the notion that most crime can be traced to a specific group of individuals. If crime is seen as a series of acts committed by a relatively small, identifiable group of people who are different from the majority of law-abiding citizens, then the objective of changing their behaviour as a result of their experience in prison should lead to a reduction in the amount of crime that they commit after they are released. If one holds that this small group of people are responsible for a disproportionate amount of crime, then any reduction in their rate of committing crime will lead to an overall reduction in crime. This argument has proved attractive to politicians who need to find a way of responding to public fear of crime.

The general principle that human beings can be encouraged to change their patterns of behaviour for the better is a sound one but whether this can be achieved in conditions of captivity is very problematic. Personal change comes as a result of a personal decision; it is not something which can be imposed against an individual's will. In the constrained environment of the prison it is very difficult for an individual to make a truly free decision. Even when prisoners have a degree of personal choice, they have to weigh carefully the consequences of any decisions they make. Agreement to take part in a particular course or programmes or refusal to do so, may mean that they will be given more or fewer privileges, or be transferred from one prison to another or that their date of release may be affected. In the words of an oft-quoted aphorism, people cannot be trained for freedom while in conditions of captivity.

The reality is that the prison is essentially a world set apart from normality. The prisoner's links with the social structures which the rest of us take for granted are at best tenuous. It would be wrong to create the impression that someone who has had problems at home, problems at school, problems in the workplace, problems in social relationships, as many prisoners have had throughout their lives, could be changed by a few months in a prison and then sent back to the world from which he or she came as a changed person. It is true that in many prisons some staff carry out sterling work in attempting to provide prisoners with opportunities to change themselves and their behaviour. A few individuals may be changed for the better by their experiences in prison, but they will always be a small minority and it can be argued that such change comes about despite the prison environment rather than because of it.

Public protection

Another stated purpose of imprisonment is to protect the public from those who commit crime, particularly in a persistent way. 'Prison works', so the argument goes, because during the time that offenders are in prison they are prevented from committing other crimes. The argument is known as incapacitation. In some respects this argument is valid, particularly in respect of specific neighbourhoods where a significant proportion of crime is being committed by identifiable individuals. However, this type of crime tends to be low level, attracting relatively short prison sentences. The person concerned may be taken out of their community for a short period of time but they are likely soon to return. This is not a new problem. In the first half of the twentieth century it was resolved by preventive detention, which involved persistent offenders being given additional sentences because of the repeat nature of their offending. The legal provision for this was eventually rescinded because it was seen to be unjust and also ineffective in the long term. An added problem is that many of the crimes which destabilize communities are not resolved by removing one or two individuals. For example, when drug dealers are removed from a local neighbourhood it will often be a matter of days, if not hours, before they are replaced by new drug dealers.

There is also an issue of public protection in respect of those people whose behaviour is such that it presents a serious threat to the safety of society. Some of them may already be in prison, convicted of serious crimes, particularly of violence against the person, and still give every indication that, if they were to be released, they would continue to present a real threat to the public. Thankfully there are very few of these people. Even in a country of 55 million people most of them are known by name, given the terrible nature of their crimes. It may well be necessary that these people should be in prison for as long as they present a threat to the public, however long that may be and for around 20 of them, it has been decided that this should be for the rest of their natural lives. There is an issue about who should make decisions about detaining a prisoner serving an indeterminate sentence for natural life. Successive Home Secretaries took this decision in respect of particularly notorious prisoners. Their decisions were open to the criticism that, whatever the rights or wrongs of a particular case, the Home Secretary could be influenced by political considerations as well as those of public safety. It is important that decisions about the detention or release of these persons should be made by a properly constituted judicial body and that they should have a recognized avenue of appeal against any such decisions. It is not appropriate that decisions of this nature should be made behind closed doors by executive or political agencies. The House of Lords confirmed this in a judgement in 2002 (R v. Secretary of State for the Home Department, ex parte Anderson, [2002] UKHL 46).

A more problematic group includes those who have not committed a serious crime but have been identified by experts as likely to do so. This group may also include some persons who are serving determinate sentences but who are considered still to present a very serious danger to the public even when their sentences have ended. This is a problematic issue, with experts expressing concern about the basis on which decisions affecting such a person might be made.

An even more contentious group included the small number of persons who were held in prison until early 2005 without charge, conviction or sentence, under the Anti-Terrorism, Crime and Security Act of 2001. In order to justify holding these men in indefinite detention the United Kingdom, alone among its signatories, had to derogate from Article five of the European Convention on Human Rights, which guarantees the right to a fair trial. In due course the House of Lords ruled that detention under these circumstances was illegal (R v. Secretary of State for the Home Department, ex parte A and others, X and another, [2002] UKHL 56) and the Home Secretary subsequently released the persons involved and made them subject to control orders in the community.

Other factors affecting the use of imprisonment

There is relative clarity about the purposes of most of the key institutions of society. For example, the purpose of the school is to educate; the purpose of the hospital is to cure illness. There is no comparable clarity about the purpose of the prison. We have just described four of its stated general purposes. The Criminal Justice Act 2003, Section 142 (1) has the following to say about the purposes of sentencing:

Any court dealing with an offender in respect of his offence must have regard to the following purposes of sentencing:
    (a) the punishment of offenders,
    (b) the reduction of crime (including its reduction by deterrence),
    (c)the reform and rehabilitation of offenders,
    (d)the protection of the public, and
    (e)the making of reparation by offenders to persons affected by their offences.

However, judges who sentence people to prison are not required to indicate in individual cases the specific reason for sending an offender to prison, whether it is for punishment, for deterrence, for reformation of for protection of the public. In so far as they consider these matters in detail, judges might well be of the view that several of the purposes apply in any one case: the seriousness of the crime which has been proved requires that a prison sentence be passed. At the same time, the judge wishes to convey a signal to the rest of society about what behaviour is tolerated and what is not. Similarly, even though the immediate purpose of sending an offender to prison is punishment, the judge may well intend that the experience of being in prison will lead somehow to a process of personal reform. Finally, the judge may take the view that for whatever period of imprisonment is set, society requires to be protected from the offender who has just been convicted.

Anyone who has observed the proceedings in a court, particularly the lower courts where most sentences are passed, quickly discovers that sentencing is not an entirely objective or rational process. In passing sentence on an offender the court takes account of many other factors, which are very difficult to assess in an objective manner. While magistrates and judges are deemed to be completely independent in matters of individual sentences, it is clear that they are influenced in their sentencing practices by many external factors. The Home Office has shown how rises and falls in levels of imprisonment can be linked to traumatic events which touch the national consciousness, such as the murder of young Jamie Bulger in 1993, or to statements by Home Secretaries at political party conferences (Home Office 2003a: 6). In a similar way, one needs to find something other than objective sentencing patterns to explain the different use of imprisonment by courts in broadly similar regions of the country for comparable offences. For example, Roger Hood's study of courts in the West Midlands (Hood 1992) drew attention to disparities between neighbouring courts in respect of the sentencing of offenders from different racial backgrounds.

In England and Wales prisons are not merely places to lock up particular types of offenders for specified periods. It needs to be understood that the prison also holds a symbolic place in modern English public life. As we shall discover in the next chapter, its development owes much to the Christian theology of sin, guilt, punishment, expiation and redemption. Even in modern secular Britain, these concepts are central to the principles on which imprisonment is based, including the notions that people who are in prison have done wrong, need to be punished and through that punishment will be given the opportunity to become better human beings, to be 'reformed'.

Central to the use of imprisonment is a decision by a society about how much punishment it wishes to inflict on those who act in a certain way. This decision is based on political, and sometimes on social factors, rather than on matters of criminal justice, such as rates of crime. It is this factor which goes some way to explaining the discrepancy in rates of imprisonment between countries which do not appear to have any noticeable difference in crime rates. This fact has been acknowledged by the Council of Europe, an organization which is made up of 46 members states, including the United Kingdom. The report which it published following a conference of heads of European prison administrations (European Committee for Crime Problems 2002: 1) drew the following conclusion:

> In the course of this conference we have been reminded several times that the way prisons are managed in individual countries is linked closely to the social structures within each state. Prisons do not exist in a vacuum. To a large extent, they reflect the values to which each society adheres. One example of this is the use which society makes of imprisonment. Several speakers . . . expressed the opinion that levels of imprisonment in each country are usually influenced much more by political decisions than by levels of crime or rates of detection of crime. A society can choose to have a high or low rate of imprisonment and this choice is reflected in the sentencing patterns adopted by individual judges. In recent years a number of European countries, especially in the West, have decided, either consciously or by default, to have higher rates of imprisonment. They have done this through the introduction of more punitive legislation or as a result of politicians and the media encouraging judicial authorities to send more people to prison for longer periods of time.

We shall see in the following chapters that imprisonment is based on the concept of exclusion from society. This suggests that societies which make a high use of prison are also likely to be ones which have a lower standard of inclusion. Put another way, they are less likely to be tolerant of those who do not conform to the norms of the majority of society. This argument appears to be reinforced by the fact that the United Kingdom government has in recent years focused on problems caused by 'social exclusion' rather than on the need for social inclusion. We will discuss in due course the fact that prisons in all countries are full of those who are marginalized in their societies. England and Wales is no exception to this, with prisons holding an over-representation of ethnic minorities, the mentally disturbed, the homeless and persons who abuse alcohol and drugs. In other words, they are 'the other', people who are different from the majority.

So, when considering the degree to which society makes use of imprisonment, it is not sufficient to analyze the direct purposes of imprisonment. It is also necessary to examine these other social factors. Finland provides a good case study of how rates of imprisonment can be subject to influences other than crime rates. In the 1950s the Finnish rate of imprisonment was one of the highest in Western Europe, four times higher than its Nordic neighbours, at about 187 prisoners per 100,000 of the population. Over succeeding decades its rate of imprisonment fell significantly: to 154 in 1960, 113 in 1970, 106 in 1980, 69 in 1990 and 55 in 2000. This did not happen by accident. Rather, the decrease was the result of deliberate, long-term and systematic policy choices (Lappi-Seppälä 2002). In the first place, there was clear political will and consensus to bring down the prisoner rate. This involved key politicians, government officials and academics. The judiciary was closely involved in developing the changes and in a number of respects sentencing practice changed in advance of new legislation. It should be noted that crime control has never been a party political issue in election campaigns in Finland. Finally, the role of the media was of crucial importance, with a general absence of populist reporting on criminal justice matters. It should be noted that the rate of imprisonment in Finland has begun to creep up slowly over the last year or so and in 2005 stood at 71 per 100,000 (Walmsley 2005), half the rate of England and Wales.

In England and Wales influences such as these may go part of the way towards explaining why the use of imprisonment has increased so dramatically since the beginning of the 1990s, despite the fact that there has been no comparable increase in crime rates. It is certainly true that individual judges are quite independent when making sentencing decisions about the individual offenders who come before them. But judges do not live in ivory towers. In addition to their legal independence, they have a part to play in interpreting the current views of society, views which are often expressed through political channels and by the media.

In a similar manner, the actual content of imprisonment is influenced by the views which a society has about how harsh the punishment of imprisonment should be. In some countries imprisonment involves merely deprivation of liberty, with few other restrictions. There are examples from India of prisons which are open camps, where the prisoners' families also live and prisoners can go out to work each day to support their families (Shankardass 2000). There are other instances where prison means almost total isolation from all outside contact. The very high security prisons in the United States of America, known colloquially as 'supermaxes' are an example of this type (Human Rights Watch 1997). A number of features which are regarded as integral to the concept of imprisonment in England and Wales are not part of prison punishment in other countries. Reference was made above to limitations on family contact and in chapter six we will raise the question of voting in elections, which is not allowed for convicted prisoners in the United Kingdom. In subsequent chapters we will also discover how the nature of imprisonment has substantially changed in this country over the years.

International standards and regulations

The manner in which prisons are regulated in England and Wales is subject to domestic legislation. This means primarily the Prison Act 1952, as subsequently amended, and also the Prison Rules, which are laid out in a Statutory Instrument, that is in secondary legislation. In addition, there is a whole range of international covenants, treaties and standards to which the government of the United Kingdom is a signatory. Some of these standards, such as those set by the United Nations, are universal in their application. Others, such as those of the Council of Europe, have regional application.

It is important to stress that these international standards have not been imposed on the United Kingdom by foreign powers. Rather, this country has been one of the driving forces behind many of the international human rights covenants, particularly the original ones drawn up in the aftermath of the Second World War. The United Kingdom was one of the prime drafters of the Universal Declaration of Human Rights (UDHR), which was adopted by the General Assembly of the United Nations in December 1948. The UDHR is not a legally binding instrument but its provisions are held to constitute general principles of law or to represent elementary considerations of humanity. The International Covenant on Civil and Political Rights was adopted by the General Assembly in 1966 and came into force in 1976. It has the legal force of a treaty for the states which have ratified it. The United Kingdom has done so. Article 10 of the Covenant requires that:

> All persons deprived of their liberty shall be treated with humanity and with respect for the inherent dignity of the human person.

Other UN conventions which are relevant to the treatment of people deprived of their liberty include the Convention against Torture and Other Cruel, Inhuman or Degrading Treatment or Punishment (1984), the Convention on the Elimination of All Forms of Racial Discrimination (1966) and the Convention on the Elimination of All Forms of Discrimination against Women (1979). These conventions are not theoretical or academic treatises. They comprise a body of international law which must be respected by the community of nations and they have direct relevance to the management of prisons in this country.

The general principles which are contained in the covenants and conventions mentioned above are covered in more detail in a number of international instruments which refer specifically to prisoners. These include the United Nations Standard Minimum Rules for the Treatment of

Prisoners (1957), the Body of Principles for the Protection of All Persons Under Any Form of Detention or Imprisonment (1988), the Basic Principles for the Treatment of Prisoners (1990), and the Standard Minimum Rules for the Administration of Juvenile Justice (1985). There are also a number of United Nations instruments which refer specifically to staff working with people who have been deprived of their liberty. They include the Code of Conduct for Law Enforcement Officials (1979) and the Principles of Medical Ethics Relevant to the Role of Health Personnel, Particularly Physicians, in the Protection of Prisoners and Detainees against Torture and other Cruel, Inhuman or Degrading Treatment (1982). All of these documents are crucial to any understanding of the principles which should apply to the current practice of imprisonment. Anyone who wishes to consider them in greater detail should refer to Coyle (2002c).

At a regional level, the European Convention on Human Rights (ECHR) makes specific reference to punishment and to those deprived of their liberty. The decision to incorporate this Convention into domestic law through the Human Rights Act 1998 attracted considerable public comment. Some of the criticisms give the impression that incorporation involved imposing the will of a foreign power on a sovereign state. This is ironic, given the fact that the United Kingdom played a key role in drafting the ECHR, which was signed in 1950 and came into force in 1953. Its provisions include many of the principles which our forebears fought so strenuously to defend in two world wars. Some of these are of specific relevance to prisoners. Article 3 deals with the right not to be tortured or to be subjected to inhuman or degrading treatment or punishment. Article 6 deals with the right to a fair trial and to preparation of defence. Article 8 deals with the right to respect for private and family life. Chapter six provides detailed references to a number of the judgements which the Court has made in respect of prison matters in the United Kingdom.

For many years the Council of Europe has also taken an interest in prison issues and has agreed a wide ranging set of standards which it encourages member states to implement. These take the form of formal recommendations from the Council of Ministers. The most important of these is Recommendation R (87) 3 on the European Prison Rules. Others include:

- Recommendation (89) 12 on education in prison.
- Recommendation (92) 16 on the European Rules on community sanctions and measures.
- Recommendation (93) 6 concerning prison and criminological aspects of the control of transmissible diseases including AIDS and related health problems in prisons.
- Recommendation (97) 12 on staff concerned with the implementation of sanctions and measures.
- Recommendation (98) 7 concerning the ethical and organizational aspects of health care in prison.

- Recommendation (99) 22 concerning prison overcrowding and prison population inflation.
- Recommendation (2000) 22 on improving the implementation of the European Rules on community sanctions and measures.
- Recommendation (2003) 22 on conditional release (parole).
- Recommendation (2003) 23 on the management by prison administrations of life sentence and other long-term prisoners.

The place of prison in society

All of the issues we have discussed so far lead us towards a realization that decisions about the use of prison are not purely a matter of criminal justice priorities. They are also affected by views about social justice and about the nature of society. In general terms there is not a great deal of public interest in imprisonment and its use, other than when politicians or the media raise the subject, usually with the suggestion that increasing the number of people in prison will help to reduce crime rates. However, in England and Wales there is a long tradition of informed debate about prisons within a wide variety of penal reform and pressure groups.

The oldest of these is the Howard League for Penal Reform, named after John Howard, of whom we shall learn more in the next chapter. The Howard Association was established in 1866 with the objective of promoting the most efficient means of penal treatment and crime prevention and the reformatory treatment of offenders. In 1921 it merged with the Penal Reform League to become the Howard League for Penal Reform. The Howard League now campaigns on a wide variety of penal reform issues, including prison overcrowding, opposition to sending children to prison, the high level of prison suicides, the need to provide prisoners with opportunities for 'real work' and the development of community alternatives to imprisonment. The biggest non-statutory organization working in the penal field in England and Wales is the National Association for the Care and Resettlement of Offenders, now known as NACRO, the crime reduction charity. NACRO has become mainly a service provider, managing extensive programmes for former offenders and other people in disadvantaged communities. The Prison Reform Trust is a relatively young organization, having been founded in 1981. It is politically aware and, while it campaigns on many of the same issues as the Howard League, it has been particularly successful in involving the media in the debate about the use of imprisonment, raising specific issues such as the justification for depriving prisoners of the right to vote in elections and the increasing number of foreign nationals in prison, as well as the needs of women prisoners and the treatment of remand prisoners. There are also a number of smaller organizations which campaign on specific issues, such as the need to provide support for prisoners' families, to improve prison education and to provide employment for released prisoners.

People will take up this book because they wish to understand more about prisons. This first chapter has demonstrated an important principle which readers should keep in mind as they read what follows. Prisons do not exist within a vacuum, nor is their use determined in an entirely dispassionate manner by the courts of justice. They are symbolic institutions and the level at which they are used has much to say about the attitude which a society has towards the acceptable limits of punishment, about punishment as a social phenomenon, about approaches to the treatment of people while they are being punished and the international legal framework within which prisons should operate. These fundamental issues set the context for the remainder of the book. We can now go on to discover how prisons as we know them today came into being.

Further reading

Cavadino, M. and Dignan, J. (2001) *The Penal System: An Introduction*. London: Sage.

Cohen, S. (1985) *Visions of Social Control*. London: Polity Press.

Duff, A. and Garland, D. (1994) *A Reader on Punishment*. Oxford: Oxford University Press.

Faulkner, D. (2000) *Crime, State and Citizen: A Field Full of Folk*. Winchester: Waterside Press.

Garland, D. (1985) *Punishment and Welfare*. Aldershot: Gower.

Garland, D. (2001) *The Culture of Control: Crime and Social Order in Contemporary Society*. Oxford: Oxford University Press.

Maguire, M., Morgan, R. and Reiner, R. (eds) (2002) *The Oxford Handbook of Criminology*, 3rd edn. Oxford: Clarendon Press.

chapter two

The history of the modern prison

The beginnings of the modern prison

The etymology of the word prison comes from the Latin word meaning to seize. The place itself is defined as a building to which people are legally committed for custody while awaiting trial or punishment. Based on that definition, prisons have been with us for many centuries. Until the seventeenth century they were used to hold people who were in the midst of a legal process. This included waiting to be tried, being held until an amount of money was paid for a debt or a fine, waiting to be sent into exile or until execution. There is broad agreement among prison historians that before the seventeenth century the notion of sending offenders to prison as a punishment in itself rarely occurred (Fox 1952) although some commentators have suggested that this did happen, at least from the thirteenth century for 'fraud, contempt, disobedience to authority, failure in public duty and petty crime' (McConville 1981: 2).

Occasionally, individuals who posed a particular threat to the local ruler or state might be deprived of their liberty for a long period. Such men or women would be held in prisons or keeps which belonged to the local ruler, frequently attached to his castle or palace (Morris and Rothman 1995).

The building used as a prison for ordinary criminals was often an annexe of the court and the jailer was frequently an officer of the court, such as a bailiff (Cameron 1983). Other prisons were in prominent locations in the centre of towns. This was no accident. Rather, it was intended to send a very clear message to all citizens about the consequences of wrong doing. The presence of these forbidding buildings in their midst was meant to remind people of the folly of a life lived outside the law and to deter them from any thought of crime. Often, however, the reality did not match this principle. Prisons were places of public coming and going, with family and friends being allowed to visit prisoners on a daily basis, prisoners purchasing food and drink from local shopkeepers, often with the jailer acting as middleman for a fee.

From the late sixteenth century in England there was a network of houses of correction or bridewells around the country. Morris and Rothman (1995: 83) reckon that by the early seventeenth century there were 170 such institutions. These were used primarily for vagrants and those who were unable to support themselves and they operated on the principle of encouraging industrious habits. They were not generally used for ordinary criminals.

The use of prison as a direct punishment of the court can be linked to reduction in the use of transportation in the early nineteenth century and its end in 1867. Transportation to an overseas colony involved exile from one's community, often for a period of seven or ten years (Shaw 1966) and sometimes for ever (Hughes 1987). The increase in the use of prison as a place of punishment was an extension of this notion of exile. Instead of being transported to the colonies, prisoners were now to be punished for their crimes by being exiled behind the high walls of the prison. The punishment of the court consisted of deprivation of liberty and the authorities had little concern for what went on inside the prison. Physical conditions in most prisons were often appalling. One of the five national Inspectors of Prisons appointed in 1835 reported that 'the picture that gradually unfolded itself before my eyes was far worse than anything I had anticipated' (Hill 1893: 120). Hill found that discipline was virtually non-existent, that the prisoners spent most of their days in idleness, that there was little cleanliness and virtually no instruction.

The development of prisons in their modern sense can be traced to two sources. The first came in the second half of the eighteenth and early part of the nineteenth centuries as a result of growing concern among a number of influential persons who were appalled at the terrible conditions which were prevalent in existing lock-ups and jails. The best known of these individuals was John Howard, who first became aware of the problem in prisons during his tenure as High Sheriff of Bedford. Howard decided to tour English counties in the expectation of finding a good example for Bedford gaol to follow. Instead he was horrified to find that the appalling conditions in Bedford were common all over England and Wales. In addition there was widespread corruption among gaolers. For example, some would not allow prisoners to leave prison, even if they had been found innocent, unless they or their families paid for their release (Howard 1792). Howard later extended his inspection to other European countries (Howard 1791). He died of typhus, known at the time as 'gaol fever', while inspecting prisons in what is now Ukraine and his portrait still hangs in the training school for prison staff in that country. Other people involved in this early movement for prison reform in the early nineteenth century were Elizabeth Fry, Joseph Gurney and Thomas Buxton. Many of these reformers were inspired by their Christian beliefs and they pressed the notion that prisons should not be places of depravity and inhumanity but that they should be decent and austere, with the prisoner subjected to positive rather than negative influences. A full description of prisons in this period can be found in McConville (1981).

The second source of reform was related to the first. Until Howard and others began their work, no respectable person would consider working in a prison. The task of turnkey was often carried out by a junior court official or was done on a part-time basis, often by people who were themselves of little standing in society, as described in chapter five. With the introduction of these reforms work in prisons, at least at a senior level, came to be considered as a more reputable form of public service. The person in charge of the local bridewells had frequently been described as the governor, a title common in many similar public institutions, such as the poor house, at the time. By the middle of the eighteenth century the person in charge of most prisons was described in this way. The position across the country was uneven but in some towns he was a person of considerable standing in the local community, on a par with the justices of the peace.

One consequence of these new appointments was that some of the persons involved began to take their work seriously and to consider whether they could be more than jailers and whether the experience of being in prison could be used to help reform those who were sent there. One of the foremost of these was William Brebner, who was governor of Glasgow bridewell and prison between 1808 and his death in 1845 (Coyle 1991). During the early years of his tenure Brebner transformed the regime in the bridewell, as was favourably noted in a Report of the Select Committee of the House of Commons on Scottish Prisons (1826). He placed the prisoners in single cells and required them to work from six o'clock in the morning until eight at night. He extended his influence beyond the prison boundary by setting up a house of refuge for released prisoners and a rudimentary form of aftercare. He also set about training his staff, improving their rates of pay, requiring regular hours of attendance and giving them annual leave. In effect, he established what was to become known as the separate system of imprisonment when it was set up subsequently in the United States. When William Crawford, Inspector of Prisons for the Home District was sent to assess the American systems of imprisonment he discovered that

The Eastern Penitentiary is, in fact, with some trifling difference in its arrangements, but a counterpart of the Bridewell at Glasgow, a prison which was in operation five years before the erection of the prison at Philadelphia.

(Quoted in the Report of the General Board of
Directors of Prisons in Scotland 1840: 23)

The separate system and the silent system

The notion that imprisonment might provide an opportunity for reform of the prisoner developed along two strands. One concept was built on the value of industrial work as a reforming experience. In this model prisoners were put to work in large communal workrooms but were forbidden to talk to each other and were punished harshly if found doing so. The second tradition was based more on the strict model of Christian monasticism. Prisoners were confined to individual cells. They were given work to do on their own. Sometimes this had some purpose to it, such as cobbling or sewing. At other times it had no purpose other than to occupy the prisoner and might involve endless turning of the crank or stepping on the treadmill (McConville 1981: 350).

In the north-east of the United States these two systems were developed respectively in New York and Pennsylvania and came to be known by the names of the prisons in which they operated. The silent system was favoured in Auburn jail in New York while the separate system was used in Philadelphia penitentiary in Pennsylvania. In England the silent system was favoured in the Middlesex House of Corrections at Cold Bath Fields, while the separate system found favour in Millbank Penitentiary, opened in 1816, and later in the new Pentonville prison, both of which had cellular accommodation as opposed to the previous ward structure. An interesting dynamic in the struggle for primacy between the two systems is one which has resonances in today's prison system. The silent system emphasized the importance of hard labour with the intention both of underlining the unpleasant nature of imprisonment and teaching the discipline necessary for an honest member of the working class. The separate system on the other hand was much more concerned with changing the mindset of prisoners. It was based on a belief that criminals could be reformed by the very experience of imprisonment. They were to be left on their own in their cells to contemplate the error of their ways. In between the work which they were given to do they were encouraged to read the one book which was allowed to them, the Bible. They were not allowed to come into contact with other prisoners, nor to talk to staff. The only people who visited them daily were the governor and the chaplain, 'good people', who were to have a beneficial influence on them. Some of the behavioural programmes which were popular in some prisons in England and Wales at the end of the twentieth century, and which are described further in chapter six, would have fitted well into the separate system of the early nineteenth century.

In the short term, the separate system won out over the silent system. It proved simply impossible to enforce complete silence on prisoners who worked side by side each day. Similarly, requiring them to wear hoods when exercising together in yards, could not prevent communication between them, even in the face of draconian punishments. It was also impossible to get prisoners to produce work of a high enough standard to defray the expense incurred. The separate system was easier to enforce, since it was premised on not allowing prisoners to come into contact with each other, but this virtual segregation affected the mental state of many prisoners. The high moment of the separate system was probably in 1837 when the governor of Millbank penitentiary resigned in protest against the strict way that he had to enforce it. The Home Secretary filled the resulting vacancy by appointing the chaplain, who was a fervent supporter of the system, as governor. Within a few years concern was being expressed about the strict religious regulations which were being applied and about the number of prisoners who were being driven mad because of the extended periods of total separation. Shortly after the opening of the new model prison at Pentonville in 1843, Millbank, the symbol of the separate system, ceased to be used as a penitentiary. Although the principle of total separation became discredited and ceased to be applied indiscriminately, it remained on statute until new Prison Rules were enacted in 1930.

The Gladstone Report

As we shall learn in the following chapter, a national Prison Commission for England and Wales was set up in 1878. By the end of the nineteenth century there was increasing criticism of the autocratic style of the Chairman of the Commission. There was also concern about a number of specific matters, such as the shortage of prison places in the London area. These issues led to the establishment of a committee under the chairmanship of Herbert Gladstone MP to inquire into several issues, including accommodation in local prisons, the treatment of juvenile offenders, prison labour and occupations, the treatment of habitual criminals and the classification of prisoners. The committee went about its task with vigour. As happened with many similar committees in later years, it decided that it could not be constrained by its terms of reference but needed 'to enter upon a comprehensive examination of the conditions under which prisoners are confined' (para 6).

The most famous conclusion of the Gladstone Report of 1895 was that 'We start from the principle that prison treatment should have as its primary and concurrent objects deterrence and reformation'. This principle and the subsequent attempts to implement these two 'primary and concurrent objects' have been blamed for much of the uncertainty and confusion which bedevilled the prison service throughout the succeeding century. Some commentators have argued (Thomas 1972: 117) that it is contradictory for an organization to have two primary objectives, especially two which are not at first sight compatible. It is not possible to maintain a balance between the object of deterrence, which implies a punitive and coercive environment, and that of reformation, which implies an environment which encourages individual development and change. The attempts to achieve this impossible balance have resulted, so it is argued, in uncertainty and frustration among prison staff about their role, a lack of clarity about how prisoners are expected to behave, and confusion on the part of governments and the public about the purpose of imprisonment.

The Gladstone Report led to the Prison Act of 1898 which finally unified the convict and local prison systems, limited the use of corporal punishment, created three classes of prisoner and introduced remission of sentence for local prisoners. The following year the rule of total silence was abolished.

The Liberal government which came into office in 1908 continued the process of reform inspired by the Gladstone Report. The Probation of Offenders Act of 1907 introduced what was to become the probation system and the Prevention of Crime Act in the following year introduced two important changes to the prison system. The first was preventive detention, which allowed courts to impose an additional sentence of between five and ten years on habitual offenders. The provision remained on statute until the Criminal Justice Act of 1967. The second was the introduction of a sentence of between one and three years for young men between the ages of 16 and 21 years, with the date of release being dependent on good conduct and response to progress through a series of 'grades'. The first unit for young men under this new sentence was opened in Borstal prison in Rochester. Thereafter, the sentence became known as Borstal training. The development of the Borstal system and other sentences for young offenders is described in chapter four.

The progressive era

The process of liberalization of the treatment of prisoners which was ushered in with the Gladstone Report continued throughout the first half of the twentieth century. Bennett (2003: 2) has suggested that, although he was Home Secretary only between February 1910 and October 1911, Winston Churchill had a significant influence on confirming the liberalization of penal policy during this period. Certainly, one of the most frequently quoted references in prison history is his statement in the House of Commons that 'The mood and temper of the public in regard to the treatment of crime and criminals is one of the most unfailing tests of the civilization of any country' (Home Office Supply (Report), H.C. Debates, 5th Series, vol. 19, col. 1354, 20 July 1910). Bennett describes his penal legacy as including 'the use of imprisonment only in those cases where it is necessary, proportionality, identifying alternatives to imprisonment and resettlement of offenders' (2003: 5).

In the 1920s the practice of obliging prisoners to have close cropped hair was abolished, the broad arrows were removed from prisoners' uniforms and prisoners were allowed to converse while at work. In the 1930s the practice of paying prisoners a small amount of 'wages' for working was introduced, as was the opportunity for those who were in prisons far away from their homes to return once a year to a prison near home in order to receive visits. The 1930 Prison Rules finally abolished the practice of separate solitary confinement for the first months of a long sentence. In 1936 the first open prison was set up at New Hall Camp near Wakefield.

These developments were not without their problems. In 1932 there was a serious mutiny in Dartmoor prison which was resolved by armed police being called in. The government set up an inquiry into the mutiny by an eminent King's Counsel. The published report (Du Parq Report 1932) concluded that the improved treatment of prisoners had not contributed to the mutiny, although it offered no other explanation for it. Thomas (1972: 159) is of the view that the report was wrong in drawing this conclusion, which he attributes to the influence of Alexander Paterson on the chairman. As one of the driving forces behind better treatment of prisoners, Paterson did not wish it to be suggested that this had contributed to a breakdown of order.

In the years after the end of the Second World War the number of open prisons increased considerably (Fox 1952). In the 1950s a new scheme was introduced in Norwich prison which had three main elements. Specific prison officers were given responsibility for the care of small groups of prisoners; there was an increase in the weekly hours for work; and all convicted prisoners were allowed to eat in communal dining areas instead of in their cells. This development was significant because it introduced formally into the adult prison system some of the principles which underpinned the Borstal system and it also gave a key role in this work to ordinary prison officers. A scheme allowing long-term prisoners who were coming to the end of their sentences to go out of the prison to work on a daily basis was also introduced in several prisons.

The growth of criminology and its effect on the use of imprisonment

What one might describe as the growth of the science of prison management was related to the parallel development of what, in due course, came to be described as the new academic discipline of criminology. Academics, public officials and others were turning their attention to the phenomenon of crime, how it was to be defined, who committed it, the reasons why they committed it and, in due course, how might they be prevented from doing so (Ignatieff 1978). In the second half of the eighteenth century there was a series of influential commentators on these issues, including Cesare Beccaria in Italy, and Jeremy Bentham and John Howard in England (Garland 2002). Throughout the course of the following century this overlap between theory and practice in the whole field of what was seen as deviant human behaviour continued to expand. This was also the era of the large institution and the growth of prison building was matched by that of large mental asylums. The notion of the person who committed crime and the mentally ill as deviant persons became fashionable. The development of social anthropology in this field, particularly Cesare Lombroso's writings on phrenology (1876), suited the political and social spirit of the time. David Garland (2002) summarizes the historical development of criminology as a distinct discipline in his essay 'Of Crimes and Criminals: The Development of Criminology in Britain' in the *Oxford Handbook of Criminology*. A recognition of how criminology came to be accepted as a proper academic discipline in the United Kingdom is an important prerequisite for understanding how the place of the prison has taken such a firm hold in British social life in the last two-and-a-half centuries. Garland underlines the importance of acknowledging that our definitions of what constitutes crime and deviance are based on 'established conventions and not on unchallengeable truths' (page 13). The development of criminology did not take place in an academic ivory tower, nor was it based on eternal principles. Rather, he argues, it was grounded in specific institutional practices, political movements and cultural settings. In brief, the practice fed on the theory and the theory fed on the practice. Garland traces the history of these developments in Britain through the late nineteenth and early twentieth centuries, on to the establishment of the Home Office Research Unit and government support for what was to become the Institute of Criminology at Cambridge University (page 40). The use of academic research to evaluate and justify official policy and its application is still a significant feature of British criminology. It can be argued that this has had a direct influence on the way imprisonment is used and the consequent increase in the size of the prison population.

The suggestion from academics that crime was an aberration from the norm and that, rather like a young tree which is growing in a crooked manner, people who committed crime could be trained to live law-abiding lives suited the new structures of imprisonment which were being applied in Great Britain throughout the second half of the nineteenth century. It led to the growth of what became known as the theory of rehabilitation, the concept of restoring people to their previous good reputation (Garland 1985). In the course of the next fifty years a new breed of experts who began to work in prisons, social workers, probation officers, teachers, psychologists, psychiatrists and assistant governors, took on the task of rehabilitating men and women who had originally been sent to prison as punishment for the crime they had committed.

The notion that people could be trained out of criminality in the prison setting, like plants forced on in a greenhouse, was an attractive one on several counts. It raised the possibility that crime might eventually be eliminated. It gave governments a justification for an expansion of the machinery of criminal justice. It gave courts a justification beyond that of mere punishment for imposing sentences of imprisonment. It also gave prison administrators the chance to claim a professional status which went beyond that of mere jailer. The optimism which resulted was voiced by Sir Alexander Paterson, one of the foremost prison administrators in the early part of the twentieth century. Giving evidence to the Persistent Offenders' Committee in 1931, he noted, 'The problem of Recidivism is small, diminishing, and not incapable of solution' (Ruck 1951: 55).

If there was a real possibility that the experience of imprisonment could turn men and women who had committed crimes into law-abiding citizens, then that became a justification for sending more people to prison. By the end of the nineteenth century there had been a quantum leap from the dank 'thieves' hole' to the high-minded notion of the prison as a place of social training. The magistrate or judge faced with the dilemma of what to do with the young man who persisted in petty offending or the old man who was consistently drunk and disorderly now had a positive solution. To the former he said, 'I will send you to prison where you will be trained to lead a law-abiding life'. To the latter he said, 'I will send you to prison for your own good'.

If it was accepted that imprisonment had a positive potential then there was an argument for imposing it early in a criminal career rather than when all other options had failed. The earlier in a criminal career one began the process of reform, the greater the likelihood of successful rehabilitation. If one could identify those who were likely to become serious offenders in the future, the logical thing would be to send them to prison at an early stage so as to begin the process of reform. In addition, it made sense that young criminals should be kept apart from the bad influence of older criminals and should be held in special prisons, where the emphasis would be on reform and training. This was the thinking which led to the creation of prisons for juveniles and, in due course, of Borstal institutions, as will be described in chapter three. So, to the original notion of the prison as a place where people were sent as punishment for crimes which they had committed was added the notion that prison could also be used as a tool for the control and prevention of crime by diverting those who were sent to prison from a life of future crime.

The suggestion that one of the purposes of the prison was to reduce the likelihood of future crime led on to the concept that the length of time which men and women were to spend in prison should be determined not merely by the gravity of the offence they had committed but also as a result of an assessment of the likelihood that they might commit further crime in the future. It was possible to base this assessment on two factors. The first took account of past actions: the number of similar crimes which the person had already committed could be used as an indication of the probability of more offending in the future. This was the justification for preventive detention which was introduced by the Prevention of Crime Act 1908. The second factor was based on an assessment, undertaken in prison, of the likelihood of future offending after release. As a consequence, the length of time that a man or woman would spend in prison would be determined, not by the sentencing court, but by some form of administrative or quasi-judicial process according to how the person responded while the sentence was being served. This led to the introduction of the indeterminate sentence in its many forms and to the concept of conditional release or parole. The implications of these developments for the system of criminal justice did not go unnoticed. As one well-placed commentator noted, 'There can be no doubt that the increase in the control of the Executive over the offender after he has been sentenced has been one of the major features of twentieth century penal history in this country' (Cross 1971: 27).

The legacy of history

The way that imprisonment is used today in England and Wales has been influenced a great deal by its history. In the course of a few hundred years there was a movement from the 'squalor carceris', the squalor of the prison, which was overseen on a part-time basis by persons who wished they had a more reputable means of earning an income, to the prison as an institution for reform, run by a new group of managers who presented themselves as masters of a new profession. The prison was no longer merely a place to await an outcome of the judicial process or a place of punishment. Instead it was presented as a place of rehabilitation, with an objective of reducing recidivism among criminals. This positive view of the prison suited the practitioners who, for understandable reasons, wished to be seen, not merely as jailers who deprived people of their liberty, but as professionals who changed the most difficult and problematic of human beings into law-abiding citizens. Nils Christie has described why what he called 'the denial-of-existence strategy', in which prisons were called institutions and prisoners were referred to as inmates, has proved popular:

> First, it makes life somewhat easier for the personnel within these institutions. The hangman's job was never very popular. Those who got a chance slipped into the doctor's role as fast as possible. There is a need for a defence. Major strategies are to claim that what one is doing to other people does not hurt, is intended to help, or actually is very efficient in helping them even though it might hurt a bit in the beginning – just like so many good cures.
>
> (Christie 1978: 181)

The concept of the prison as a place of reform also suited other players. Christie again:

> Study after study has shown how penal measures and long-term incarceration have been made more acceptable to society if they were disguised as treatment, training or pure help to suffering individuals in need of such measures. The more the element of intended pain has been kept out of the picture, the easier it has been to evade justice and legal protections.
>
> (Christie 1978: 181)

The concept of personal reform as one of the purposes of imprisonment was discussed in the previous chapter. In recent years this concept has been expressed in a much narrower sense as 'reducing re-offending' among those released from prison (Blunkett 2004). The implications of making this an objective of imprisonment will be discussed in greater detail in the next chapter.

Important moments in recent English prison history

A number of the key moments in the history of prisons in England and Wales in the 1990s, especially those which are of organizational significance, are recorded in chapter three. Chapter seven, which deals with issues of security and good order, refers in some detail to the period relating to the publication of the Mountbatten Report in 1966 and its aftermath.

The period which is likely to prove significant in historical terms began with a riot at Strangeways prison in 1990 and ended with the follow-up to the reports into the escapes of high security prisoners from Whitemoor and Parkhurst prisons in 1994 and 1995 respectively. These events are worthy of more detailed examination.

Strangeways and the Woolf Report

On Sunday 1 April 1990 what was to become the worst riot in English prison history broke out in Strangeways prison, Manchester. Coyle (1994: 148) has described the succeeding events as follows:

> When it ended 25 days later, one prisoner had died in circumstances which may have been connected with the disturbance. One officer had died of pneumonia. Later another prisoner who had played a prominent part in the riot took his life in another establishment. 47 prisoners were injured. 147 members of staff received injuries or were affected by smoke or fumes. The cost of repairing the blackened shell of what remained of the prison was estimated at £60 millions.

While the riot was still in progress the Home Secretary appointed Lord

Justice Woolf, a distinguished High Court judge who was later to become Lord Chief Justice of England and Wales, to undertake an inquiry into what had gone wrong at Strangeways and the six other prisons at which rioting also took place. Nine months later Woolf produced what was to become one of the most comprehensive reports ever produced on prisons in the United Kingdom. The first half of the report was a description of and commentary on the events of April 1990. As with so many other reports on prison issues, Woolf went on to say that the riots could not be understood without reference to the general state of imprisonment and the way prison was used in England and Wales. In the second part of the report, written with the assistance of Judge Stephen Tumim, the Chief Inspector of Prisons, he provided a masterly analysis of these issues.

Woolf's key conclusion was that a stable prison system should be built on three interdependent pillars: security, control and justice (para 9.19). Security recognizes the need to ensure that prisoners do not escape. Control ensures that prisons are safe places for those who live and work there. Within the term 'justice' Woolf encompassed the need to treat prisoners with humanity and fairness and to help them prepare for their return to the community.

In sum, Woolf made 204 proposals and included 12 main recommendations (Section 15). The main recommendations (para 15.5) were:

1 Closer co-operation between the different parts of the Criminal Justice System. For this purpose a national forum and local committees should be established.

2 More visible leadership of the Prison Service by a Director General who is and is seen to be the operational head and in day-to-day charge of the Service. To achieve this there should be a published 'compact' or 'contract' given by Ministers to the Director General of the Prison Service, who should be responsible for the performance of that 'contract' and publicly answerable for the day-to-day operations of the Prison Service.

3 Increased delegation of responsibility to Governors of establishments.

4 An enhanced role for prison officers.

5 A 'compact' or 'contract' for each prisoner setting out the prisoner's expectations and responsibilities in the prison in which he or she is held.

6 A national system of Accredited Standards, with which, in time, each prison establishment would be required to comply.

7 A new Prison Rule that no establishment should hold more prisoners than is provided for in its certified normal level of accommodation, with provisions for Parliament to be informed if exceptionally there is to be a material departure from that rule.

8 A public commitment from Ministers setting a timetable to provide access to sanitation for all inmates at the earliest practicable date not later than February 1996.

9 Better prospects for prisoners to maintain their links with families and

the community through more visits and home leaves and through being located in community prisons as near to their homes as possible.

10 A division of prison establishments into small and more manageable and secure units.

11 A separate statement of purpose, separate conditions and generally a lower security categorization for remand prisoners.

12 Improved standards of justice within prisons involving the giving of reasons to a prisoner for any decision which materially and adversely affects him; a grievance procedure and disciplinary proceedings which ensure that the Governor deals with most matters under his present powers; relieving Boards of Visitors of their adjudicatory role; and providing for final access to an independent Complaints Adjudicator.

The government's response to the Woolf Report was published as the White Paper, Custody, Care and Justice (Home Office 1991). This was a positive document which was generally welcomed at the time. The Home Office had previously accepted all but one of Woolf's principal recommendations, the one that would have placed an obligation on the Home Secretary to seek parliamentary approval to allow a prison to hold more prisoners than it had places for. The Woolf Report and the subsequent White Paper ushered in what was to prove to be an all too brief moment of optimism in the history of prisons in England and Wales, which coincided with the enactment of the Criminal Justice Act 1991. For a short period crime was not the major political issue of the day and other matters claimed the attention of the tabloid press. The slow rise in prison numbers throughout the early 1980s began to level off by the middle of the decade and by 1991 the number of people in prison was beginning to fall. There was a positive atmosphere among those who worked in prisons and external agencies involved with them and a sense of anticipation that, after the trauma of Strangeways, a period of real reform was about to begin, typified by debates about issues such as the community prisons which are referred to in chapter eight.

The main concern of some commentators at the time was that the White Paper did not include a timetable for implementation and that, in due course, because of political priorities or for some other reason, some of the more radical recommendations of the Woolf Report would be quietly shelved. This was indeed what happened. There was a change in the political climate, with a government becoming increasingly vulnerable to attacks from the opposition about law and order issues. Most importantly, there were two high-profile escapes in quick succession from maximum security prisons and the political response to these events was quite different to that after Strangeways.

The escapes from Whitemoor and Parkhurst prisons

In September 1994 six exceptional-risk category A prisoners, five IRA terrorists and one man who had been involved in a previous armed prison escape escaped from the Special Security Unit at Whitemoor prison. All six prisoners were recaptured within a short distance of the prison. In January 1995 two category A and one category B prisoner escaped from the sports hall at Parkhurst prison on the Isle of Wight. They were taken back into custody five days later, still on the Isle of Wight. (The various security classifications for prisoners are described in detail in chapter seven.) These two sets of escapes influenced the direction of the prison service until the end of the decade.

Following the Whitemoor escapes, Michael Howard, the Home Secretary, set up an inquiry, headed by Sir John Woodcock, a former HM Chief Inspector of Constabulary, to investigate the events surrounding the escape. The Woodcock Report (1994) was published in December 1994 and included 64 recommendations on how to improve security. The Home Secretary accepted all of the recommendations. He appointed General Sir John Learmont to undertake a general assessment of prison security and, following the Parkhurst escape, extended his terms of reference to include this event. The Learmont Report (1995) was published on 27 September 1995 and contained 127 recommendations. Woodcock and Learmont focused entirely on the narrow terms of reference which they had been given and neither saw any need to frame their reports within a wider context. For them, and especially for Learmont, security was all that mattered. This was to set the tone for the management of the prison service for most of the remainder of the 1990s.

The riot in Strangeways prison at the beginning of the decade and the two escapes of groups of high-security prisoners in the middle of the decade were the most traumatic series of events in the history of the prison service in the 1990s. The fact that they were dealt with so differently had profound effects on the prison service. There were three important differences. The first was between the personalities who led each of the inquiries. Woolf was a senior judge, highly experienced in conducting inquiries and knowledgeable in the subject, who set about placing the particular events into which he was inquiring into a more general context. Woodcock and Learmont were not at all interested in Woolf's insistence on the need for a balance between considerations of security, control and justice. They were much more concerned to allocate blame for what had happened than to understand why it had happened. This was understandable, given the other two factors which were in play, but one is left wondering how different matters might have been had Woolf inquired into the Whitemoor and Parkhurst escapes and Woodcock and Learmont into the Strangeways riot.

The second difference between the two sets of inquiries was the political atmosphere of the time. In 1990/91 none of the main parties tried to make party political capital out of what had happened or how it was being dealt with. This was a period of relative confidence in the way criminal justice was organized and of political consensus. By 1995 the atmosphere had changed. The government was under considerable pressure from the opposition and the events at Whitemoor and Parkhurst presented another opportunity to score political points, as the debates in the House of Commons showed.

The third difference related to changes which had occurred by 1995 in the way the prison service was managed. At that point the Director General was a commercial businessman. As we shall see in the next chapter, his appointment had attracted considerable comment both inside and outside the prison service and he had a much higher personal profile than many of his predecessors. One consequence of this was that when the Home Secretary's personal position came under threat he felt able to divert pressure on to the Director General in a manner that would not have happened previously and which resulted in the dismissal of the latter.

The period since 1995

In the years immediately following the Woodcock and Learmont Reports the prison service concentrated its attention and resources almost entirely on security issues. The Director of Security was appointed as Director General, the first time that this post had been filled by a former prison governor.

The period covered by the late 1990s and early 2000s was marked by an increasing politicization in the use of imprisonment in England and Wales and as a consequence by a significant increase in the numbers of people being held in prison. Instead of being regarded as a place of last resort, prison became an important tool in the government's 'war on crime'. The increase in the number of offenders being sent to prison was most marked among women and children. Although relatively small in total numbers, the increase in these two groups was much more striking than that among adult males. These issues are dealt with in more detail in chapter four.

This brief look at the history of the prison in England and Wales has demonstrated what one writer has called the lack of inevitability (McLachlan 1974) about how its use has developed and how this has been driven more as a response to unexpected events, by the influence of forceful personalities or by political necessities. With this understanding, we can now go on to consider how the prison service is organized.

Further reading

Foucault, M. (1975) *Discipline and Punish: The Birth of the Prison*. Middlesex: Peregrine.

Ignatieff, M. (1978) *A Just Measure of Pain*. London: Macmillan.

Morris, N. and Rothman, D. (1995) *The Oxford History of the Prison: The Practice of Punishment in Western Society*. Oxford: Oxford University Press.

McConville, S. (1981) *A History of English Prison Administration, Vol. I*. London: Routledge & Kegan Paul.

Rusche, G. and Kirchheimer, O. (1939) *Punishment and Social Structure*. New York: Russell and Russell.

Stern, V. (1993) *Bricks of Shame*. Middlesex: Penguin.

chapter three

The organization of the
prison system

The system before 1877
The Prison Commission
Organizational dissonance
1963 to 1990
1990 to the present
Privatization
Independent monitoring and inspection
The future
Further reading

There are three main prison systems in Great Britain, those of England and Wales, Scotland and Northern Ireland, reflecting the different legal and historical traditions of the United Kingdom. In this text we are concerned with the largest of the three, that in England and Wales.

The system before 1877

The national prison system in England and Wales dates from the Prison Act 1877. Before that date local prisons, holding accused persons who had been remanded in custody to await trial or sentence and convicted persons who were serving short sentences, were generally under the control of local magistrates (McConville 1981). As described in the previous chapter, many of them were in a terrible condition and this was what had spurred John Howard and others to begin their work of prison reform (Howard 1792).

The first real steps to set up a national control of prisons came with the Prisons Act of 1835, which established five Inspectors of Prisons, whose task it was to visit every prison in the country and to publish reports on what they found. Like those of their modern successors, many of their reports were trenchant, drawing attention to the appalling conditions which they found and the lack of any proper management or structure.

From the 1840s the number of convicts being transported to penal servitude in the overseas colonies began to reduce significantly and there was a proportionate increase in those serving penal servitude in the United Kingdom. In 1857 the distinction between transportation and penal servitude was abolished and in 1867 transportation finally came to an end (Shaw 1966). Throughout this period many of the convicts who would previously have been transported were held in the former convict hulks or in separate prison accommodation and employed on public works, such as the creation of dockyards and harbours (McConville 1981). This explains why today there are prisons in places like Parkhurst, Portland, Portsmouth and Rochester. Partly in response to the criticisms of the Inspectors of Prisons and because of the need to cope with the numbers of convicts being held in this country, the government began to build central prisons, the first of these being opened at Pentonville in London in 1842. In 1850 the Directorate of Convict Prisons was established to administer these central prisons. The three successive chairmen of the Directorate were all serving soldiers: Lieutenant Colonel (later promoted to Major General and knighted) Joshua Jebb, Colonel Edmund Henderson and Captain Edmund Du Cane.

The Prison Commission

The middle of the nineteenth century was a time when national commissions were very much in vogue. In addition, the 1870s were a period when successive governments were determined to reduce the burden of taxation, particularly at a local level and this was to prove a significant factor in the creation of a national prison system, financed from central taxes rather than local rates (McConville 1981).

When what was to become the Prison Act 1877 was being debated in parliament, the government under Disraeli faced two conflicting fiscal pressures. The first was about whether to retain the relatively new system of national income tax, which was proving very unpopular and which the Conservative party had promised to abolish while in opposition. The second pressure was to reduce the burden of local taxation. The Hansard records of the parliamentary debates before the legislation was passed show that the two main arguments presented in favour of centralization were the need for an improvement in the discipline within prisons and better fiscal control (Thomas 1972). With the increasing involvement of central government in the inspection of prisons and the management of the growing number of convict prisoners, there was a strong body of opinion that if local rate payers were to be subject to this degree of central oversight they should no longer have to carry the financial burden of prisons. For political reasons this argument won the day and, despite the natural antipathy of the Disraeli government to any centralizing tendency, the Prisons Act 1877 was introduced.

The fact that a national prison system was established in England and Wales for reasons that had less to do with good prison management and more to do with public expenditure confirms the point made at the end of the previous chapter about the development of the modern prison system in England and Wales being influenced by external factors at specific points in time as much as by any coherent concept about the nature and use of imprisonment. This is a point which should be borne in mind when we come to discuss more recent organizational changes at the end of this chapter.

The Prisons Act which came into force on 1 April 1878 conferred on the Secretary of State the responsibility for every aspect of prison administration in England and Wales. He took over all the powers which had previously been vested in local justices of the peace in this respect, including the prisons themselves, the appointment of all staff and the control of the prisoners. A new body, the Prison Commission, was set up to manage all of these matters on behalf of the Secretary of State, although the latter reserved certain powers. Although the local and convict prisons retained their separate identities, within the Commission the traditions of the former Convict Directorate took precedence. Du Cane, the former Chairman of the Convict Commissioners and by then a lieutenant colonel, was appointed first Chairman of the Prison Commissioners and remained in office until 1895. During this period he retained his military commission and was, in due course, promoted to Major General and knighted. Du Cane dominated the world of English prisons throughout this 20-year period. Like many of his subordinate staff, he was an officer in the Royal Engineers. This explained the origins of the tradition of recruiting staff from the armed forces, which was to stay with the prison service until the middle of the twentieth century.

The publication of the Gladstone Report in 1895, which was described in the previous chapter, came at the same time as the retirement of Du Cane. Although he had reached superannuable age and was also unwell, the coincidence of his departure at the same time as the publication of a report which was seen as largely critical of his stewardship of the prison service has largely coloured subsequent assessments of his work. He was succeeded as Chairman by Evelyn Ruggles-Brise, the first of what was to be a long succession of career civil servants in charge of the prison system. Ruggles-Brise had strong political connections, not least of which was his friendship with his former school friend, Herbert Gladstone, who subsequently became Home Secretary in 1908 (Ruggles-Brise 1921).

The English Prison Commission lasted from 1877 until 1963. Throughout that long period there were some major changes in the organization of the adult prison system but in general terms its management did not figure high on the political or public agenda. At the start of this period prisons were places of regimentation and discipline was strictly enforced. Until the end of the nineteenth century little was expected of prisoners other than that they should do what they were told. The principles on which prisons were run were simple and easily understood by staff and prisoners. After the changes introduced when Churchill was Home Secretary they were generally regarded as places of 'last resort'; that is, they were to be used only when the court considered that it had no other reasonable disposal available. The official view of how prisoners were to be treated became more liberal after the publication of the Gladstone Report and as a result of the influence of some key individuals such as Alexander Paterson, who was a Commissioner for 25 years from 1910.

Organizational dissonance

Within a few years of centralization in 1877 there were signs that the prison service was a dysfunctional organization (Thomas 1972), signs which became stronger as years went by and which persist today. There were tensions between prisons, which were known in Home Office terms as 'outstations', and central management. Staff in prisons at all levels were generally concerned with daily operational matters, whereas the administrative and policy staff in the Home Office had to have one eye on the requirements of Ministers, Parliament and the Treasury. Some commentators attribute the tensions to the fact that from the outset the highest level of the organization was based in the Home Office, a central government department which does not have a history of managing large organizations successfully. The Secretary of State, through the Home Office, was accountable to Parliament for prisons and the treatment of prisoners. He determined penal policy and expected the Commissioners to implement it. However, the Prison Commissioners regarded their work as 'self-contained' and that they were 'primarily responsible for both the formulation and application of policy' (Fox 1952: 78).

Within a few years of the Prison Commission being set up there were complaints that administrative civil servants in the Home Office were bypassing the Commissioners. In particular, key issues affecting personnel, rates of pay, decisions about transfer from one prison to another and allocation to prison housing, were decided within the Home Office (Thomas 1972: 102–21). The Commissioners' main concern was with the treatment of prisoners, as was that of prison governors. Decisions about personnel matters were made by anonymous persons in the Home Office and were passed down the line to staff. There was little opportunity for upward communication and governors were seen to have little influence over the conditions of employment for staff. In respect of prisoners, on the other hand, both governors and commissioners were seen to be making decisions directly, often to the benefit of the prisoners. This was the start of the negative attitude towards 'management', which still persists among some staff today. These matters are discussed further in chapter five.

In the decade after the Second World War the majority of people at the highest levels in the Commission were administrative civil servants. Staff in the Commission with experience of working in prisons generally concentrated on 'operational' roles, such as that of Director of Prison Administration. Within prisons, increasing bureaucracy meant that the civilian staff who carried out administrative and clerical duties began to communicate directly with 'Head Office' rather than through the prison governor.

1963 to 1990

By the early twentieth century central government departments were becoming frustrated with the system of boards and commissions which administered many large public institutions at arms length from government. In 1914 the Royal Commission on the Civil Service expressed opposition to this system (Coyle 1991: 187). Change to the way prisons were managed came first in Scotland, where a Prison Commission for Scotland had also been set up in 1877. In 1926 the post of Secretary for Scotland was upgraded to Secretary of State. As part of the consequent Reorganisation of Offices (Scotland) Act 1928, the Scottish Prison Commissioners ceased to hold office and in 1929 they were replaced by the Prisons Department, which came under the direct control of the new Secretary of State. It had been intended to introduce parallel legislation in England but the enabling Bill of 1938 was abandoned at the outbreak of war. A similar Bill ten years later was withdrawn by the Home Secretary at the committee stage because of strong opposition (Evans 1980: 110).

The plan was quietly resurrected, tucked away in Section 23 of the Criminal Justice Act 1961. In February 1963 in the House of Commons the Home Secretary moved that the Prison Commissioners Dissolution Order 1963 should be approved. The proposal met with strong opposition in the Commons, in the press and in other circles. The government stood alone in supporting the proposal, enthusiastically backed by its officials (Evans 1980: 110). As was the case forty years later, the government majority was so large that its will was bound to be approved by parliament. This indeed happened and on 1 April 1963 the Prison Commission was dissolved. The former Chairman became Assistant Under Secretary in charge of the new Prisons Department in the Home Office.

Many critics predicted that the abolition of the Prison Commission and the absorption of the prison service into the Home Office would have a detrimental effect on the relationship between staff and the central headquarters and on the way prisons were managed. There was concern that the Home Office would simply swallow up what had previously been an autonomous and identifiable organization. Writing on this subject in 1980, Peter Evans noted:

> Though the old Prison Commission was not without its faults (some prison officers thought it autocratic), MPs defending it felt it had the overriding virtue of independence and was a depository of practical experience that won for it in its time a far higher reputation than is now possessed by its more bureaucratic successors.
>
> (Evans 1980: 112)

Over the years since the Commission was abolished, some commentators, particularly from inside the prison system, have harked back to the halcyon days of the Prison Commission, whose members 'understood what prison was about and stood no nonsense from anyone' (Miller 1976: 185). This is too simple an explanation. There is clear evidence that the morale of staff was low before 1963, although it undoubtedly suffered more after that date. In 1966 the Mountbatten report, which is described in some detail in chapter seven, identified low staff morale as a major contributory factor to the service's operational failure. Structural problems were also present in the days of the Prison Commission and it may well be that the root fault was committed in 1878 by the creation of a monolithic national service to manage prisons which were essentially local institutions. Subsequent organizational changes have tried to deal with this issue by creating four regions in 1968 and then replacing them with 12 areas in 1990 but, as will be discussed in chapter nine, it may be that the real solution is to dismantle the national prison service.

Throughout all of this time comparatively little changed in the way prisons themselves were managed. In general terms prison governors were left to govern their prisons as they saw fit, provided they observed the Prison Rules and Standing Orders. This began to alter from about 1990.

1990 to the present

The years after the Strangeways riot and the subsequent report by Lord Justice Woolf, described in chapter two, were ones of significant change in the management of prisons and the prison system. During this period all public services were subject to a new drive towards efficiency and effectiveness and the prison service was no exception. The period since 1990 has been characterized by an increasing emphasis on how the prison service is organized and on managerial process. This began in prisons before the Strangeways riot with the production in 1989 of the *Review of Organisation and Location above Establishment Level* (Home Office and PA Consulting Group, unpublished). In a debate that was reminiscent of the discussions in 1963, this review was prompted by a concern that the four existing regional directors, each with substantial support structures based in regional offices, were operating in too autonomous a fashion and were no longer under the control of the central department. The solution was to replace them with twelve area managers, who were to be based in central headquarters and to operate largely as individuals with the remit of ensuring that the edict of the centre was observed in each prison.

Area managers were given a series of 22 corporate objectives against which the performance of each prison was to be measured. This was the first attempt at creating a consistent set of performance measurements across the prison service and was a progressive development in that, for the first time, it provided prison governors with a set of objectives against which they could measure their performance and that of their prisons. Its weakness was that the corporate objectives were concerned with process, that is, with how things were done, rather than with what was being done. It also failed to take into account the variety of tasks which faced different kinds of prisons.

In 1993 the prison service was re-defined as an 'agency' of the Home Office. This was an attempt to separate the operational management of prisons, which was the responsibility of the new agency, from government policy relating to the use of imprisonment, which was to remain within the main Home Office. Until this point the post of Director General of the prison service had traditionally been filled by a senior Home Office civil servant. Having set up the prison service as an agency, the government decided that there should be an open competition for the post of Director General. The senior civil servant who had been Director General for two years was given the opportunity to apply for his own job but in the event was not appointed. Instead, a businessman who had previously been, among other appointments, the finance director at the Ford Motor Company and chief executive of Granada, was appointed to head the prison service.

The new Director General, Derek Lewis, built on the efficiency arrangements introduced by his predecessor but also moved quickly to introduce a different style of management. As part of the new arrangements introduced when it was preparing for agency status the prison service had produced a set of documents, including a corporate plan, which described in general terms what it planned to achieve over a three-year period, and a business plan, which gave details of its planned activities for the following 12 months. The prison service soon found itself with a 'statement of purpose', a 'vision', a set of six 'goals' and eight 'key performance indicators' against which achievement of its goals was to be measured.

These documents are now part and parcel of the life of prison management and are updated on a regular basis. The most recent versions (HM Prison Service 2003) are:

Statement of purpose
Her Majesty's Prison Service serves the public by keeping in custody

those committed by the courts. Our duty is to look after them with humanity and help them lead law-abiding and useful lives in custody and after release.

Principles

1 Deal fairly, openly and humanely with prisoners and all others who come into contact with us.
2 Encourage prisoners to address offending behaviour and respect others.
3 Value and support each other's contribution.
4 Promote equality of opportunity for all and combat discrimination wherever it occurs.
5 Work constructively with criminal justice agencies and other organizations.
6 Obtain best value from the resources available.

Aim

To deliver effective execution of the sentences of the courts so as to reduce re-offending and protect the public.

Objectives

1 To protect the public by holding in custody those committed by the courts in a safe, decent and healthy environment.
2 To reduce crime by providing constructive regimes, which address offending behaviour, improve educational and work skills and promote law-abiding behaviour in custody and after release.

The prison service now has 14 key performance indicators or targets which are reinforced by 45 key actions and outcomes. It has become increasingly difficult to pick one's way through the complexity of aims, objectives, targets and indicators which are set for the prison service by the government and its various departments.

In moving in this direction, the prison service was being required to adopt a much more managerial approach to running prisons and the application of many of the principles which had long been adopted in the business world. One can understand that the prison service should account for the way in which it spends public money and should be measured by how it meets the objectives which have been set for it by government. However, one disadvantage of this has been an increasing emphasis on what has become known as managerialism, that is, a concentration on process, on how things are done, rather than on outcome, that is, what is being achieved.

In April 2003 a new 'benchmarking programme' was introduced (HM Prison Service 2004) 'to improve and reward performance in the Prison Service'. This allocated every prison to one of four levels of performance and these have inevitably become known colloquially as league tables. Level four prisons are 'exceptionally high performing, consistently meeting or exceeding targets, no significant operating problems, achieving signifi-cantly more than similar establishments with similar resources'. Level three prisons are 'meeting the majority of targets, experiencing no significant problems in doing so, delivering a reasonable and decent regime'. Level two are 'basically stable, secure and providing a limited but decent regime; experiencing significant problems in meeting targets and/or experiencing major operational problems'. A level one prison is 'failing to provide secure, ordered, or decent regimes and/or has significant shortfalls against the majority of key targets'.

The benchmarking is reviewed regularly, with prisons being promoted or relegated according to how they have performed since the previous assessment. Those in the lowest category are described as 'failing prisons' and can be subjected to 'special management measures' and ultimately may be 'market tested', as described in the next section.

One benefit of the increasing focus on how prisons and the prison service are managed has been a growing recognition of the complexity of prison management. In 1991 the chief executive of British Aerospace was asked by the Home Secretary to carry out a review of the organization of the prison service. In his report he concluded that 'The Prison Service is the most complex organisation I have ever encountered and its problems some of the most intractable' (Lygo 1991: 2).

What has been added in recent years has been an increased political and public accountability. The highest profile example of this was the fall out following the escape of high security prisoners from Whitemoor prison in 1994 and from Parkhurst prison in 1995, which resulted in an unseemly tussle between the Home Secretary and the Director General of the prison service, fought out on various battlefields, including the floor of the House of Commons (House of Commons Hansard, 16.10.95, [264] col. 30–43). An added feature was the fact that the Director General at the time was the businessman who had been appointed in 1993. It is doubtful whether a traditional civil servant would have challenged a Home Secretary in such a public manner, nor indeed would a Home Secretary have hidden behind one of his officials when reporting to Parliament. The first casualty of the argu-ment was the governor of Parkhurst prison who was initially removed from his post and shortly after that resigned from the prison service. The second casualty was the Director General who was dismissed from his post in a very public manner in October 1995, although he subsequently took successful action for wrongful dismissal against the Home Secretary (Lewis 1997).

One consequence of this affair has been the reluctance of any business person since then to take on the role of Director General. Following the dismissal of Derek Lewis, for the first time a former prison governor was appointed to the post. When he retired in 1999 there was a shortage of candidates from inside or outside the prison service. In the course of giving evidence to a public inquiry, the person who was subsequently appointed claimed that he had only got the job because no one else would take it (Zahid Mubarek Inquiry, 8 February 2005, written transcript: 80–81).

Privatization

Until the eighteenth century a number of prisons in England and Wales were run for the private profit of individuals. In the course of the following century the government gradually took over the management of all prisons. When transportation to the American colonies ended in 1775, the government first responded by holding the convicts in floating prisons boats or hulks in the Thames. For a short period these hulks were placed under the control of a private contractor (McConville 1981: 106). For the next 200 years and more all prisons in the United Kingdom were under government control. It would have been as inconceivable for prisons to be in private hands as it would have been to have a mercenary army or a private police service. Over the last 20 years this situation has changed and the United Kingdom has now become what one private prison company has described as 'the second largest private correctional market in the world' (Press release: 'The GEO Group Inc. announces opening of head office in the United Kingdom', 1 December 2004).

The description 'prison privatization' is normally used to describe one of two models of prison management. The first is where the entire operation of a prison is contracted to a commercial company or a not-for-profit organization. In this case the state builds and continues to own the prison buildings and enters into a contract with the company about the way in which the prison is to be managed. Thereafter the state takes no part in the daily management, other than to ensure that contractual commitments are being met. The second model involves a commercial company taking a prison from drawing board to final operation. This includes its design, its construction, its financing and its management.

The modern notion of prison privatization in the United Kingdom was first advocated by the Adam Smith Institute in 1984 with a proposal that the government should privatize the building and management of prisons on the grounds that 'it would overcome both the spiralling costs of the prison system and the shortage of places by using innovative managerial and technological methods and by concentrating resources on capital investment rather than increased labour costs' (*Omega Report on Justice Policy* 1984).

Two years later the House of Commons Committee on Home Affairs visited two private prisons in the United States as part of an inquiry into the state of prisons in England and Wales. In its subsequent report, the committee concluded that

> the Home Office should, as an experiment, enable private sector companies to tender for the construction and management of custodial institutions ... We also recommend that tenders should be invited in particular for the construction and management of new

remand centres, because it is there that the worst overcrowding in the prison system is concentrated.

(*Contract Provision of Prisons*. Fourth Report from the Home Affairs Committee, Session 1986/87, 6 May 1987)

This recommendation was accepted by the government and enabling legislation was included in the Criminal Justice Act 1991. Shortly thereafter the security firm Group 4 was awarded a contract to manage the newly built Wolds prison, which had 320 places for male remand prisoners. The prison opened in April 1992. In February 1993 the application of the Criminal Justice Act 1991 was extended to include existing prisons as well as new ones.

The mechanism for implementing the private construction and management of new prisons, as with other public institutions, has been the Private Finance Initiative (PFI) or Public Private Partnership (PPP). While in opposition, the Labour party strongly opposed these developments. In 1995 the shadow Home Secretary, Jack Straw, stated that

It is not appropriate for people to profit out of incarceration. This is surely one area where a free market certainly does not exist . . . at the expiry of their contracts a Labour government will bring these prisons into proper public control and run them directly as public services.

(Labour gives pledge to end prison privatization, *The Times* 8 March 1995)

After it came to power in May 1997 the Labour party continued and expanded the previous government's programme of prison privatization. In 1998 the Home Secretary announced that all new prisons in England and Wales would from then on be privately built and managed. At the end of January 2005 there were 6881 people held in private prisons (see Table 3.1 for details) out of a total prison population of 74,103; that is, a proportion of 9.3% (HM Prison Service monthly population bulletin January 2005). In Scotland, one private prison holds 600 prisoners, something less than 10 per cent of the total number of prisoners.

The government has also embarked on exercises with existing prisons to 'test the market' in prison management. A market testing exercise for Manchester prison in 2000 resulted in the prison service successfully tendering against commercial companies to retain the management of the prison in public hands. As mentioned in the previous section, the government has on a number of occasions stated its intention to market test, that is, offer for private management, prisons which it considers to be 'failing'. In 2001 the market to manage Brixton prison was tested but was found not to exist when no commercial company submitted a bid (Nathan 2003). In 2005 the government announced its intention to subject three prisons on the Isle of Sheppey in Kent to a single market test.

Table 3.1

Prison/YOI	Opened	Operator	Prisoners
Public build, private management:			
Wolds	1992	GSL	390
Blakenhurst	1992	UKDS	873
(Returned to prison service management in 2001 after re-tendering)			
Doncaster	1994	PPS	1,105
Buckley Hall	1994	Group 4	330
(Returned to prison service management in 2000 after re-tendering)			
PFI contracts to design, construct, finance and manage for 25 years:			
Parc	1997	Securicor	943
Altcourse	1997	GSL	900
Lowdham Grange	1998	PPS	495
Ashfield	1999	PPS	290
Kilmarnock (Scotland)	1999	PPS	596
Forest Bank	2000	UKDS	1,027
Rye Hill	2001	GSL	600
Dovegate	2001	PPS	792
Bronzefield	2005	UKDS	407
Peterborough	2005	UKDS	840

In 1996 the Home Office published the results of academic research which contrasted Wolds prison with public sector prisons including Woodhill, opened around the same time as Wolds. The research found that

> similar and, some might argue, better achievements are to be found in some new public sector prisons, showing that the private sector has no exclusive claim on innovation or imaginative management able to deliver high quality regimes to its prisoners.
>
> (Home Office Research Findings No. 32 1996)

This research was subsequently published separately in an expanded form (James, A., Bottomley, K., Liebling, A. *et al.* 1997).

In 2001 the National Audit Office published a generally positive report on PFI prisons (National Audit Office 2001). However, a further report in 2003 was much more cautious. The second report (National Audit Office 2003) made three major points. First, the performance of private prisons in delivering what is in the contract 'has been mixed' (page 6). Some private prisons have delivered and others have not. Second, private prisons 'span the range of prison performance' (page 7). The best are better than many of the public prisons. The worst are at the bottom amongst the least well performing public prisons. Third, private prisons have brought some innovation in the use of technology and the way they recruit and use their employees but 'little difference in terms of the daily routine of prisons'.

The report concludes that the use of private prisons 'is neither a guarantee of success nor the cause of inevitable failure' (page 9).

There is an increasing literature on prison privatization, some ideological and some pragmatic, some laudatory and some critical. Examples are Ryan, M. and Ward, T. (1989), Matthews, R. (ed.) (1989), Logan, C. (1990), McDonald, D. (1990), Harding, R. (1997), James, A., Bottomley, K., Liebling, A. *et al.* (1997), Coyle, A., Campbell, A. and Neufeld, R. (eds) (2003), Posen, D. (2003). The international spread of private prisons is quite limited, restricted largely to English-speaking countries. The debate so far has been largely polarized and limited to a discussion about the contrasting benefits and disadvantages of private and public prisons. The 2003 National Audit Report concludes that there is now little to choose in practical terms between the two models.

The real issue is not about whether private prisons are managed more effectively and efficiently than public ones, or vice versa. The fundamental change which has come about with the introduction of privatization is the concept of prison as a 'marketplace' and a business which will inevitably expand. Private prisons have been introduced as a response by governments to rising prison populations, to shortage of prison places and to limited public funding to maintain existing prisons and to build new ones. The requirement that all new prisons should be provided by the private sector has meant that the financial and social costs of an increasing use of imprisonment have not been subject to public scrutiny. Many of the costs of increased imprisonment are hidden in the short term. In fiscal terms, high capital expenditure can be converted into long-term revenue expenditure, which reduces current financial costs while increasing future costs to the public purse. In social terms, the government has not encouraged public debate about why so many additional prison places are needed, being content to argue that it will provide as many places as are necessary to protect the public.

Independent monitoring and inspection

HM Chief Inspector of Prisons

By their nature prisons are closed institutions, where men and women are deprived of their liberty, largely out of public view. Yet they are managed on behalf of society as a whole and society has a right and an obligation to be aware of what is done in its name behind the walls or fences of its prisons. One way of doing this is by ensuring that they are subject to independent monitoring and inspection. This can be done through statutory or voluntary mechanisms.

We read in chapter two that the first involvement of central government in locally managed prisons came in 1835 when five government inspectors were appointed to inspect and report on the conditions of prisons throughout the United Kingdom. For the next forty or so years they published a series of critical reports describing in detail what they found and what needed to be done to put matters right. When all prisons were taken under the control of central government in 1878 the inspectors were incorporated into the prison system. Their reports were no longer published separately and their criticism became much more muted. This remained the position broadly for the next 100 years.

The report of the May Committee of Inquiry (May Report 1979) recommended, in the face of the evidence submitted by the Home Office opposing this, that there should once more be a system of independent inspection of prisons throughout the United Kingdom. This recommendation was accepted by the government and in 1981 an independent inspectorate was set up, headed by Her Majesty's Chief Inspector of Prisons for England and Wales. HM Chief Inspector of Prisons' responsibilities are set out in Section 5A of the Prison Act 1952 as inserted by section 57 of the Criminal Justice Act 1982. A similar body was established in Scotland. The statutory terms of reference of the Chief Inspector were to:

- inspect or arrange for the inspection of prisons in England and Wales and report to the Home Secretary;
- in particular, report to the Home Secretary on the treatment of prisoners and conditions in prisons;
- report to the Home Secretary on matters connected with prisons in England and Wales and prisoners in them as the Home Secretary directs; and
- submit an annual report to the Home Secretary, in a form that the Home Secretary determines, to be laid before Parliament.

The Inspectorate has the right to visit all parts of every prison at any time, whether giving notice in advance or not. It is this authority to inspect places where citizens are deprived of their liberty that sets the Inspectorate of Prisons apart from all other public inspectors. It has no executive power, being unable to order that any of its recommendations must be implemented. Over the last 25 years the Inspectorate has developed in such a way that it is now probably the best example of a national independent monitoring mechanism in the world. It was not inevitable that this should happen. Although independent of the prison service, the Inspectorate is based within the Home Office and the Chief Inspector is appointed on royal warrant on the recommendation of the Home Secretary for a five-year term of office, which can be renewed. The success of the Inspectorate can be attributed to two main factors. The first is the quality and credibility of the individuals appointed as Chief Inspector, particularly the most recent three, who have been respectively a judge, a General and a human rights activist. The second is the fact that they have developed the tradition of publishing their reports in their entirety. The most common reports are those following inspections of individual prisons. There have also been a number of reports highlighting particular matters of concern, such as suicides (1999a), health care (1996), women (1997, follow-up report in 2001), young prisoners (1997) and juveniles (2004). Although some of the reports have been complimentary, many have been highly critical and have attracted widespread media attention. The Chief Inspectors are also frequent commentators on general matters to do with prisons and penal reform.

Independent Monitoring Boards

When prisons were centralized in 1878 local magistrates were given residual powers to visit at will the prisons which served their court for the purpose of ensuring that they were being managed according to legislation. Under the provisions of the Prisons Act 1898 visiting committees were reformed into Boards of Visitors, this time with a much wider local representation, although there was still a requirement that two members of each board should be magistrates. In 2003 the Boards of Visitors were renamed Independent Monitoring Boards.

The Boards have been subject to criticism that in some instances they have identified too closely with prison staff and have ignored clear examples of abuse and improper behaviour. In some of these cases Boards have responded that they did identify abuses and drew them to the attention of the prison service or ministers, who then ignored their alarm calls. The manner in which Boards deal with complaints from individual prisoners is described in chapter six. At their best, the Independent Monitoring Boards are an expression of the British tradition of people volunteering for public service without pay in a committed and dispassionate manner.

European Committee for the Prevention of Torture

In common with the other 45 members of the Council of Europe, the United Kingdom is subject to independent monitoring of all places where people are deprived of their liberty by the European Committee for the Prevention of Torture and Inhuman or Degrading Treatment or Punishment, commonly known as the CPT. The Committee is made up of one representative from each of the member states. Inspections are usually carried out by a small number of members accompanied by one or two experts. They have the right of access at any time to any place where people are deprived of their liberty, to all documents and to interview prisoners in private. Reports are subsequently submitted in confidence to the government concerned. The custom is that the government in due course invites the Council of Europe to publish the Committee's report along with its own response.

When the Committee visited the United Kingdom for the first time in 1991 it concluded that the combination of overcrowding, insanitary conditions and lack of regime which it found in Brixton, Leeds and Wandsworth prisons amounted to inhuman or degrading treatment (CPT 1991).

In the report which the Committee published following its visit to the United Kingdom in 2001 it concluded that 'much remains to be done to achieve the prison service's objective of holding all prisoners in a safe, decent and healthy environment' (CPT 2002). It made specific references to what it had found in the prisons it visited and, for example:

- recommended that staff at Pentonville should be reminded that force should only be used as a last resort;
- expressed concern at inter-prisoner violence and bullying at Feltham YOI;
- confirmed the basic requirement that prisoners should receive at least one hour's exercise each day and expressed misgivings about the very flexible wording of the relevant Prison Rule; and
- underlined the importance of monitoring systems in private prisons to ensure that the state remains in a position to discharge all its obligations to persons deprived of their liberty.

The future

Since the nineteenth century there has been debate about the need to relate the efforts which are made to reform individuals while in prison with the experience which they face after release. In recent years one focus of this discussion has been the relationship between the prison service and the probation service. There has been general recognition of the need for much greater collaboration between them, especially to ensure that released prisoners are given appropriate supervision and support with a view to increasing the likelihood that they will, in the words of the Prison Rules 'lead a good and useful life on discharge' or, in more modern parlance, that their re-offending will be reduced.

With a view to creating greater coherence between the two services the government began to refer to them jointly in the late 1990s as correctional services and in 2003 it set up an inquiry into their organization. In January 2004 the Home Office published the report of this inquiry (Carter 2004). This recommended the establishment of a National Offender Management Service (NOMS) to replace the prison and probation services, with a single Chief Executive who would be accountable to Ministers 'for punishing offenders and reducing re-offending'. On the day the report was made public the Home Secretary also published his response in which he announced that a National Offender Management Service would come into being in June 2004 (Blunkett 2004). This duly happened and a Chief Executive, a National Offender Manager and 10 Regional Offender Managers were appointed. The Chief Executive of the service expressed the following ambition, 'The establishment of the National Offender Management Service, covering both the prison and probation services, provides us with the opportunity to achieve even more to protect the public and reduce re-offending' (Home Office 2005a: 3).

These organizational developments have raised a number of concerns. One is that they view people only as offenders, their only identifying feature that they have committed an offence. This is emphasized by the tactic of observing every other feature of their humanity through the prism of their offending. These include family relationships, accommodation needs, employment, social links, health and use of alcohol or drugs. Instead of being features of human existence these become, in the quasi-professional terminology used in some quarters, as 'criminogenic needs'. As a result of a conviction, people are transmogrified into 'offenders, and all their relations with other people are henceforth to be identified solely in terms of offending. They are no longer fathers, mothers, brothers, sisters, sons or daughters. They become 'the other', people to be dealt with, people to be 'managed in a seamless way, end to end', although it is not quite clear what this end might be.

The absence of context means that it is very difficult to discuss the potential strengths or weaknesses of the NOMS model. It has no reference point to the sort of society we are striving for and whether that is meant to be inclusive or exclusive, nor to who the offenders are and what is their place in a wider society, nor to general criminal justice issues, such as the overall fall in the rate of crime. In his 2003 report HM Chief Inspector of Probation for England and Wales referred to what he called 'signs of strain' in the probation service:

> The *Criminal and Probation Statistics* indicate that over the last decade offenders who would formerly have been fined are today receiving community penalties and, through a similar process of ratcheting up, short custodial sentences have increasingly displaced community penalties. The proportion of offenders supervised by the Probation Service, who are first time or summary offenders, has increased and the proportion convicted of serious indictable offences or who have previously been sentenced to imprisonment, has fallen. Which is to say that the Probation Service caseloads of recent years are silting up with lower risk offenders.
>
> (HM Chief Inspector Prisons 2003: 5)

Without a clear understanding of the framework within which NOMS will operate, it seems likely that this process of 'silting up' may well continue as the business of the criminal justice agencies expands. The unexpected and unexplained resignation of the first Chief Executive of NOMS in autumn 2005 has been interpreted by some as evidence of increasing high level political uncertainty about the wisdom of establishing this new structure.

Further reading

Clemmer, D. (1965) *The Prison Community*. New York: Holt, Rinehart and Winston.

Coyle, A. (1994) *The Prisons We Deserve*. London: Harper Collins.

Cressey, D. (ed.) (1961) *The Prison: Studies in Institutional Organisation and Change*. New York: Holt, Rinehart and Winston.

Jacobs, J. (1977) *Stateville: The Penitentiary in Mass Society*. Chicago: University of Chicago Press.

King, R. and McDermott, K. (1995) *The State of Our Prisons*. Oxford: Oxford University Press.

Sykes, G. (1958) *The Society of Captives: A Study of a Maximum Security Prison*. Princeton: Princeton University Press.

The prisoners

In England and Wales at the end of 2005 there were about 77,000 men, women and children in prison. Who were these people and why were they in prison?

There is a tendency to consider prisoners as a homogeneous group, defined primarily by the fact of their imprisonment. In reality, the criminal justice profile of individual prisoners is a wide one, as are their personal profiles.

Those at the edges of society

The social and economic groupings in society are not evenly represented in the prison populations. In most countries one can discover which are the marginalized groups of society by analyzing the prison population. Invariably a disproportionate number of prisoners will come from minority groups. In Australia it will be Aboriginals; in New Zealand, Maori; in Central Europe, Roma people. England and Wales is no exception to this norm. In society as a whole less than 9 per cent of the population is from an ethnic minority group (Office for National Statistics 2001), whereas

22 per cent of the male prison population and 29 per cent of the female prison population are from ethnic minorities. In addition, 11 per cent of the prison population is made up of people who are nationals of another country (Home Office 2003a).

The marginalization is not confined to ethnic groupings. In 2002 the Social Exclusion Unit (SEU) of the Cabinet Office described in some detail the disadvantaged social and educational profile of prisoners in England and Wales. The SEU reported that, compared to the population as a whole, prisoners as a group are:

- 13 times more likely to have been in care as a child.
- 10 times as likely to have been a regular truant from school.
- 13 times more likely to have been unemployed.
- 2.5 times more likely to have a family member who has been convicted of a criminal offence.
- 6 times more likely to have been a young father.

These statistics paint a disturbing picture of the personal backgrounds of those offenders who are sent to prison, demonstrating how dysfunctional many of their lifestyles are. They also indicate the complex interventions and support which are needed if they are to be helped to organize their lives in a manner which will reduce the likelihood of further involvement in crime.

The SEU also examined the basic skill levels of prisoners and discovered that:

- 80 per cent have the writing skills of an 11-year-old.
- 65 per cent have the numeracy skills of an 11-year-old.
- 50 per cent have the reading skills of an 11-year-old.

This indicates that a high proportion of people who are in prison have, in some way or another, failed within the mainstream educational system. It means that they do not have many of the skills which are necessary to survive within modern society: filling in forms or applications to register for access to health care, to apply for housing or employment benefit and so on. Far less are many of them capable of applying for and following the process necessary to find employment. In 2002 the government estimated that 65 per cent of prisoners were 'essentially unemployable in the case of 96 per cent of all jobs available in Job Centres' (Narey 2002b).

The general health profile of prisoners is also poor. This is only to be expected, given the above statistics about the disadvantaged nature of the prison population as a group. Prisoners are more likely not to be registered with a general practitioner. Many have untreated health conditions. A high proportion of them are addicted to one or other form of drug abuse. Estimates of the proportion of drug-users in European prisons vary, with suggested figures of 47 per cent in Sweden, 32 per cent in France and between 38 per cent and 70 per cent in Portugal. The figure given for England and Wales is between 15 and 29 per cent (Stöver 2002: 24–5).

The 2002 SEU report found that 70 per cent of prisoners had abused drugs before coming into prison. In the light of these figures, it is not surprising that rates of infection with hepatitis B and C, tuberculosis or HIV are also much higher than in the community. The SEU found, for example, that in England and Wales the incidence of HIV positive is 15 times higher among prisoners than among the general population.

Mental ill-health is a major problem among prisoners. The SEU found that 70 per cent of all prisoners suffer from at least two mental disorders. This was in keeping with the findings in 1997 of the Office for National Statistics that 78 per cent of male remand prisoners, 64 per cent of male sentenced prisoners and 50 per cent of female prisoners were suffering from a personality disorder (Office for National Statistics 1998).There has always been a close link between prisons and mental health institutions. As was discussed in chapter two, the nineteenth century was characterized by the construction of large institutions to take 'undesirables' out of society and to hold them in environments where they could be personally reformed by being subjected to positive experiences. Prisons and mental asylums were prime examples of such institutions and often had overlapping clients.

From the middle of the twentieth century the science of psychiatry began to move away from the principle of holding large numbers of mental patients in big institutions, often far removed from centres of population. Instead, priority was given to helping these patients to recover from their illness as close as possible to their own communities, in what was known as 'care in the community' (Scull 1984). In some cases this involved them living in small supervised units. In others it meant them living on their own with appropriate professional support. In principle these arrangements were progressive and very few people regretted the passing of the large mental hospitals, which frequently mirrored penal institutions, both in the buildings and in the regimes to which the patients were subjected. However, in many instances the reality of care in the community did not match the aspiration. The mental hospitals were closed before proper community care and support had been put in place (Barham 1992). Within a few years there was the spectacle in a number of cities of people who were clearly mentally ill sleeping rough during the night and hanging around in shopping centres and elsewhere by day. In 1999 the government became so concerned about this development that it established a body called the Rough Sleepers Unit, which is now based in the Office of the Deputy Prime Minister, to deal with this new phenomenon. It was little surprise that a large proportion of these people found themselves in trouble with the law and ultimately being sent to prison persistently for minor offences. From the time of the bridewells of the sixteenth century prison-like institutions had the role of 'asylum', that is, places of safety for the vulnerable and marginalized. This is a role which prison still fulfils and which, despite all government initiatives, it seems likely to have to continue to exercise.

In mental and emotional terms people react to prison in different ways. For some it can indeed be a place of safety, where there is warmth and security, known faces and little expected in terms of personal responsibility. For others, it can be a very frightening and disorienting place, especially at point of first entry. The Director General of the prison service (Wheatley 2002b) has acknowledged this:

> We are greatly at risk of individuals in the prison being completely dehumanized – it's a very big machine that is churning away – as individuals, they are not very important to it and they feel the weight of imprisonment at that point and it looks like a very scary world they are entering.

The feeling of loss of personal control can be felt most keenly by men and women who are already emotionally disordered. Another of the factors listed in the SEU report is that 20 per cent of male prisoners and 37 per cent of women prisoners have previously attempted suicide. Little wonder then that the incidence of suicide and self-injury in prisons is disturbingly high. This has been a matter of concern for a number of years (Liebling 1992), as is described in more detail in chapter six. The prison service has developed increasingly sophisticated formulae for alerting staff to the danger that individual prisoners might harm themselves or attempt to commit suicide but these have done little to stem the tide of deaths and self-injuries.

In 2004 there was a total of 94 deaths in prison service custody. In December 2004 the Parliamentary Joint Committee on Human Rights warned that suicides had reached 'shocking' levels and criticized the 'over-reliance' on custodial sentences which had boosted the prison population (Joint Committee on Human Rights 2004). Its report argued that increased resources and a reduction in the use of imprisonment were necessary to tackle the problem. Speaking at the launch of the report, the Committee chairperson said, '. . . throughout our inquiry we have seen time and again that extremely vulnerable people are entering custody with a history of mental illness, drug and alcohol problems and potential for taking their own lives. These highly vulnerable people are being held within a structure glaringly ill-suited to meet even their basic needs' (http://news.bbc.co.uk/1/hi/uk_politics/4093349.stm).

Remand prisoners

About 18 per cent of prisoners are on remand, awaiting trial on a broad spectrum of charges. This means that in the eyes of the law they remain innocent and should not be treated as offenders. About 20 per cent of remand prisoners are found not guilty and of those who are found guilty 50 per cent of men and 41 per cent of women receive a prison sentence (Home Office 2003a). In international terms the proportion of pre-trial prisoners in England and Wales is not particularly high. The country with the highest proportion of pre-trial prisoners is Paraguay, at over 92 per cent. Other examples of countries with high rates are India at 70 per cent, Nigeria at 64 per cent and Turkey at 49 per cent. In Western Europe, France has over 35 per cent and the Netherlands 35 per cent (ICPS 2005). These figures generally say more about the speed of the criminal justice processes and the likelihood that courts will remand accused persons in custody than they do about prison administration.

Given their legal status, which is that they have not been found guilty of any offence, remand prisoners should be treated differently from convicted prisoners. In the first place, they should have separate accommodation. There is strong justification for arguing that, since they are legally innocent, they should have the best prison conditions available. The reality is often the reverse. Prisoners in England and Wales who are detained while awaiting trial are generally taken from court where they have appeared to the nearest local prison. These prisons often suffer from the worst overcrowding in the system. The Chief Inspector of Prisons has published a thematic report drawing attention to the problems of remand prisoners and the treatment which they receive (HM Chief Inspector of Prisons 2000b).

Overcrowding brings with it several negative consequences. In the first instance, many prisoners are required to share a cell designed for single occupancy with another person who is a complete stranger. The Prison Rules say that remand prisoners cannot be obliged to work, but should be given the opportunity to do so if they wish (Rule 31.5). In practice, because of shortage of facilities and resources, most remand prisoners do not have access to many of the facilities which are available to convicted prisoners. In addition to being unable to work, their access to education will be limited, if it exists at all. An important consequence of these restrictions is that many remand prisoners have to spend the majority of each day, sometimes more than 20 hours, locked in their small cells. Chapter six provides a description of what this might involve, including sharing the restricted space with a stranger.

A further important consideration is that, unlike convicted prisoners, those on remand are not assessed for security category, unless they are perceived as being very high risk. In principle this is as it should be but in practice the result is that all remand prisoners are kept in relatively high-security conditions, regardless of the offence with which they are charged. Persons charged with shoplifting might well find themselves sharing a cell with someone who has been charged with grievous bodily harm. In all cases they will be held in prisons where they have to be escorted by staff wherever they go. They will all be subject to random drug testing, telephone calls will be monitored and correspondence may be scrutinized. It is certainly true that a small number of remand prisoners will be facing very serious charges and will ultimately be convicted of them. These prisoners may well pose a threat to the safety and security of other people and they need to be held in high security conditions. However, they will constitute a small minority of remand prisoners. The need to treat them in this way does not justify holding all remand prisoners in high-security conditions. As mentioned in chapter seven, the Woolf Report (para 1.206) recommended that, unless there was good reason for treating them otherwise, all remand prisoners should be regarded as equivalent to security category C rather than category B but this recommendation has never been implemented.

Some prisons make provision for the needs of remand prisoners to prepare adequately for their court cases. All will allow unlimited and uncensored correspondence with legal advisers and most will have special arrangements for them to visit their clients in private. A number of prisons also have schemes to provide remand prisoners with information about how to apply for bail if they have not been able to do so at court.

The general arrangements for prisoners to have contact with their families and friends are dealt with in chapter six. The Prison Rules entitle remand prisoners to receive as many visits as they wish, subject to any limits and conditions imposed by the Secretary of State (Rule 35.1). The normal arrangements are that these visits will take place in very confined conditions and will last for a very short period, sometimes little more than 15 minutes, on most weekdays. This arrangement can put an impossible strain on a young mother who might face a journey of several hours by public transport with two or more small children in tow each day, simply to sit in a large, public and friendless visiting room with her partner for 15 minutes. The problems faced by women who are in prison in respect of visits are often more acute, as is mentioned below.

Convicted prisoners

On 30 June 2003 the 53,967 sentenced prisoners in England and Wales had been convicted of the following groups of offences:

Violence against the person		11,668
including murder	3464	
Sexual offences		5283
Burglary		8922
Robbery		7197
Theft and handling		4282
Frauds and forgery		917
Drugs offences		8724
Other offences		5941
Not recorded		1002
In default of payment of a fine		31

(Home Office 2003a)

In 2001, 15 per cent of sentenced adult male prisoners and 34 per cent of sentenced females had no previous conviction. At the other end of the spectrum, 47 per cent of sentenced adult male prisoners and 24 per cent of sentenced females had seven or more previous convictions.

In the decade between 1992 and 2002 the average length of sentence increased. In 1992, 42 per cent of prisoners were serving four years or more, while by 2002 this had risen to 48 per cent. In 1992 42 per cent of prisoners were serving between 12 months and four years, while in 2002 that proportion went down to 38 per cent. The proportion serving less than 12 months also decreased slightly.

These statistics indicate that the rise in the prison population in England and Wales has been caused, not only by the fact that more people are being sent to prison, but also that people are being sent there for longer periods. One consequence of this latter fact is that the age profile of prisoners is also moving upwards. Between 1992 and 2002 the proportion of sentenced prisoners aged 30 years or more rose from 41.7 per cent to 48.5 per cent (Home Office 2003a). The Chief Inspector of Prisons reported that in 2004 the number of prisoners in England and Wales over the age of 60 had risen threefold to more than 1500 in the previous 10 years (HM Chief Inspector of Prisons 2005).

The arrangements for deciding the level of security to which each convicted prisoner needs to be subjected is described in chapter seven and the general routine which they will experience throughout their sentence is covered in chapter five.

Women prisoners

> Overall, our reports record the extent of the distress and vulnerability in the women's prison population. This is most evident in the local prisons that receive women directly from court; but managing severely damaged and self-harming women is part of the core business of all the closed prisons we inspected. It is hard to meet that level of need – as the number of self-inflicted deaths among women testifies. It is equally hard to provide a positive, interactive regime for less damaged women who nevertheless need support to overcome their difficulties.
>
> (HM Chief Inspector of Prisons 2005: 52)

In Western Europe, the average proportion of women prisoners is around 6 per cent. In Northern Ireland it is 2.8 per cent; in the Republic of Ireland 3.2 per cent; in France 3.8 per cent and in the Netherlands 8.8 per cent. England and Wales comes in around the European average with 5.9 per cent of convicted prisoners (ICPS 2005).

Prisons are primarily male institutions:

- the majority of prisoners are men;
- the majority of prison staff are men;

- the regulations about how prisoners are to be treated are drawn up with male prisoners in mind.

Given the ratio of male to female prisoners, it is understandable that the prison system is organized from a male perspective. It is important to be aware that in the real world of the prison this has specific consequences, usually disadvantageous, for the relatively small number of prisoners who are women. A report by the Fawcett Society (2004) illustrated the extent to which the prison system is designed to contain male offenders, with the result that the problems of women are not adequately addressed.

Although the overall ratio of female to male prisoners remains low, the proportionate rise in the number of women in prison in recent years has been much larger than that for men. The Prison Reform Trust (2004) reported that in 1992 there were 1811 women in prison (3.5 per cent of the total), compared to 4671 in April 2004 (6.2 per cent). Over that same period the number of women being imprisoned or on remand has increased by 252 per cent compared with a 91 per cent rise for men. The House of Commons Home Affairs Committee (2005) noted that the huge rise in the female population was largely due to a significant increase in the severity of sentencing and went on to comment that the vast majority of women are in prison for non-violent offences and have never been a danger to the public.

The profile of women prisoners is quite different to that of men. In 2002 almost one-third of all women sentenced to immediate custody were convicted of shoplifting (Home Office 2004). The majority were held for non-violent offences, with 41 per cent being held for drug offences. Some 40 per cent were serving three months or less, with almost 75 per cent serving 12 months or less (Home Office 2003a).

Over half of women prisoners say they have suffered domestic abuse (compared to one-quarter of men) and one in three has suffered sexual abuse (compared to one in ten men) (Office for National Statistics 1998: 276). Some 40 per cent of women have received help for a mental health problem in the year before imprisonment, double the proportion of male prisoners. Male prisoners have a tendency to vent their frustration, anger and fear on other prisoners, staff or buildings. Female prisoners, on the other hand, tend to turn inwards, demonstrating stress by deliberately injuring themselves or attempting to commit suicide. In 2003, 30 per cent of women prisoners deliberately injured themselves, compared to 6 per cent of male prisoners (HM Prison Service 2004), and women accounted for 14 out of 94 suicides in prisons that year. In all, 61 women have committed suicide in prison since 1990.

The imprisonment of a woman will often have significant consequences for other family members, especially since many of them are likely to have been the primary carers. The Home Office estimates that 66 per cent of women in prison have children and more than half have a child under 16. Each year, 17,000 children are separated from their mothers by imprisonment (Prison Reform Trust 2004). Just 5 per cent of the children of women prisoners remain in their own home once their mother has been sentenced (Prison Reform Trust 2000).

There is a general understanding that the closer to home prisoners can be held, the better their chance of maintaining links with their family and of reintegrating into society on release. Because of the small numbers involved, it is much more difficult to achieve this with women prisoners than with men. Most prison systems use one of two arrangements. The first is to have prisons which hold only women. The advantage of this is that in principle it will be easier in a dedicated environment to create facilities which are more appropriate for the needs of women. This can apply to the buildings and the living arrangements, as well as to resources for education, health care and work. The disadvantage is that there will only be a few of them and many of the women will therefore be held far away from their own home areas. The alternative is to have units for women within larger prisons for men. While this may allow them to be nearer their homes, it is also likely to mean that they will have access to far fewer facilities within the prison, since the needs of the male prisoners are likely to predominate.

Historically, the choice in England and Wales has been to opt for separate prisons for women. In March 2004 there were seven local prisons, six closed prisons and two open prisons for women (HM Prison Service 2004). Because of the uneven geographical spread of these prisons, one-half of all women are in prisons more than 50 miles from their home and a quarter are more than 100 miles away (Prison Reform Trust 2004). This has far-reaching consequences for visiting arrangements, for regimes within the prison and for arrangements to help the women settle after release.

It is clear even from this brief overview that the needs of women prisoners are quite different from those of male prisoners. The dilemma which faces those who try to deal with those needs within an organization which is geared to deal with male prisoners has been well documented in books such as that by Rock (1996), which charts the history of the development of the new Holloway prison in the 1970s. The design of the prison as originally conceived was based on the admirable premise that women prisoners were more in need of care and support than of coercion and restriction. As the design and building proceeded this concept changed and more traditional principles about imprisonment came to the fore. The outcome was the building which now exists, one of the largest prisons for women in Western Europe and despite the best efforts of all involved with it, remains subject to constant criticism (HM Chief Inspector of Prisons 1997, 2001; Ramsbotham 2004). While Holloway as a single prison epitomizes the problems of women's imprisonment in England and Wales, there are also major organizational issues.

Following pressure from the Chief Inspector of Prisons (1997), the prison service set up a functional department to manage all women's prisons and to develop policy to do so. In April 2004 this decision was reversed and the management of women's prisons was handed back to the geographical area managers, although a small central policy group was retained (HM Prison Service 2005: 118). These changes and their reversal highlight the dilemma of whether to manage women as a separate group of prisoners, with the danger that they are offered fewer resources than their male counterparts, or to include them in general management arrangements, with the danger that their specific needs are overlooked. As long as women prisoners are dealt with inside what will inevitably always be primarily a male environment, there are likely to be persisting and specific problems about the way they are dealt with. The final chapter of this book raises the possibility that prisons in the future might be structured and organized in a different way.

Children and young people

People can only be detained in prison if they are legally deemed to be of an age at which they can be held to be criminally responsible for their actions. The ages of criminal responsibility vary from country to country. In England and Wales penal measures are applied to children from the age of 10 years. Scotland has one of the lowest ages of criminal responsibility at 8 years, whereas in Belgium, Luxembourg and Portugal it is 16 years. Detaining children and young persons in any form of institution is usually avoided whenever possible. When the institution is a prison, detention is even more problematic. The International Covenant on the Rights of the Child has been ratified by the United Kingdom government and is, therefore, binding in law. Article 37(1) requires state parties to ensure that 'The arrest, detention or imprisonment of a child shall be in conformity with the law and shall be used only as a measure of last resort and for the shortest appropriate period of time'. In many countries children who need to be detained are held in reformatory or welfare institutions. The conditions in many of these institutions are very poor, as can be seen from a reading of the country reports produced by the Committee for the Prevention of Torture. However, they are not legally prisons. England and Wales stands apart from other European countries in respect of the extent to which it delivers children into prison service custody.

The prison system is one of the last major institutions in the country which recognizes 21 as the age of majority. Prisoners below that age are held separately from those of that age and above, who are classed as adults. As was explained in chapter two, the historical basis for this comes from the Gladstone Report of 1895, which reflected the view of the time that the best hope for young people who had strayed from the lawful path was to give them an experience as close as possible to that of a good boarding school, where they would be subjected to a rounded experience of education, giving them a grounding in basic educational and work skills, together with a sense of corporate identity, very much the notion of 'a healthy mind in a healthy body'. This led to the establishment of the Borstal system following the Crime Prevention Act of 1908. The Criminal Justice Act of 1961 reduced the minimum age at which Borstal training could be imposed to 15 years. Commentators have argued that this change contributed to a shift in the reformative ethos to one which was much more punitive and a confusion about the functions of care and control (Muncie 1999: 292).

In the years immediately after the Second World War there was a sentiment that one way of dealing with young men who were on the verge of a life of crime was by subjecting them to the experience of the military detention centre or 'glass house'. This led to the concept of the 'short sharp shock' or detention centre. The theory was that if a young man who was convicted of a first crime was given a short period of intense regimented activity from morning till night, with everything done 'at the double', the experience would give him such a shock that he would give up any idea of a life of crime. Detention centres for training young offenders between the ages of 14 and 21 years were introduced by the Criminal Justice Act 1948. The Prison Commissioners at the time were uneasy at the prospect of taking on responsibility for offenders under the age of 17 years. Previously they had been the responsibility of the Home Office Children's Department (Home Office 1984: 57). The Criminal Justice Act 1961 introduced more of a training and reformative element into what had originally been intended to be a purely punitive regime.

The new Conservative government in 1979 decided to establish a tougher detention regime in two centres. Speaking at his party conference that year the Home Secretary announced, '. . . these will be no holiday camps and I sincerely hope that those who attend them will not ever want to go back there again' (quoted in Home Office 1984: 1). An evaluation carried out a few years later by the Home Office (1984) found that, compared to the standard detention centres, the tougher regimes had virtually no effect on the future behaviour of those who underwent them.

In 1982 Borstal institutions were re-designated as youth custody centres. The Criminal Justice Act 1988 replaced the sentences of Borstal and detention training with a single sentence of detention in a young offender institution for all males under the age of 21 but not less than 14 years and for females under 21 but not less than 15 years. One reason for these changes was the introduction of a greater consistency in the treatment of young persons. Another was the removal of the indeterminate nature of the Borstal sentence. All prison service institutions holding those under the age of 21 were renamed young offender institutions. The Criminal Justice Act 1991 raised the age threshold for detention in a young offender institution to 15 years. The Criminal Justice Act 1994 increased the maximum length of detention in a young offender institution for 15- to 17-year-olds from one year to two. The Crime and Disorder Act 1998 replaced the sentence of detention in a young offender institution with a Detention and Training Order.

At the end of December 2004 there were 2203 young people aged 15 to 17 years and 8073 young adults in prisons. Young adults are defined as those between 18 and 20 years and also 21-year-olds who were 20 or under on conviction and who had not been re-classified as part of the adult population (Home Office 2005b).

For many years the vast majority of those held in young offender institutions were 18 years or over, with a small number aged between 15 and 17 years. A major change in recent years has been the significant increase in the number of those in prison service custody who are under the age of 18 years. This increase can be traced, at least in part, to a harsher sentencing climate. Also, new arrangements were introduced with the establishment in 1997 of the Youth Justice Board (YJB), which now oversees the management of all young persons under the age of 18 years who come within the purview of the criminal justice process. One of the objectives of the YJB is 'purchasing places for children and young people remanded or sentenced to custody' (Youth Justice Board 2005). From the age of 12 years a child in England and Wales may be held in a secure establishment before his or her trial and from the same age a child may be given a 'detention and training order' for up to two years. Half of this time must be served in custody and half under supervision in the community. The YJB is responsible for allocating each of these young persons to a particular institution. In doing so it has three main options. It can send them to local authority care, to secure training centres which are managed by private companies or into the care of the prison service.

Until the end of the twentieth century the prison service was reluctant to have charge of any offender who was still of compulsory school age; that is, below the age of 16 years, although it frequently held a small number of 15-year-olds. In more recent years it has prided itself on its ability to deal with damaged children who have fallen foul of the law and has sought to expand its activities in this 'business'.

Speaking at the Prison Service Conference in 2002, the Director General said,

> Three years ago at this conference the majority of people in this room ... suggested we should not care for those aged seventeen and under. I was one of those who disagreed, believing passionately that we could care for this most difficult age group with firmness and compassion so long as we got some of the significant funding from the deep coffers of the Youth Justice Board ... At every single juvenile establishment huge progress has been made. At a fraction of the cost of a place in a local authority secure unit or a Secure Training Centre, young people's lives are being changed. Those permanently excluded from school, who total 75 per cent and more of the juveniles in some of our places are getting their first ever education.

As a consequence of this aggressive approach by the prison service in competing with local authority secure units and Secure Training Centres, almost 21 per cent of all young offenders are now under 18 years. This is 3.9 per cent of all prisoners. This rate is greater than that of all other Western European jurisdictions, with the exception of Northern Ireland (Council of Europe 2003). In absolute numbers England and Wales has the greatest number of prisoners under the age of 18 years, with 2206 in March 2005 (Home Office 2005c). Some of the differences from other countries can be explained by different sentencing practices. The fact that in a number of countries offenders under 18 years are sent into a welfare system rather than the prison system is also a significant factor.

Until 1997 all male offenders in prison service custody under the age of 21 years were held together in young offender institutions. When the YJB came into being it required that all those under the age of 18 years should be held separately from those over that age. The prison service responded to this by designating certain units in some young offender institutions for this group of prisoners and in addition by designating four young offender institutions as exclusively for what were termed 'juveniles'. The YJB pays the prison service for these places and has the authority to define the standards of care to be given to these young people. It was initially quite dissatisfied with the standards in a number of instances but gradually this improved as new finance became available. A negative consequence of the improvement in the conditions for those under the age of 18 years was that conditions for those between the ages of 18 and 20 years were shown to be quite inadequate (Prison Reform Trust 2004).

The treatment of women prisoners under the age of 21 years has always been problematic because of the small number involved and there have never been any dedicated institutions for this small group. Instead they have been held either in separate units in the larger female prisons, or even simply accommodated with the adult women. In March 1999, the Home Office declared its commitment to remove sentenced 15- and 16-year-old girls from prison service accommodation, but this has not been done. The Youth Justice Board indicated its intention to remove all under 17-year-old girls from prison service accommodation during 2003 but this did not happen. Instead the government announced its intention to create five small units for girls under the age of 17 years (HM Chief Inspector of Prisons 2004).

The issue of prison suicides is dealt with in chapter six but there has been special concern about the number of prisoners under the age of 18 years who have taken their own lives. This is a problem which has stretched back for many years. The Parliamentary Joint Committee for Human Rights reported that, between 1990 and 1994, 25 children took their lives while in prison service care. In 1990 17-year-old Simon Willerton hanged himself in Leeds prison while the following year 14-year-old Jeffrey Horler hanged himself in Feltham Young Offender Institution (Stern 1998: 155). In March 2002 Joseph Scholes hanged himself in Stoke Heath Young Offender Institution one month after his sixteenth birthday. This tragic event led to a call by Joseph's mother and others for a public inquiry.

Introducing a debate in the House of Lords to support this call, Lord Dholakia described Joseph's death as 'an example of how society failed to protect a vulnerable young boy' (House of Lords Hansard, 1 April 2004, cols 1564–84). The government minister responded to the debate by saying that there were no plans to hold a public inquiry but that there would be 'a comprehensive summary of the lessons learned by the various agencies involved'. He went on to point out that

> There have been no apparent self-inflicted deaths of juveniles since that of the 17-year-old Ian Powell at Her Majesty's Prison Parc on 6 October 2002. The recent reduction in self-inflicted deaths of juveniles may be attributed to a number of key improvements for the care of juveniles. These are increased safety and a more controlled estate, coupled with increasingly active regimes, including more time out of cell and higher levels of purposeful and structured activities.

On 20 January 2005, 16-year-old Gareth Price hanged himself in Lancaster Farms Young Offender Institution, as mentioned in chapter six.

The treatment of juvenile prisoners in England and Wales has also been criticized by the UN Committee on the Rights of the Child. Speaking in November 2004, the chairman of the committee asked why Britain tolerated the unnecessary jailing of juveniles (*The Guardian* 29 November 2004). He said,

> Urgent action is required to remedy the plight of children in custody ... many children are officially classed as too vulnerable for prison service custody, and there are continuing and grave concerns about children's access to education, health care and protection. My committee recommended in 2002 that detention should only be used as a last resort, yet the UK still locks up more children than most other industrialised countries. Why is this tolerated?

This criticism echoed earlier concern expressed by the Parliamentary Joint Committee on Human Rights (2003) about the government's rejection of the UN criticism and in particular the government's acceptance of the need to incarcerate between 2000 and 3000 children at any one time and the appropriateness of holding them in prison service custody.

Life sentence prisoners

In England and Wales the increased use of life sentences can be traced to the abolition of the death penalty for murder by the Murder (Abolition of the Death Penalty) Act 1965, which introduced the mandatory life sentence for the crime of murder. In the years immediately after the act was passed the number of convictions for murder increased considerably. There was no evidence that this was because of an increase in the murder rate. Instead it was more likely that juries, which had previously been unwilling to convict an accused person of murder in the knowledge that the likely consequence would be execution, now had this inhibition removed. In 1957 there were 140 life sentence prisoners in England and Wales, in 1970 730, in 1980 1535 and in 1990 3095 (Cavadino and Dignan 2002: 31). In 2002 this figure had risen to 5150 (Home Office 2003a). England and Wales now holds the dubious honour of having more life-sentenced prisoners than the rest of Western Europe combined.

As well as an increase in numbers, there has been a constant rise in the length of time these prisoners have to serve in prison before being conditionally released. Between 1900 and 1950, the average period served by life-sentenced prisoners in England and Wales was eight years, with a few prisoners serving less than three years (HM Inspectorates of Prisons and Probation 1999). The mean length of time served by mandatory lifers released in 2002 had risen to 13.7 years (Home Office 2003a). This figure will increase in the future since the Criminal Justice Act 2003 introduced tariffs of 15 years, 30 years and whole life for a murder conviction.

Mandatory, discretionary and automatic life sentences

The steep increase in life-sentenced prisoners in England and Wales is partially a consequence of new legislation that has expanded the number of crimes for which life imprisonment is a potential punishment. Until fairly recently one could be relatively certain on coming across a life-sentenced prisoner that he or she had been convicted of murder and was serving a mandatory sentence. This is no longer the case. Since the 1950s judges have had the discretion to impose a life sentence for certain serious crimes, particularly if it was felt that the convicted person was unstable or too dangerous to be given a determinate sentence. There are now over 70 offences for which discretionary life sentences can be imposed, including serious sexual and violent offences such as manslaughter, grievous bodily harm and rape (Solomon 2004: 8–9). In 1997 the law was amended to require judges to give life sentences to people convicted of a second or subsequent, serious violent crime or sex offence, unless there are exceptional circumstances relating either to the offence or the offender (Crime (Sentences) Act 1997). According to the Home Office's most recent figures, about 30 per cent of life sentence prisoners have been convicted of crimes other than murder (Home Office 2003a).

The management of life sentence prisoners

Life sentence prisoners do not, as a whole, present disciplinary problems. They often have better disciplinary records than prisoners serving much shorter sentences. There is no evidence that prisoners serving life sentences are likely to be more disruptive or to pose a threat to good management merely because of the nature of their sentence. Frequently, life sentence prisoners are older than the mainstream population. They are often first-time offenders who have never previously committed violent acts. Typically, their victim will be someone they have known previously. Because their final date of release will, at least in part, depend on how they respond in prison, they have an interest in not causing disturbances. In England, life sentence prisoners are spread over almost half of all prisons, including a number of low security facilities.

Most life sentence prisoners begin their sentences in high-security prisons. They will then proceed to prisons with a medium level of security. In the case of what are known as domestic murderers, if it is decided that the prisoner presents little risk to the community, this may happen within a few years. Several years before anticipated release the prisoners will be transferred to a low-security prison where they will have the opportunity to leave the prison from time to time, sometimes for days at a time, as part of the final preparation for return to the community.

Authority for release

The 'life' element of the sentence for most 'lifers' is divided into two parts. The first part is served in prison. The second part, which lasts for the rest of the person's natural life, is served under supervised licence in the community. Arrangements for authority to move from the first to the second part are quite complex.

At the point of sentence the judge sets a tariff, which is the period that the offender must serve in prison as the punitive part of the sentence. Since a House of Lords judgement in 1993, mandatory lifers are entitled to be told the length of the tariff and to make representations against it (R. v. Secretary of State for the Home Department, ex parte Doody. 1994. 1 AC 531). Once the tariff period has been served, life sentence prisoners are eligible to be considered for release on parole. In the case of discretionary lifers, the Parole Board sets up a panel, chaired by one its judicial members, which conducts an oral hearing, which prisoners are entitled to attend, at which they can be legally represented and to which witnesses can be called. The Parole Board itself makes the final decision about when persons serving discretionary life sentences are to be released. These arrangements also apply to prisoners who have received an automatic life sentence under the Crime (Sentences) Act 1997, as well as to those found guilty of murder when under the age of 18 who are given an indeterminate sentence of imprisonment 'during Her Majesty's Pleasure'. Following a House of Lords judgement in 2002 (R v. Secretary of State for the Home Department, ex parte Anderson, [2002] UKHL 46), these arrangements are also followed in respect of those serving mandatory life sentences.

As well as tending to be better behaved than other prisoners inside prison walls, life sentence prisoners also tend to have lower reconviction rates after release. In England and Wales, just 9 per cent of the 1587 life sentence prisoners released between 1972 and 1994 had been re-convicted of any offence within two years. This rate is in stark contrast to the overall figures, which show that 59 per cent of all prisoners discharged in 1999 were re-convicted of an offence within two years of release (Home Office 2003a).

Early and conditional release

Very few prisoners actually serve the full sentence which is passed on them by the court. There are three main grounds for release before the end of sentence. They are automatic release, better known as remission, discretionary release, usually known as parole, and home detention curfew, a relatively recent innovation.

Automatic release

The practice of remitting part of a sentence can be traced to the time of transportation when convicts who had been of good behaviour were given a ticket of leave from their sentence (Livingstone and Owen 1999: 328). The good behaviour was calculated by a system of marks, which entitled a convict to a set number of days of remission according to his behaviour. This system was, in due course, applied to those convicts who served their sentences in England rather than in the colonies (McConville 1981: 101). The Prison Act of 1898, which has already been referred to, applied remission to local prisoners as well as to convicts.

As a reward for good behaviour, remission was originally something that was to be earned by each prisoner. Throughout the course of the twentieth century there was a gradual shift in the way it was applied until there was a presumption that all prisoners would be given remission unless their bad behaviour in prison warranted that some of it should be removed. In parallel with this, there was an increase in the length of sentence that was to be remitted. Over the years it was increased from one-sixth to one-quarter (1891), to one-third (1940) and in 1987 to one-half for all sentences of 12 months or less. From 1973 the time spent on remand in England and Wales (but not in Scotland) counted towards the length of sentence and also of eligibility for remission. These changes were largely a response to concern about the increasing prison population.

After 1948, during the remitted proportion of the sentence the released prisoner was not subject to any form of supervision in the community. The Criminal Justice Act 1991 altered this arrangement for those prisoners serving over 12 months. Since then those serving over 12 months but less than four years have been automatically released at the half-point of sentence but been subject to supervision in the community for the period up to the three-quarters point of their sentence. Those serving over four years have been automatically released at the two-thirds point but also subject to supervision until the three-quarters point. Although the release itself has been automatic, its continuance is conditional on the person not being convicted of any further offence during the outstanding period of sentence. If there is a further conviction, the court dealing with the subsequent offence may activate the remitted part of the original sentence.

The Criminal Justice Act 1991 finally abolished the term 'remission', recognizing its automatic nature. The power of the authorities to reduce remission was replaced by the power to 'add days'. The procedures for doing this are explained in chapter seven of this text.

Discretionary release

Conditional or discretionary release under a supervision licence for prisoners serving longer sentences was introduced by the Criminal Justice Act 1967. The introduction of what was known as parole was partly a pragmatic response by government to the need to manage the size of the prison population and partly an expression of the concept that the rehabilitation of prisoners could be aided by early release coupled with support in the period immediately thereafter (Windlesham 1993). The White Paper which preceded the legislation talked explicitly about long-term prisoners reaching 'a recognisable peak in their training at which they may respond to generous treatment, but after which, if kept in prison, they may go downhill' (Home Office 1965: para 5).

The parole system came into operation on 1 April 1968 and applied to all prisoners serving determinate sentences. They were eligible to be released on licence after serving one-third of their sentence or twelve months, whichever was the longer. In practice, this meant that parole applied to prisoners serving over 18 months. There was a three-tier arrangement for reaching decisions about early release. In each prison which held eligible prisoners there was a Local Review Committee (LRC). The membership of this committee had to include a probation officer from outside the prison, a member of the Board of Visitors, a prison governor and two independent members appointed by the governor of the prison. One member of the LRC and the prison governor interviewed the prisoner whose case was being considered and the committee then made a recommendation to the national Parole Board. The Parole Board considered the report from the LRC and made a recommendation for or against early release to the Home Secretary. In most cases the Home Secretary was represented by the Parole Unit within the Home Office and civil servants within that unit made the final decision. In high-profile or problematic cases the unit would refer the final decision to a Home Office Minister or to the Home Secretary himself. The function of the Parole Board was purely advisory: the Home Secretary could not grant parole without a positive recommendation from the Parole Board, but was not bound by a positive recommendation to grant parole.

This arrangement continued without any significant variation until 1983 when the Home Secretary introduced three changes to existing policy

(Hansard, Sixth Series, xlix (1983), Written Answers, cols 505–8). The first was that early release for prisoners serving more than five years for sexual, drug, arson or violent offences would be granted only in exceptional circumstances and then only for a few months before the end of sentence. Secondly, certain cases of life sentence prisoners would be required to serve a minimum of 20 years before being considered for parole. Thirdly, the minimum qualifying period for parole was to be reduced to six months.

The operation of the parole system continued to cause concern, with the judiciary being uneasy about the effect of the lower threshold, coupled with the new arrangements for automatic early release, on those serving shorter sentences. In 1987 a committee under Lord Carlisle was appointed to review the parole system. The report of the Committee (Carlisle Report 1988) recommended a series of far-reaching changes. With the exception of a recommendation that the Parole Board and not the Home Secretary should take the final decision on release of all prisoners serving determinate sentences (he retained the decision on those serving seven years or more, increased to 15 years or more in 1998), the recommendations of the committee were accepted by the government and found their way eventually into the Criminal Justice Act 1991.

In addition to the automatic release arrangements for those serving determinate sentences and the release arrangements for those serving life sentences which have been described above, the 1991 Act introduced a discretionary conditional release system for prisoners serving determinate sentences of four years or more. These prisoners were now eligible to apply for conditional release on licence for the period between half and two-thirds of their sentence. The Local Review Committees were abolished and a more transparent system was introduced. Prisoners were given the right to be interviewed by a member of the Parole Board before a decision was taken. They were also allowed to read the report of that interview and of all other documents on which the Board made its decisions, but not to know the reasons for the decision itself.

The 1991 Act entitled the Home Secretary to set criteria which the Parole Board had to apply when considering a prisoner for discretionary release. He did so in 1992 and again in 1996, when the Parole Board became an independent executive Non-Departmental Public Body under the Criminal Justice and Public Order Act 1994. The criteria place great importance on the prospect of future offending, and safeguarding the public is given a higher priority than any benefit to the prisoner. The Board is also required to take account of the prisoner's willingness to deal with his 'offending behaviour'. This is a subjective criterion, open to a variety of interpretations by those responsible for reporting to the Board. There are also specific concerns about whether prisoners who refuse to admit their offence would be likely to be granted parole. There has been a progressive reduction in the levels of eligible prisoners being granted parole since 1992 and the evidence suggests that the new guidance has had a strong restraining influence. Between 1992 and 1995, 70 per cent of eligible prisoners were given parole. This rate has since dropped to 48 per cent (Hood and Shute 2000: x).

Home detention curfew

The third type of early release is Home Detention Curfew (HDC), which was introduced under the Crime and Disorder Act 1998. Under this scheme prisoners serving sentences of three months or more but less than four years can be released up to 90 days early, either conditionally or unconditionally, depending on the length of sentence. During this period they are subject to various conditions, including a home curfew of at least nine hours a day, enforced by electronic monitoring. Decisions about release under HDC are made on the basis of risk assessments carried out by prison and probation staff. Authority lies formally with the Home Secretary but in practice is delegated to prison governors, although in at least one high-profile case, that of Maxine Carr, it was reserved to the Home Office.

Honesty in sentencing

The arrangements for early and conditional release as they currently exist are complicated. They are not easy to explain to those who are involved in them, far less to members of the public. When offenders are convicted in open court and sentenced to 12 months in prison, an observer might think that they would then go to prison for one year. In fact, there are a variety of possibilities. They will in reality only have to serve six months in prison. However, if they have already been in prison on remand for four months, they will actually serve two months and if they have been six months on remand, they will be released immediately. Since the sentencing magistrate does not explain that in court at the point of sentencing, neighbours and others will be surprised to see the person walking about free the following day. In similar circumstances, offenders sentenced to three years in prison will be released after 18 months, or after 12 months if they happen to have spent 6 months on remand, or after 9 months if they are subject to home detention curfew. The situation with longer sentences is even more complicated to explain.

All of this has led to a demand for what politicians have called 'honesty in sentencing', a phrase first use in recent times by Michael Howard at the Conservative Party conference in 1995. This implied that prisoners should 'do real time'; that is, they should serve the full length of sentence passed by the court. Supporters of conditional release have argued that it has at least two sets of benefits. The first is that it provides an incentive for prisoners to put their time in prison to good advantage by learning new skills or facing up to the behaviour which led to their offences. While prisoners should be encouraged to do this in any event, the possibility that such a response might lead to earlier release will encourage them to do so. Linked to this is the perverse incentive that if they do not obey the rules of daily living in prison they might well face the prospect of days being added to their sentence. The second benefit is that conditional release means that former prisoners will be subject to supervision in the community during the period immediately after release when they might be most at risk of committing further offences. The paradox which this creates is that a prisoner who does not conform to prison discipline or seek to improve his behaviour while in prison and who, therefore, might be the one who most requires supervision after release will not be subject to it because he has had to serve his full sentence.

Supporters of the honesty in sentencing argument respond that early release decided by the executive is an interference in the sentencing powers of the court. It undermines the credibility of the judicial process, in the eyes of the public in general and victims in particular.

What is never clarified in this argument is just what honesty in sentencing might mean. Politicians appear to suggest that what it means is that if the judge passes a 12 months sentence, then the offender should go to prison for 12 months from that date, rather than, in the example above, have the possibility of being released immediately or within a few months. If this were to happen there would be a sudden need for a significant increase in the number of prison places, a fact which politicians, at least while they are in opposition, do not regard as a problem. The truth is that, when passing a prison sentence, the judge is well aware of the actual length of time which the offender will have to spend in prison. Although periods of early release or possible conditional release should not be taken into account in individual cases, it is likely that overall tariffs do take account of this factor.

This confusion about lengths of time to be served can be traced back to the competing purposes of imprisonment which were described in chapter two. Until there is much greater clarity about these, there is unlikely to be a resolution about whether prisoners should or should not be eligible for early or conditional release.

One immediate and simple contribution to honesty in sentencing would be if there were to be a statement from the court at the point of sentencing about what the sentence might actually mean in practice. This would reduce the implication that somehow the executive was subverting the wish of the court.

Further reading

Carlen, P. (1983) *Women's Imprisonment*. London: Routledge & Kegan Paul.
Genders, E. and Player, E. (1989) *Race Relations in Prison*. Oxford: Oxford University Press.

Hoskison, J. (1998) *Inside: One man's Experience of Prison*. London: John Murray.
Liebling, A. (1992) *Suicides in Prison*. London: Routledge.
Social Exclusion Unit (2002) *Reducing Re-offending by Ex-Prisoners*. London: Office of the Deputy Prime Minister.
'Zeno' (1968) *Life*. London: Macmillan.

chapter five

Prison staff

The early days
The evolution of the role of the prison officer and the influence of
   the trade union
The role of the prison officer today
Recruitment of prison officers
Training of prison officers
Prison governors
Leadership
The other groups of personnel who work inside prisons
Diversity and equality
Further reading

Prisons are primarily dynamic institutions in which the most important elements are the human beings who live and work within them. As we saw in the previous chapter, much has been written about those who have to live in prisons, the prisoners. Considerably less attention has been paid in academic literature to the other large group of prison people, the staff who work there. There is a relatively shallow pool of research literature about their role and experiences. From North America this includes work by Kauffman (1988), which focused on staff in the Massachusetts Department of Corrections, and by Lombardo (1981). A number of works on general prison issues have dealt with staff matters in a more general context. The first of these was Sykes' classic (1958) text *The Society of Captives*, which analyzed the dynamics of Trenton Prison in New Jersey. Another important contribution was Jacobs' (1977) work on the Illinois state penitentiary, *Stateville*. Staff issues were also included in DiIulio's *Governing Prisons* (1987). Vinson's illuminating account of his experiences in the New South Wales Department of Corrections (1982) inevitably focused strongly on staff issues. In the United Kingdom the first piece of sociological research which included extensive comment on prison staff was the 1963 study by Morris and Morris, *Pentonville*. This was followed by a number of works which dealt to a greater or lesser degree with staff issues, such as King and Elliott (1980). The one British work which focused primarily on the role of the prison officer was that of Thomas (1972), *The English Prison Officer since 1850*. More recently Alison Liebling, sometimes in collaboration with colleagues, has published a number of pieces of research on prison officers, including *The Prison Officer* (2001), while Elaine Crawley has written *Doing Prison Work: The public and private lives of prison officers* (2004).

As far as the public is concerned, much of the ambivalence which it feels about prisons is transferred onto its attitude about prison staff. On the one hand, the public recognizes that the prison officer carries out an important task by protecting it from dangerous criminals. On the other hand, there is unease that the main task of the prison officer is to deprive other human beings of their liberty. What kind of person would choose to spend their working life doing such a job? Indeed, what does their job entail? Are they primarily turnkeys, whose main task is to make sure that prisoners do not escape? Is their role to deliver punishment on behalf of society to convicted criminals? Or are they social workers in uniform, whose main task is to support prisoners and to help them to become law-abiding citizens?

The majority of prison staff look after prisoners directly on a daily basis. In some jurisdictions they are described as guards, wardens or correctional officers. In the United Kingdom they are known as prison officers. In England and Wales there are approximately 25,000 of them and some will spend a professional lifetime, 30 or more years for some, working in prisons. In general terms work in prisons does not have a high public profile. It is not the sort of employment which career guidance teachers will normally recommend to school leavers or graduates. In many countries, there is a pattern of prison staff being poorly paid, badly trained and attracting little public respect. Yet in order to understand how prisons function, it is essential to know something about the kind of people who work in prisons and what they do.

The early days

We discovered in earlier chapters that the modern prison is a relatively recent invention. The responsibility of looking after those who were temporarily held in prisons was originally given to whichever low level public servant was available. The parish constable often took it on as part of his general duties, with his wife providing food for the prisoners, often only on payment. Very often the fees paid by prisoners were the main source of income for jailers (McConville 1981). In the 1830s the newly appointed Inspector of Prisons for Scotland found that the jailer of Alloa combined his duties with that of chimney sweep and commented, 'Judging from his appearance, I should presume that he carries out an extensive business'. In nearby Linlithgow, the Inspector discovered that the jailer was a blind man (Coyle 1991: 25).

The beginning of the modern prison system in England and Wales came with the setting up of the Convict Prison Commission in 1850. The Commissioners were mainly military officers, often from the Royal Engineers, and not surprisingly they recruited former soldiers to be convict guards. This tradition continued when the Prison Commission was set up in 1877. The deliberate intention of the first Commissioners was to eliminate the disorder of the former local prisons and to create a highly regimented structure. For this reason it made a great deal of sense to recruit former military men, particularly non-commissioned officers who would be accustomed to arranging large groups of men in an orderly fashion. This tradition remained until well into the twentieth century.

Throughout this period prisons remained largely secretive places, with little public attention paid to the way they were organized. As a consequence, not much was known from external sources about the staff who worked in prisons. Different groups of interested commentators had differing views about them. The daughter of a Scottish prisoner described them as being 'specially chosen from the army, the police force and from mental hospitals, for their hardness and brutality' (Milton 1973: 126), while the Chairman of the Prison Commissioners wrote of the same period that 'discipline with kindness is the watchword of our Prison Staff' (Ruggles-Brise 1921: 10).

What was clear throughout the nineteenth century and the early part of the twentieth was that the task of the prison officer, or warder as he was then known, was solely to supervise prisoners: to make sure that they did not escape and that they were always where they were meant to be, doing as they were instructed. Prison staff were forbidden to have any conversation with prisoners, other than to issue necessary instructions. This philosophy was based partly on the hierarchical structure of the prison system and also on a fear on the part of senior staff that 'in a community of wrongdoers (the prison officer) is open to corruptive influences' (Grew 1958: 187). The mistrust of junior staff by senior management was a theme which was to permeate the prison system and to lead to many of the tensions which still exist today. It also created an environment in which staff were discouraged from using any initiative and urged to concentrate solely on ensuring that nothing went wrong. This led a committee of inquiry into the pay and conditions of service of prison staff in 1923 to observe of the prison officer that it was 'especially impressed with the monotony of his life' (Stanhope Report 1923: para 11).

The first suggestions that the role of the prison officer might become more than that of a simple turnkey or guard came with the introduction of Borstal institutions in the early twentieth century, as described in chapter three. From the outset Borstal officers were expected to get to know the 'boys' under their care and to help them to develop skills to cope with life after their release. The Borstal officers were required to work closely with the house masters to create a positive atmosphere within their 'houses'. Some staff were recruited directly to work in Borstals. Others were transferred from prisons. As staff were promoted, they were appointed on an interchangeable basis between the two types of establishment. In the early years prison staff tended to look down on Borstal staff, regarding their work as not being equal to the hard task of working with difficult adult prisoners. The reality was that work with problematic young men was every bit as demanding as working with adults, sometimes more so. While it would not be true to say that the ethos of the Borstal officer, with his civilian clothes instead of a uniform and his less regimented attitude, ever permeated the adult prison, it did introduce the possibility that staff could work more proactively with prisoners.

The first half of the twentieth century was marked by the introduction of a variety of specialist staff into the prison service. They included welfare officers, work instructors, teachers, psychologists and assistant governors. These staff were recruited as a result of the increasing emphasis on the principle of rehabilitation or reform of prisoners so that they could be prepared to live law-abiding lives after release. For many prison officers, the recruitment of these new staff merely served to emphasize that their own task remained primarily a custodial one. They were there to do the difficult work, to ensure discipline and to impose control and to inflict punishment when required. The view of the wing principal officer that, if a prisoner was to be given bad news, he would be the one to convey it, but that if the news was good, the assistant governor or welfare officer would arrive to pass it on, may have been cynical but it was not always far from reality.

Throughout all of this period there was a growing dichotomy between what was said officially about the role of the prison officer and what in practice he was expected to do. J. E. Thomas refers to the developments as 'crystallising a conflict' (Thomas 1972: 162). Throughout the early twentieth century official rhetoric emphasized the importance of providing prisoners with opportunities for reform. This was driven by a number of charismatic persons at the most senior level. As was discussed in chapter three, one of the most important of these was Alexander Paterson. Following the introduction of the Borstal system there was a growing belief that adult prisoners also could be reformed by the experience of imprisonment if only they were subjected to the correct pressures. This was to be achieved by two main initiatives. In the first place the absolute regimentation of the prison was to be modified and prisoners were to be treated in a more humane manner. For example, the requirement for close cropped hair was abolished and prisoners were allowed to talk and to mix with each other. Secondly, the new staff were to work with prisoners during the day in classrooms, workshops and interview rooms to help them develop their personalities and skills.

The consequences for prison officers were also twofold. In the first place, they felt that their tasks of controlling the prisoners, minimizing the risk of escape and ensuring that there was always good order, were made considerably more difficult by the changes which were being implemented by senior authorities who, at least in the eyes of the officers, knew very little about the reality of daily life in a prison and the need to maintain firm discipline. Secondly, officers felt that their role was undervalued by governors and senior administrators. A distinction was drawn between the men (and in those days they were almost all men) 'in suits', that is civilian clothes, and those in uniform. There were two groups in uniform: the prisoners and the prison officers. Officers often felt that senior staff drew little distinction in their attitude to them and to the prisoners.

The evolution of the role of the prison officer and the influence of the trade union

The defining feature of all modern prison systems is the relationship between prison officers and the prisoners for whom they are responsible. The uniformed staff unlock prisoners in the morning and lock them up last thing at night. In between these two moments, they deal with prisoners when they are at their best and at their worst, at their strongest and at their weakest. There is a relationship of mutual dependency between prisoners and prison staff. One group cannot exist without the other. Their joint behaviour dictates whether the prison has a humane or an inhumane environment. On a day-to-day basis what makes prison life either tolerable or unbearable for prisoners is their relationship with staff.

Prison staff often regard themselves as the forgotten members of the criminal justice system. They do not have the public profile of judges, prosecutors or members of the police service. In many countries prison staff are poorly trained, badly paid and have little respect in their communities. Even in the United Kingdom until very recently there was a reluctance on the part of some prison staff to let neighbours or friends know where they worked. It was almost as though some of the guilt of prisoners rubbed off onto the prison staff. This ambivalence on the part of prison staff about the value of their work was exacerbated by their symbiotic relationship with governors and senior management described above. This malaise at the heart of the work of the prison service was identified in the Woolf Report which commented on:

i) the high calibre and deep commitment of the majority of Prison Service staff at all levels. They have an immense sense of loyalty. They have a warm sense of camaraderie with their colleagues. They want to see improvements within the prison system; and

ii) the dissension, division and distrust which exist between all levels of Prison Service staff. They labour under a blanket of depression.

They lack confidence in the value of what they do. They harbour a deep sense of frustration that the effort which they are devoting to the Service is not appreciated.

(Woolf Report 1991: para 12.1)

One result of this 'dissension, division and distrust' has been that since the early years of the twentieth century prison officers have turned inwards, looking for support not to management but to their trade union, the Prison Officers Association, the POA. The antecedent of the POA was the clandestine National Union of Police and Prison Officers, which had been set up illegally in 1914. Following industrial action by some police and prison staff in 1918 legislation was introduced which forbade police and prison staff to strike and the Police Federation and the Prison Officers Representative Board (PORB) were established as in-house consultative bodies. From the outset there was a strong current of opposition to the PORB on the part of some staff and in 1920 the unofficial *Prison Officers' Magazine* came into being under the editorship of a former prison officer who used the pseudonym E. R. Ramsay.

Ramsay became a folk hero to an earlier generation of English prison officers. His influence on them, and ultimately on the prison system, was enormous. He became the mouthpiece of staff discontent, and built their grievances into a staff culture. He set the tone of the *Prison Officers' Magazine* for all time.

(Thomas 1972: 146)

Finally, in 1938 official approval was given for the foundation of the Prison Officers' Association to replace the largely discredited PORB. The experience of the early years has affected the way the POA has represented its members ever since. Although the POA members who now consult their leadership in the union's offices in Cronin House, named after a long-serving general secretary of the association, may not know of the struggles of the 1930s and 1940s, the legacy of that period has burrowed deep into the psyche of the association and its membership and even today affects its relationship with senior management in the prison service.

In the absence of much job satisfaction, of acknowledgement from the public for the service which they carried out or of respect from senior management, over the years the POA concentrated efforts on behalf of its members on improving pay levels and safeguarding conditions of employment. Traditionally, prison officers have sought parity of pay with police officers. Yet in the eyes of the public and of the government prison staff lag well behind the police in terms of status and public recognition. Successive committees of inquiry have refused to place prison officers' pay on a par with that of police.

Throughout the course of the 1970s there was ongoing conflict, sometimes at national and at other times at local level, between prison management and the POA. In some prisons the POA committee virtually constituted an alternative management for the prison. One of the techniques used by prison staff to get round what they regarded as their low level of basic pay was to find opportunities for high overtime payments, often with the collusion of local management. Industrial relations broke down in late 1978 when the POA threatened widespread industrial action. The Home Secretary responded by setting up the May Committee of Inquiry. In its Report in 1979 the Inquiry drew attention to the multiplicity of over-time and other payments made to prison staff through what were known colloquially as 'Spanish practices' (King and McDermott 1995: 29).

The May Report did little to resolve the underlying problem of staff pay and by the mid-1980s almost one-third of the prison service staff pay bill was spent on overtime (Coyle 1991: 139). This was a situation which satisfied no one. Officers were discontented that they had to work such long hours in order to take home what they considered to be a decent rate of pay. At the same time, management were faced with an arcane set of working practices which guaranteed virtually unlimited overtime in some prisons and no flexibility in the allocation of staff. The situation could not continue and in 1987 a new structure for pay and conditions of service called Fresh Start was introduced. This abolished all overtime payments, increased basic salaries and unified the former separate grading structures for prison officers and governors into a single structure. This new structure was at first opposed by the POA but management refused to be moved and in due course the changes were accepted. Some commentators (Wilson and Bryans 1998: 11) have argued that since that point the power of the POA has been significantly reduced.

In many respects the manner in which the POA developed over the years is a case study in poor industrial relations. Twenty-five years after it was officially recognized the authors of one of the first sociological studies of an English prison were in no doubt about its negative influence:

> The characteristics of the POA at a national level are such as to create for prison administrators a stereo type of conservatism. The Associ-ation tends to be exceptionally suspicious of change, authoritarian in its penal views and given to tenacious bargaining over comparatively small details. Above all, it is a militant association.
>
> (Morris and Morris 1963: 217)

Yet, this gives only one side of the picture. The prison service was not the sort of organization which by its nature attracted militant left wingers and wreckers. The men and women who joined the prison service were, and remain, broadly speaking, people with a sense of public service who were seeking a secure form of employment. That many of them subsequently resorted to industrial action through their trade union says as much about the management of the prison service as it does about staff. A report by a senior businessman in 1991 into the management of the prison service concluded, 'Difficult unions fill the vacuum left by ineffective management and all managements are ineffective if they are not allowed to manage'

(Lygo 1991: 6). In writing this, Lygo was pointing to the fact that the national management of the prison service was located in the Home Office, which imposed a bureaucracy and centralization on individual prisons which made them difficult to manage efficiently. Reference was made to this in chapter three.

It would be wrong to dismiss the role and influence of the POA as entirely negative. Over the years the senior echelons of the union have included a number of individuals who contributed positively to the development of the prison service. In 1963 the POA published a memorandum entitled 'The Role of the Modern Prison Officer'. This was one of the first real attempts to analyze the role of the prison officer and to present a vision of what this might become in the future. In some respects this document was ahead of its time but its detailed proposals were never likely to have the wholehearted support either of all its members or of the Home Office. Thomas (1972: 208) suggested that the main motivation for producing the memorandum was as an attempt to prevent the erosion of the status of the prison officer as more and more specialist staff were being introduced.

The poor state of industrial relations which continued through the 1980s and early 1990s led to the enactment of Section 127 of the Criminal Justice & Public Order Act 1994 which banned prison officers from striking. In subsequent years relationships between the POA and prison management, especially at national level, improved. The two sides agreed a legally enforceable voluntary collective agreement that precluded prison officers from inducing or taking part in industrial action. In March 2005 the government obtained parliamentary approval to disapply Section 127 of the 1994 Act and restored full trade union rights to the POA.

The role of the prison officer today

At the beginning of this chapter we posed the question as to what kind of person would choose to spend his or her life locking up other human beings. We also need to turn this question on its head and to consider the kind of person to whom society would wish to entrust the task of locking up other human beings. The answer to this question depends on what we decide the key features of this task should be. The task of the teacher is to educate young people; the task of the nurse is to help people to maintain good health and to help them to care of themselves when they are ill. What is the task of the prison officer? The fact that it is difficult to give a clear and unambiguous answer to this question is a reflection of the fact that, as was discussed in the early chapters of this book, society remains uncertain about the purpose of imprisonment.

Until the beginning of the twentieth century the task of prison staff was relatively straightforward. It was to guard prisoners in such a way as to prevent them from escaping and to ensure that they behaved in an orderly fashion throughout the course of their imprisonment. In order to carry out this task the prison system needed to recruit people who would be meticulous in carrying out what was a very mundane set of duties, who would be capable of imposing strict discipline and who would themselves obey orders without question. Former members of the armed forces fulfilled these requirements very well. The fact that many of the senior personnel in the prison system were former military officers added to the logic of filling the ranks of the prison guards with former 'other ranks'. Throughout this period also there was a steady supply of soldiers and others who were looking for work as their period in the armed services came to an end.

During the middle five decades of the twentieth century the basic skills required of the prison officer became increasingly difficult to define in a simple manner. This was exemplified with the change of title from 'warder' to 'prison officer' in 1921. According to the *Oxford English Dictionary*, the word 'warder' derives from the old French word meaning 'to guard', making the attached responsibility quite clear. The title 'prison officer' carries no comparable clarity. The former tasks of guarding and imposing good order remained but there was also an attempt to introduce the concept that staff should in some indefinable way be responsible for reforming prisoners. The lead in this work was to be taken by the new groups of staff mentioned above but it was recognized that prison officers also had to be involved in this work. Writing in 1930, Alexander Paterson described the qualifications required of a prison officer as 'an aptitude for leadership, a desire for service, a private life above suspicion, and sufficient intelligence to understand the guiding principles and grasp the details of a penal system' (Ruck 1951: 103). Some twenty years later the Chairman of the Prison Commissioners defined the qualities which the prison system required in its officers as 'Humanity, fairness, self-responsibility, self-control and complete integrity' (Fox 1952: 160).

Despite the high personal qualities demanded of those who were to become prison officers, there was never any real clarity on the part of the authorities about how the reforming role of the prison officer was to be achieved. Inevitably this led to confusion on the part of the staff about what was expected of them. It was suggested that the two strands of the work of the prison officer, security and control on one hand and reformation of the prisoner on the other, were incompatible. In principle that did not have to be the case as the two functions could have been placed within a single context which showed that they were complementary rather than in competition with each other. In practice, the absence of a clear definition about what the two functions involved and the relation between them resulted for a long time in a perception that it was impossible to maintain a balance between them.

In recent years, in addition to focusing on specific elements of the prison officer's work, there have been attempts to analyze what have been described as the qualitative aspects of the work. One of the most important of these has been that of Liebling and Price which set out to produce an 'appropriately sympathetic analysis of the often neglected or stereotyped prison officer' (2001: 1). This 'sympathetic analysis' was based on field-work carried out by the writers over a number of years in several prisons, using what they termed a process of appreciative inquiry into the work which prison officers actually do. The research confirmed the centrality of the relationship between prisoners and prison staff.

The authors observed that in inward-looking institutions, like the prison, small matters of detail assume a significance far in excess of what would be usual in more normal societies. A consequence is that members of these institutions develop a finely tuned awareness of what is fair and what is not. This applies in the prison setting and prisoners place a high import-ance on consistency in their dealings with staff. The unpopular prison officer is not necessarily the one who is the strictest nor the most lenient. The unpopular officer is the one who is inconsistent; saying 'Yes' one day and 'No' the next in very similar circumstances. Expressing this in the language of everyday human relationships, what the authors point out is that the good prison officer is one who treats each prisoner as an individual and as a human being rather than as a cog in a machine.

Within this context Liebling and Price identify one of the significant skills of the good prison officer as being a regular underuse of power and instead a concentration on using discretion in many situations. They iden-tified the importance of this discretion being exercised in a consistent manner. Conscious decisions have to be made on a daily basis about which rules to insist on and which to overlook. This is not to say that staff will simply avoid confrontation by avoiding application of rules but rather that the good officer appreciates that more can be achieved by sensible decisions about when to enforce compliance with rules and when not to do so. In many respects what the authors have discovered is that the rules which govern normal life for all of us, what they call the trad-ition of good relationships, are no different in the prison setting. Liebling has gone on in a subsequent publication (2004) to expand her arguments about what she calls the 'moral performance' of prisons and prison staff. What she seeks to do in her work is to provide a counterbalance to meas-urements of the work of the prison officer which apply merely quantita-tive criteria.

This broad theme of attempting to get under the skin of what work in prison involves has been continued by Crawley (2004) in her attempt to go beyond a description of what constitutes the work of prison officers in order to analyze the emotional demands which they face as they go about their daily duties. She concludes that prison officers are 'a very hetero-geneous group, and they respond to the demands and pressures of their work in very different ways' (2004: 252). She also reaches a dispiriting but not entirely surprising conclusion about the difficulty of prison officers achieving their desire to 'make a difference', given the day-to-day pres-sures caused by overcrowding, lack of training and lack of support by senior management.

Recruitment of prison officers

The difficulty of resolving tensions between the various demands made of the prison officer is reflected in the prison service recruitment literature, which describes the role of the prison officer as 'a complex challenge, balancing authority with a large amount of understanding and compassion'. It goes on to say:

> As a Prison Officer you will be expected to undertake varied duties and tasks, such as:
>> Carrying out security checks and searching procedures
>> Supervising prisoners, keeping account of prisoners in your charge and maintaining order
>> Employing authorised physical control and restraint procedures where appropriate
>> Taking care of prisoners and their property, taking account of their rights and dignity
>> Providing appropriate care and support for prisoners at risk of self harm
>> Promoting Anti-Bullying and suicide prevention policies
>> Taking an active part in rehabilitation programmes for prisoners
>> Assessing and advising prisoners, using your own experiences and integrity
>> Writing fair and perceptive reports on prisoners.
>> (http://www.hmprisonservice.gov.uk/careersandjobs/
>> typeswork/prisonofficer)

In many countries the task of the first-line prison officer is still regarded solely as custodial and a large proportion of new recruits may be former members of the armed services, enhancing their army pension by working as prison guards. In a number of countries in Eastern Europe there is still compulsory national service and it is possible to fulfil this by working as a prison guard for one or two years, an option which can be seen as less hazardous than being sent as a soldier to patrol dangerous borders. In this case the conscripts are often little more than teenagers, younger than many of the prisoners of whom they have charge. In these circumstances there can be a complete turnover of guards every two or three years.

These considerations do not apply in the United Kingdom but there may be other ones at play. The historical desire of prison staff to equate their duties with those of the police has already been referred to. In some instances people who have been unsuccessful in an application to work in the police service turn to the prison service as a second-best option and this is likely to influence their attitude to their future work.

Another important consideration when it comes to recruiting prison staff is the geographical location in which they will be working. Not many prisons are built in high amenity areas or within communities where there is high employment. The large local prisons that were built throughout the country in the Victorian era are often in what are now depressed inner city environs. People who live in the local disadvantaged communities would not normally consider a career in the prison service and those from elsewhere are often reluctant to travel to work in what they might regard as a threatening environment. Other prisons were deliberately built far from centres of population in order to emphasize the separation of the prisoner from his or her community. Dartmoor prison, still very much in use today, was built in the early nineteenth century on a Devon moor, far from centres of population, to house French prisoners of war. The same principle applied almost two centuries later to the construction of Whitemoor prison in the Cambridgeshire fens. The Scottish equivalent is Peterhead prison, built in that part of Scotland which stretches furthest into the North Sea. It holds prisoners who come mainly from the highly populated urban areas of the country many miles to the south, while the majority of staff come from the local farming and fishing communities. This arrangement is typical in many other countries. One of the main maximum security prisons for the state of New York is in the small town of Attica close to the Canadian border. The vast majority of the prisoners held there are black urbanites from New York City, hundreds of miles to the south, while the staff are predominantly of white farming stock from up-state.

In more recent years, the location of a new prison may be determined not by the concept of exiling prisoners but by the need to provide local employment. In Sweden, a maximum security prison was built in Kumla because the government was concerned by the need to find alternative employment for the men of the local community who had been made redundant when the shoe-making factory and the railway engineering workshops closed down (Coyle 2002a: 83). In England, the prison which opened in Doncaster in 1994 recruited many people who had previously worked in steel making, while the prison which opened in Bridgend in Wales in 1997 recruited staff made redundant from the mining industry.

A series of circumstances such as this, in which people work in prison either by default, or because they were previously in the armed services, or because they have failed in their desire to work in the police force, or simply because there is no other work available, and in which there may be a cultural divide between prisoners and prison staff does not suggest that the prison service has a clear notion of the kind of people that it wishes to recruit as first-line prison staff. In the situation where the new prison personnel had originally wanted to have jobs, such as policemen or women, which would give them respect in their communities or where they were already feeling devalued at being made redundant from their previous skilled jobs they would not necessarily come to their new role of prison officer with a sense of vocation or of being involved in an important public service.

Further proof that the prison service has no clear picture of the kind of people it wishes to recruit is to be found in the virtual absence of any requirement that they should have prior qualifications. In England and Wales new recruits to the prison service, aged between 18½ and 57 years, are not required to have any academic qualifications, while in Scotland they need to have five passes at Standard grade or three years' experience of managing people. Applicants attend an assessment centre to take part in a series of exercises designed to replicate situations that may arise in a prison environment, as well as medical, eyesight and fitness tests. After personnel have been recruited and selected, they then have to be properly trained.

Training of prison officers

If one accepts that work in the prison system is indeed a form of public service, this will affect the nature of the training that is to be given to staff. One option is to relate the training of prison staff to that given to public servants in similar fields of work. In the Netherlands, for example, the National Agency for Correctional Institutions trains its prison staff by using the standard vocational training available in general public service training facilities and educational institutes. This means that prison officers get approximately the same type of training as people working in mental health care or with child care or other social services. This has the added benefit of making the work of the prison officers a more respected job and more comparable with these other professions. This is not to suggest that the work of the prison officer is exactly the same as that of the mental health nurse, the teacher or the social worker. There are specific elements, such as the requirement to be conscious of security considerations, which make the role of the prison officer unique; but these special features are considered within the context of those other features which are common to people working in similar professions.

In contrast to this arrangement, there is little read across in England and Wales in the training given to recruits to the prison service and to those being trained for work elsewhere in the caring professions. In most of these professions new staff have to spend between two and three years in training and satisfy a process of assessment or examination before they are regarded as being fully qualified. Until the late 1990s the period of initial training for new recruits to the prison service was eleven weeks. In response to the urgent need to recruit additional staff to supervise the increasing numbers of prisoners, the initial period of training was then reduced from what might have been thought of already as a minimal period to eight weeks. Some of this training takes place in the Prison Service College and some in prisons. During this initial training some attention is paid to the development of interpersonal skills but in the short time available the main emphasis is on matters of security and discipline and on training in the techniques to control violent prisoners which are described in chapter seven.

In 1999 the International Centre for Prison Studies carried out a review on behalf of the Prison Service of England and Wales of the induction training given to newly recruited prison officers. One of the most important conclusions of this review was that there was a lack of clarity about what staff were being trained for (Coyle 2002a: 82). What was discovered was that the individual elements of the training course were very well delivered by the different groups of tutors but that there was little overall concept of what the fundamental role of the prison officer was. This confirms the comments in the previous section about uncertainty surrounding the task of the prison officer.

After eight weeks training the newly minted officers are sent to a prison to begin to supervise prisoners. The officer might be sent to a Victorian local prison, to a training prison built in the 1970s, to a dispersal prison, to a prison for women or to a prison for young offenders, some of whom will be no more than children. While it is true that the work of the prison officer has many generic features which remain the same wherever he or she is working, there is also a wide variety of skills that are specific to particular settings. The challenges of working with young prisoners are different in many ways from those which are required for working with women prisoners. The approach required of staff in a low-security prison is quite different from that in a high-security prison. Much of the initial training given to staff is aimed at the majority who will work with adult male prisoners with, at best, a short session or two given to the special skills needed for working with other groups. Working in maximum security prisons holding adult males who are serving long sentences for serious crimes often carries a special cachet and is regarded by many staff as the most demanding form of work. In some instances this may be the case, but it is frequently the case that a much higher level of skill is required to work, for example, with volatile young offenders who find it very difficult to cope with the fact of their imprisonment or with abused and damaged women prisoners, some of whom are determined to injure or even kill themselves. However, work with these groups of prisoners does not attract the same glamour as working in a high security prison. No specialized training is given to staff before they are sent to these very different working environments.

In theory the new prison officers are given further training in the specific requirements of working in a particular setting once they arrive in their first prison. They are, in theory, under supervision for the remainder of their first year. During that period their performance is assessed by senior staff and the prison's training officer has a duty to ensure that they are given appropriate support and guidance. In reality operational pressures will invariably take priority over any training demands and new staff gather their coping skills by working alongside more experienced staff.

As it took evidence for its inquiry into the arrangements for providing education for prisoners, the House of Commons Education and Skills Committee became increasingly concerned to learn that prison officers were expected to undertake their complex tasks with only eight weeks initial training and very little development training thereafter:

> The initial training period of 8 weeks for prison officers is totally inadequate. The Government must encourage the development of prison officers if prison staff are to be expected to encourage the development of prisoners. The initial training period must be significantly increased to a level that reflects an appropriate investment to enable prison officers to play a key role in the education and training of prisoners. Furthermore, prison officers should have an equivalent entitlement to training and development once they are in post.
> (House of Commons Education and Skills Committee 2005: para 329)

Since the year 2000 the prison service has encouraged staff to take National Vocational Qualifications in 'custodial care'. These have been approved by the Custodial Care National Training Organisation, a body which represents employers, both public and private, in the 'custodial care sector'. There are now over 60 units of study at NVQ levels two and three, which are intended to provide staff with the knowledge and skills needed to reach the required professional standard in their work.

The sad reality is that in recent years the pressure on everyone in the prison service to cope with operational pressures such as overcrowding, coupled with the demand to meet an increasing number of procedural targets, has meant that staff training has been given a much lower organizational priority. This has consequences for the short term and for the staff who are immediately affected. It also has more fundamental implications for the organization itself. As long as men and women, however well-intentioned they may be, with no required prior qualifications can be recruited and can begin work after only eight weeks basic training, it will be impossible to argue that the role of the prison officer is a professional one. This is singularly unfortunate as the role is undoubtedly a challenging and demanding one.

Prison governors

We have already made several references to the fact that the prison is a hierarchical institution. At the top of that hierarchy is the governor, a person appointed in terms of The Prison Act 1952 to be in charge of each prison. In earlier chapters we learned how the role of the governor developed from the mid-nineteenth century. In some respects this role has changed significantly as time has gone on. There is much less autonomy now than even a relatively few years ago, with governors having to meet increasingly detailed central demands on a wide range of issues affecting the daily management of prisons and having to report to area managers and national headquarters on performance. There is also constant oversight

from internal auditors and external inspecting bodies. Despite this centralizing tendency, the 'role of the governor in creating and shaping a good
prison is crucial' (Wilson and Bryans 1998: 137).

Even allowing for the increased involvement of central management,
governors as individuals can set the tone of an entire prison and more
fundamentally their method of governing can determine whether a prison
is a place of decency, humanity and justice. Time and again the response of
the prison service to critical reports on prisons from the Chief Inspector has
been to remove governors who are thought to have failed in their task and
to bring in new governors with the express instruction to 'turn the prison
round'. This tactic can be used excessively and there have been examples
where new governors have not been able to effect any improvement. The
most successful governors today are those who can combine the skills of
management and of leadership. Neither on its own is sufficient; both are
necessary.

Good management

Until relatively recently few prison governors regarded themselves as
managers of what are often large and complex organizations. The auto-
biographies written by former prison governors in the twentieth century
have tended to portray their authors as charismatic individuals, who
knew by instinct how to govern (for example, Rich 1932, Grew 1958
and Miller 1976). By the end of the twentieth century, however, percep-
tions were changing and it gradually became accepted that modern
prison management requires a high degree of professional skill and
awareness.

In public sector organizations in many countries the last decade or so
has been marked by an emphasis on managerial issues. The world of
prisons has not been exempt from this development. It was noted in the
1970s in the United States by Jacobs in his study of Stateville Penitentiary
in Illinois. He observed that an incoming warden 'brought to the prison a
commitment to scientific management rather than to any correctional
ideology . . . He stresses efficient and emotionally detached management'
(Jacobs 1977: 103).

In its positive sense, management is concerned with achieving something
and is a means to that end. In a more narrow sense, management can
become an end in itself. To use its own terminology, what is sometimes
described as 'managerialism' usually involves a focus on what are called
processes and outputs rather than on outcomes. In common language, this
means a concentration on how things are done and what the organization
achieves rather than on the changes which result from the activities of
the organization. There is much to be said for such an approach. Properly
used, it can ensure that organizations run more efficiently, that they
are cost effective and that they produce what is expected of them.
Nevertheless, it is important to recognize its limitations, especially in a

prison system. For example, we shall learn in the next chapter that the efficiency of the prison service is judged by use of a series of measures, or key performance indicators. One of these measures is the number of 'accredited offending behaviour programmes' which are undertaken by prisoners each year. The measure is not the effect which these programmes have on the prisoners who undertake them, which would be an outcome, but simply on the number of programmes undertaken, which is a process. This is effective in managerial terms but it may or may not be effective in real terms.

There has been some academic attempt to analyze what constitutes good prison management. In the United States of America one can point to the work of McCleery (1957) and DiIulio (1987) and more recently in the United Kingdom to Wilson and Bryans (1998). Earlier in England and Wales Rutherford (1993) approached the subject from a different perspective by analyzing the values and aspirations that shaped the work of a variety of criminal justice practitioners, including prison governors. He argued that the personal values of the persons in charge had a distinct influence on regimes in prisons. As a result of interviewing 28 individuals, five of whom were from the prison system, he identified three clusters of values and beliefs, which he called 'credos'.

> The first of these embraces the punitive degradation of offenders. The second cluster speaks less to moral purpose than to issues of management; pragmatism, efficiency and expediency are the themes that set the tone. Third ... there is the cluster of liberal and humanitarian values.
>
> (Rutherford 1993: 3)

Rutherford's approach to this subject is an important one. If one accepts the contention that prisons are places where the relationships between the human beings involved have a central role to play in determining both culture and organizational direction, an important conclusion follows. This is the need for prisons to operate within an ethical context. If one loses sight of this, there is a real danger that the perfectly proper insistence on performance targets and process delivery will encourage the ever-present danger of forgetting that the prison service is not the same as a factory which produces motor cars or washing machines. The management of prisons is primarily about the management of human beings, both staff and prisoners. This means that there are issues that go beyond effectiveness and efficiency. When making decisions about the treatment of human beings there is a more radical consideration. The first question which must always be asked when considering any new managerial initiative is, 'Is it right?'.

In managerial terms it is important that processes and outputs in prisons should be run efficiently and effectively so as to meet the legitimate expectations of governments, of civil society, of victims and of staff, prisoners and their families. If it is true that prisons reflect the most central values of a society, it is even more important that those with responsibility for prisons and prison systems should look beyond technical and managerial considerations, Rutherford's second cluster of 'credos'. They also have to be leaders who are capable of enthusing the staff for whom they are responsible with a sense of decency in the way they carry out their difficult daily tasks, Rutherford's third cluster. If this happens it is more likely that the 'outcomes' from the prison will be of benefit to all members of society.

Leadership

The notion of leadership permeates every level of the prison system but it is at its most important in individual prisons. Prison staff look to the person at the top for a lead as to what is expected in terms of attitude, behaviour and manner of working. The prisons with the most humane atmosphere, with the most positive culture, are likely to be those with the most visible leadership (Wheatley 2002a: 14). Rutherford's 'liberal and humanitarian values' are important in themselves but it is also important to recognize that they are most likely to produce efficient security systems and a safe environment for prisoners and staff.

Leadership in the prison setting can be demonstrated in a number of ways. A strong leader will generally have a recognizable charisma, which will attract trust and confidence from staff. If it is genuine leadership, it will also be linked to organizational ability in a way that ensures that it does not degenerate into idiosyncrasy. The best leaders are likely to place great emphasis on the ethos within which the prison should operate and will set very clear parameters about what is to be done and what kind of behaviour is acceptable and what is not. Having done that, the leaders will then encourage staff at lower levels to use their initiative in implementing the details of the policy which has been set.

The issue of trust is important in the prison setting. In many respects the most important consideration for prison staff is that things should not go wrong. There should be no escapes, no riots, no serious disturbances, no suicides. If success is to be measured in such a negative manner, it is understandable that prison governors and other senior managers will place a greater emphasis on ensuring that mistakes are not made rather than on giving a priority to innovative ways of working which may bring about change but which may also carry a degree of risk. What this has meant traditionally in prisons is that senior management have not trusted their staff and have spent most of their energies on preventing failures rather than on encouraging success. A real leader will have the confidence to hit the proper balance between the two and will imbue staff with a sense of belief in their own ability.

The career of the prison governor

Historically in England and Wales there have been two main routes to becoming a prison governor. The first was for men and women who had already had a first career to be appointed as junior governors. Until the middle of the twentieth century many of those appointed were former military personnel. Grew (1958: 15) describes how he was appointed straight from the Army in 1922, following a short interview, to be deputy governor of Borstal Institution in Rochester. In later years the first point of entry to the governor grade was as housemaster in a Borstal institution or as an assistant governor in a prison for long-term prisoners. Miller (1976: 20) describes his first day as an assistant governor in Wakefield prison in 1946. In the decades after the Second World War a formal system of training for assistant governors was developed in the Prison Service Staff College in Wakefield. At one point this was an eight-month course, before being converted into a two-year course, spent partly in Wakefield and partly in a prison. Coyle (1994: 8) describes how this operated in the early 1970s.

The second route into the governor grade was from that of prison officer. A few junior officers were identified each year as having special potential and were appointed directly to the assistant governor training course. Others moved up gradually through the officer ranks, until eventually being appointed to a junior governor grade, a process which could take many years.

For many years the Prison Officers Association expressed strong opposition to the high proportion of assistant governors who were appointed directly to the prison service, arguing that 'there were enough officers of suitable calibre to be promoted to this grade' (Thomas 1972: 198). In 1987 what were known as the Fresh Start working arrangements were introduced, as mentioned above (see page 88), and the two separate groupings of prison officer grades and governor grades were combined. From that point, everyone joining the main ranks of the prison service did so as a prison officer. However, even after that it was felt that there had to be special arrangements to recruit persons who could be promoted quickly to the senior levels of the service and an accelerated promotion scheme was introduced. This was aimed at attracting young graduates who would be willing to spend a few years as a prison officer before moving quickly to governor level.

In recent years the focus has been on recruiting future governors straight from university or very shortly thereafter. The current system is known as the intensive development scheme. Following an assessment process, which includes psychometric and written tests, successful candidates undertake the same eight-week training course as prison officer recruits. They then spend a period as a uniformed prison officer, working in different prisons at different grades. Throughout this period the individual undergoes extended assessment and is supported by mentors and a training programme structured according to personal needs. Within three or four years the person can expect to be appointed to a junior governor grade. There has also been a limited reversal to the system which Major Grew would have recognized, with a small number of individuals being appointed directly to senior grades, although this time mainly from a business or administrative background, rather than from the armed services.

There has been an increasing tendency for former governors to be appointed to the most senior administrative posts in the service. Since the 1990s almost all area managers have been former governors and since before then one or two members of the Prison Service Management Board have always been former governors. As was explained in chapter three, the three Directors General appointed since 1996 have been career members of the prison service.

The other groups of personnel who work inside prisons

Officers and governors constitute by far the largest group of prison staff but there are many others. In the mid-nineteenth century the chaplain ranked second only to the prison governor in importance, betraying the Christian antecedents of the modern prison system (Noblett 1998: xxx). Until the mid-twentieth century, in addition to religious duties, the chaplain was responsible for much of what was considered to be rehabilitation in many prisons, with the exception of industrial work. This ranged from controlling prisoners' access to educational facilities and to the prison library, to granting additional visits and to approval of which groups of people from outside the prison were allowed to come in for cultural activities. At that time the chaplain to each prison was by law required to be an ordained clergyman of the Church of England. For many chaplains working in prison was a career choice, bringing with it free accommodation and the possibility of transferring from one prison to another. Representatives of other Christian denominations were described as 'visiting clergymen'. Attendance at church services was compulsory until the late 1960s (Atherton 1987: 35). Representatives of other faiths were allowed to visit individual prisoners only at the specific request of the prisoner and with the approval of the chaplain.

The situation today is much more ecumenical. Registering as a member of a particular faith or religious denomination is a matter of personal choice for each prisoner, as is attendance at religious meetings or services. Attached to each prison there will be representatives of every religious grouping to meet the needs of the prisoners and each will be given facilities to observe their religious practices as required. Having said that, the primacy, at least among equals, of the established church remains. The senior chaplain in a prison will invariably be from the Church of England, as is the Chaplain General based in prison service headquarters.

If the tradition was for the chaplain to be second in the prison hierarchy, the doctor was not far behind in third place. The development of health care in prisons and the role of medical and nursing staff is dealt with in the next chapter.

The development of the role of education staff is also dealt with in chapter six.

The link between prisons and the outside community will be dealt with in chapter eight. The key members of staff in promoting links between prisoners and the outside world have successively been social workers, welfare officers and probation officers (Thomas 1972: 198). Thomas describes how the first probation officers began to work inside prisons in 1965 and how prison officers saw this change above all others as a diminution of their role in helping prisoners. The precise role which probation officers have to carry out inside prisons is likely to be changed in an as yet unidentified way with the introduction of the National Offender Management Service.

In addition to salaried members of staff, there are many different individuals and groups who work in prisons on an ad hoc basis, some for pay and some on a voluntary basis. Some of these will be mentioned in chapter eight.

Diversity and equality

Reference was made in chapter four to the disproportionately high number of prisoners from ethnic minorities (22 per cent of the male prison population and 29 per cent of the female prison population) and also to the fact that 11 per cent of prisoners are nationals of another country. These figures are not reflected in respect of staff but, when launching its joint five-year Agenda for Change in race relations in December 2003 along with the Commission for Racial Equality (CRE), the prison service announced that over 5 per cent of its workforce came from an ethnic minority background (up from 2.9 per cent in 1998). In addition, 10 per cent of fast stream graduates were black or Asian, 8 per cent of recruits to the service were from an ethnic minority background, and 7 per cent of staff promoted within the service the previous year were from an ethnic minority background. The Agenda for Change action plan was launched following a series of high-profile instances of racial discrimination against prisoners and staff which led to severe criticism of the prison service by the CRE.

There are also a number of new initiatives on other aspects of diversity and equality.

Further reading

Boin, A. (1998) *Contrasts in Leadership: An Institutional Study of Two Prison Systems*. Delft: Eburon.

Bryans, S. and Wilson, D. (1998) The Prison Governor. Leyhill: *Prison Service Journal*.

Dilulio, J. (1987) *Governing Prisons: A Comparative Study of Correctional Management*. New York: The Free Press.

Kauffman, K. (1988) *Prison Officers and their World*. Cambridge, Mass: Harvard University Press.

Liebling, A. and Price, D. (2001) The Prison Officer. Leyhill: *Prison Service Journal*.

Lombardo, L. (1981) *Guards Imprisoned: Correctional Officers at Work*. New York: Elsevier.

Thomas, J. (1972) *The English Prison Officer since 1850*. London: Routledge & Kegan Paul.

What happens inside prison

A place of routine

The prison remains a place of great symbolism in many societies. Yet very few members of the public have any real knowledge of what happens after a judge passes a sentence of imprisonment and the convicted person disappears down the stairs to the cells beneath the well of the court to be conveyed to prison. The media generally paints two contrasting pictures of prison life. One is of a dangerous environment where there is an ever-present threat of violence and brutality, coming sometimes from prisoners and on occasion from staff. This picture is reinforced whenever violence or brutality is reported, as in the case of three prison officers who were jailed in 2000 for assaulting a prisoner in Wormwood Scrubs prison, a prison which had been the subject of damning reports from the Chief Inspector of Prisons (HM Chief Inspector of Prisons 1999b). The other picture is of the prison as a holiday camp, in which prisoners can lie in bed all day if they so choose, are well fed and provided for and are given occasional days out to further relax with family and friends. One example was the description of Hollesley Bay prison as 'Holiday Bay' (*Sunday Mirror* July 2003). The daily reality in prisons in England and Wales is far removed from either of these extremes.

The British prison has its modern origins in the Victorian tradition of large institutions but its roots go much further back to a belief in the virtue of the institution as a place in which to mould human behaviour. Its sister institutions were the large army barracks and the boarding school (Foucault 1979). It also has important Christian connotations. Like the monastery, the traditional prison consists of serried ranks of cells, typically grouped around the most substantial building on the campus, which is the chapel (Hoskison 1998).

All large institutions are places of routine, where the same things happen day after day without change. Prisons are no exception to this rule. Many prisons in the United Kingdom hold 500 or more prisoners and several have over 1000 places. Institutions of this size can only get through the business of the day by following a strict timetable: staff come on duty at the same time each day, cells are unlocked and locked at regular intervals, meals are served at the same time and all other activities follow a set pattern. Once they have become used to this routine, many prisoners will often refer to the sheer monotony of daily living as one of the major features of being in prison.

Cells and sanitation

Daily life for most prisoners is typified by short periods of intense activity, followed by long periods with little to do. The main reason for this is that the timetable is determined by staff patterns of attendance. During the night there will be no more than a few staff on duty, to patrol the accommodation areas and the perimeter of the prison and also to oversee the security systems. When the main group of staff come on duty, usually around 7.00 am, they will begin their work by visually checking all prisoners through the observation window in each cell door. The cells will then be opened. Until the mid-1990s this was the signal in most prisons for the process of 'slopping out'. Prisoners would have been locked in their cells for ten or more hours with no access to a toilet, forced to use a plastic chamber pot. Immediately the cell doors were opened there was a mad rush of prisoners along the landings to the communal toilet areas, where the chamber pots were emptied into the sluice sinks and jugs were filled with water to take back to the cells for washing and shaving. This was a ritual which disgusted both staff and prisoners. The stench of urine and faeces was everywhere. Sinks were frequently blocked and overflowing. The pace of movement at the beginning of the day meant that tempers were short and there were often verbal or physical confrontations.

The Woolf Report (1991) identified slopping out as a symbol of the inhumanity which existed in prisons and recommended that the prison service should move quickly to ensure that all prisoners had continuous access to proper sanitation.

> When courts send prisoners to prison, they are entitled to expect that prisoners will be treated in accordance with the Prison Service duty to look after them with humanity . . . However, to lock up prisoners for long periods at a time with no alternative but to use a bucket for their basic needs, which then has to remain in the cell, sometimes for many hours, is manifestly inconsistent and makes a mockery of that duty. . . . It is not just. The commitment we have proposed (eliminating slopping out by 1996) would remove a practice which is a blot on our prison system and which undermines the justice of the sentence which prisoners are serving.
>
> (para 11–101)

The Home Secretary accepted this recommendation and ordered the prison service to implement it as soon as possible. For the next few years all the building effort of the service was concentrated on achieving this, by whatever means possible. The best long-term way of dealing with this would have been by taking three cells and converting the middle one into a toilet and shower area, which could be accessed by people in the adjoining cells. This, however, would have been an expensive and time-consuming business. It would also have reduced prison capacity significantly. The preferred option was simply to install toilets in existing cells.

On average, prison cells are between six and eight square metres, with just enough room for a single bed, a small table and chair and perhaps a small wardrobe or cupboard. The installation of a flushing toilet and small wash-basin in such a confined space made it even more claustrophobic. The situation was bad enough when there was one prisoner in a cell but in many cases there were two prisoners in this space, sleeping in bunk beds. In many instances the toilet was not screened from the rest of the space. A person lying on the bottom bunk would be within a few inches of another person using the toilet. In most prisons nowadays prisoners have to eat their meals in their cells. This would mean one person using the small table, while the other sat on the bed or even the toilet with his meal tray on his knees.

By the mid-1990s the prison service was able to announce proudly that slopping out had ended. But this had been achieved at a cost. During this period there had been a virtual standstill on other essential building works so that the fabric of many prisons deteriorated and other facilities, such as workshops and education units, had not been improved. While there could be little argument that using a flushing toilet rather than a chamber pot was an improvement, the improvement was relative. The comment was frequently heard that it was hard to decide whether the cell had become a bedroom with a toilet in it or a lavatory with a bed. Having spent a great deal of money at speed to install toilets in cells, it is unlikely that the prison service will have funding to provide more decent arrangements for many years to come.

As the number of prisoners has increased in recent years, every available bed space has been pressed into use. This has meant using cells which had previously been taken out of commission and had no toilets. The prison service can no longer even say that every prisoner has continuous access to toilet facilities (HM Chief Inspector of Prisons 2004a).

In Scotland in 2005 a significant proportion of prisoners still had to slop out. A remand prisoner, Robert Napier, sought a judicial review in 2001 of the decision of the Scottish prison service to detain him in what he argued were 'inhuman and degrading' conditions in contravention of Article 3 of the European Convention on Human Rights or, failing that, in conditions which infringed his right to respect for his personal and family life contained in Article 8 of the Convention. These conditions involved sharing a cell with another prisoner, where he had to use a chamber pot. In 2004 the Court of Session in Edinburgh found that the Scottish Ministers, who were responsible for the Scottish Prison Service, had 'acted unlawfully in terms of Section 6 of the Human Rights Act 1998 and *ultra vires* in terms of Section 57 of the Scotland Act 1998 by acting in a manner incompatible with Article 3 of the Convention and detaining the petitioner in conditions in which he was subjected to degrading treatment (Napier 2004).

Overcrowding

The vast majority of sleeping accommodation for prisoners is intended for single occupancy, as described above. However, for many years the rising number of prisoners has meant that two and sometimes three prisoners have had to live in cells intended for one person. The prison service annual report 2003/04 indicates that in the year 2003/2004 21.7 per cent of prisoners had to share a cell designed for single occupancy. In local adult prisons that proportion rose to 42 per cent and in male young offender remand centres to 60 per cent (Home Office 2003a).

Even when two prisoners are sharing a cell which was designed to hold one person, the prison service does not automatically describe this as overcrowding. There are no specific criteria about what should be the minimum amount of cell space for one person. Each prison has what is known as a level of 'certified normal accommodation' (CNA). This is a figure agreed between the prison and the central management about the number of prisoners who can be held without any overcrowding. This figure is reached by a process of negotiation, based on the number of single or multiple occupation cells. The CNA was used to define the number of prisoners to be held in a prison. When the current pressure on prison places began in the early 1990s the prison service initially coped with it by redefining capacity. Overnight, cells which had been built to hold one prisoner were said to be capable of holding two persons. A new classification of 'operational capacity' was introduced; this was 'a safe level of overcrowding' and over ten years on it is regarded as the norm. Only when the number of prisoners goes above the operational capacity does the prison service accept that a prison is beyond its capacity.

This measure of 'operational capacity' refers solely to sleeping space and takes no account of pressure on kitchens, on health provision, on sewage systems, or on education and work resources. In March 2005 the Howard League for Penal Reform published a list of the ten most overcrowded prisons in England and Wales (see Table 6.1).

In its report following its visit to the United Kingdom in 2003 the European Committee for the Prevention of Torture (CPT 2005: para 20) expressed concern at the way the prison service defined its capacity:

> A new Prison Service order sets out the cell occupancy levels which can be certified for operational capacity. In the CPT's opinion, the cell capacities approved by the Prison Service are too high; in particular, placing two persons in cells measuring as little as 6.5 m², including the sanitary facilities, cannot be considered acceptable.

Table 6.1

Prison	CNA	Prisoners	Occupancy
Leicester			189 per cent
Preston			180 per cent
Shrewsbury			173 per cent
Swansea			165 per cent
Bedford			161 per cent
Exeter			158 per cent
Dorchester			157 per cent
Leeds			155 per cent
Lincoln			149 per cent
Wandsworth			149 per cent

(Howard League 2005)

Food

One of the consequences of the riots which took place in Strangeways and other prisons in England and Wales in 1990 has been that since then the practice of prisoners eating in dining rooms has largely disappeared. The majority of prisoners now have to eat meals in their cells, often in the conditions described above. In a number of prisons, particularly the large local prisons, prisoners collect what is euphemistically described as a 'continental breakfast' before they are locked up in the evening. This will typically consist of a clear plastic bag with a small packet of cornflakes, some sugar and milk, a roll or bread, some margarine and jam and a tea bag. When cell doors are unlocked in the morning, prisoners can fill their tea mugs with water from hot boilers. In other prisons, breakfast is collected from a servery on the ground floor, prisoners coming down in groups to collect a tray to take back to their cells. In most cases prisoners will keep their own plate and bowl, mug, knife, spoon and fork, all made of plastic, and will wash them after each meal in the small hand basin in the cell.

The two main meals of the day, lunch and tea, are usually prepared in a central kitchen, where a few staff with catering qualifications supervise a larger number of selected prisoners to cook the food for all prisoners. A typical lunch might consist of soup, a main course and a sweet dish or a piece of fruit. There will usually be a choice of two main courses, with prisoners coming to the servery in groups which are rotated to ensure that one will have first choice every third or fourth day. In prisons where there is a low turnover of prisoners, meals are chosen up to a week in advance from a self-select menu, rather as in a hospital. In addition there will be a wide selection of 'special diets', to cater for religious and cultural needs, vegetarians and those with medical requirements. The evening meal will usually consist of one hot dish, although at weekends it may be restricted to pre-prepared cold food, such as meat or cheese.

The quality of prison food has improved significantly in recent years but a major source of complaint remains the narrow timetable within which meals are served. Lunch may be served any time between 11.00 am and 12.30 pm, while tea may be provided between 4.00 and 5.30 pm. This can leave a gap of up to 16 hours between the last meal of the day and the first of the next. If this gap is 14 hours or more, prisoners must be provided with a snack and a hot drink before the prison is locked for the night.

Exercise and time out of cell

Prisoners spend most of each day inside buildings, much of it in small spaces where there is little opportunity for exercise. In the interests of health, they should spend a minimum period each day in the fresh air. This is normally referred to in prison parlance as 'exercise'. The international standards relating to the treatment of prisoners recommend that as a minimum prisoners should have at least one hour per day in the fresh air.

> *European Prison Rule (1987) 86*
> Every prisoner who is not employed in outdoor work, or located in an open institution, shall be allowed, if the weather permits, at least one hour of walking or suitable exercise in the open air daily, as far as possible, sheltered from inclement weather.

Until recently this recommendation was complied with in England and Wales. That situation changed with the introduction of a new order in 1998 that prisoners should have daily exercise in the fresh air 'for such a period as may be reasonable in the circumstances' (Prison Service Order No. 4275). This amendment was criticized by the European Committee for the Prevention of Torture following its visits to the United Kingdom in 2001 and again in 2003:

> The CPT has previously made it clear that it regards the entitlement of at least one hour of outdoor exercise per day as an essential requirement ... During the 2003 visit, the delegation once again heard complaints that outdoor exercise could be limited to half an hour per day, especially at Pentonville. The CPT reiterates its longstanding recommendation in this respect.
>
> (CPT 2005: para 35)

The requirement to have a minimum time in the fresh air becomes more important the greater the length of time a prisoner spends in his or her cell. The reality is that in many large local prisons persons spend the bulk of the day inside their cells, coming out for less than four hours. For many prisoners, the most important time out of cell is when their visitors come to see them, as described below. A significant proportion of prisoners will also have the opportunity to take part to a limited extent in what are described later in this chapter as 'constructive activities'. All of these activities are compressed into the hours when the main group of prison officers are on duty to supervise them, usually between 9.00 and 11.30 am and 1.00 to 4.30 pm.

When prisoners have been served their early evening meal, the main group of staff who came on duty to open the cells in the morning will go off duty. A smaller contingent will return after their own tea break to supervise evening activities, which usually take place between 6.00 and 8.30 pm. This period is known colloquially as 'association' or recreation. This will vary according to the number of prisoners involved and their security status. In some cases, it may be limited to a small group of prisoners being allowed access to table tennis, a pool table or television in a room on the groundfloor of the accommodation wing for up to two hours, with each prisoner having access to this once or twice a week. In other cases, all cells in a wing may be unlocked, with prisoners allowed to move freely within the wing. This will be the period when many prisoners will take the opportunity to have a shower, do their personal washing and ironing or use the pay telephone. In some prisons there may be an educational or cultural programme or a continuation of visits for a selected group of prisoners during this period.

Staff on evening duty will hand over to night duty staff around 9.00 pm. Before this happens all prisoners will be locked in their cells and a count taken to ensure that no one is missing. By 9.30 pm at the latest the prison will be secured for the night, with no cell to be unlocked, except in case of emergency, until the next morning.

Contact with family and friends

Visits

For many prisoners, one of the most distressing features of imprisonment is separation from family and friends and contact with them is the thing that they value above all else. Since 1992 the Scottish Prison Service has carried out regular surveys of prisoners and consistently these have confirmed the high priority which prisoners give to direct contact with their families (Scottish Prison Service 2004). Family contact, of course, is important not only for the member who is in prison, but also for the rest of the family, who may be parents, children, siblings, spouses or partners. This is recognized in the international human rights standards relating to imprisonment:

UN Standard Minimum Rule 79
Special attention shall be paid to the maintenance and improvement of such relations between a prisoner and his family as are desirable in the best interests of both.

We have already discovered that the prison is by its nature a closed world and the daily restrictions of prison life make it impossible to have a meaningful family life. For that reason special efforts need to be made to ensure that prisoners can maintain and develop links with their families and friends as best they can.

The most valued form of communication is through a face-to-face visit. In virtually every country sentenced prisoners are allowed to have contact with their families and friends, although the conditions in which visits take place vary enormously. In some jurisdictions in the United States, prisoners are not allowed to have any physical contact with their visitors. They are separated by thick glass and have to talk to each other by means of a telephone system, with all conversation being monitored by staff. In several Latin American countries visits are allowed once a week for the whole day. On that day visitors can come right into the prisoners' living accommodation and in a prison holding 1500 prisoners one might find up to 3000 visitors at one time. Visitors are searched on entering and leaving the prison but otherwise there is no supervision.

Conditions for visiting also vary within Europe. In Spain prisoners who are not entitled to home leave permits may receive one family or intimate visit per month of not less than one hour and not more than three hours. All closed prisons must have suitable facilities for these family/intimate visits. A number of Scandinavian prison systems have similar arrangements for what are usually described as conjugal visits. The prisoner and the visitor are allowed to go into a room which has a bed and a shower for a period of up to three hours. It could be argued that the most humane type of visits, for prisoners and family members are to be found in Eastern European countries. In many of these jurisdictions sentenced prisoners may receive private visits from their spouses and families lasting up to three days at regular intervals. These visits take place in small flats within the security of the prison. The family visitors bring with them sufficient food for the period. There are usually communal sitting, cooking and play areas for children with separate bedrooms for up to a dozen prisoners and their partners at a time. During these few days prisoners can lead a relatively normal life with family members.

In England and Wales visits take place in a general visiting room where staff can see, but not necessarily hear, everything that is going on. In many cases prisoners are required to wear a bib or other piece of clothing which identifies them as prisoners. Visitors, including children of prisoners, are required to sit at the opposite side of a table. The room is surveyed by closed-circuit television cameras, with definition high enough to pick up small writing on wrapping paper. Visits usually last for two hours at most, even for prisoners serving long sentences. On occasion, special arrangements will be made in prisons where persons are serving long sentences to have an extended period for visiting so that parents can be with their children in a less formal setting.

Despite the fact that private or intimate visits are commonplace in many comparable countries, the governments of the United Kingdom have so far set their face firmly against any such arrangement. The argument for this restriction is not usually based on security considerations. A number of prison governors have indicated that they see no security objection to private visits, while others have indicated support for them. Instead the government appears to be fearful of criticism from the media and the public, that this would be the ultimate in turning the prison into a hotel. Whatever else they may be allowed to have, prisoners should forfeit the right to sexual relations by the fact of imprisonment. This is to take a very narrow view of private visits. The family visits lasting two or three days, which are common in Eastern Europe and also in Canada, are meant to strengthen family ties. The visitors may indeed be spouses or partners, but they may also be parents and children and the family intimacy should not be seen solely as sexual. Such visits are as beneficial to the visitors as to the prisoners and are intended to meet the requirement of Article 8 of the European Convention on Human Rights, which guarantees the right to family life to all.

In recent years increasingly severe restrictions have been imposed in a number of countries on high security prisoners when they meet family or friends. In England and Wales these prisoners are separated from their visitors by a glass screen. They are allowed no physical contact and all conversations are monitored. Prisoners may be in this category because of the seriousness of their offence or because of previous attempts to smuggle drugs or other items in through the visit room.

Letters

Given the relative infrequency of visits, many prisoners set a high store on correspondence with their family by letter. In England and Wales there is no limit to the number of letters prisoners may send or receive, nor on their length.

Until the mid-1990s all correspondence to and from prisoners was read by staff. There were two justifications for this. The first was on security grounds. By checking all letters, staff hoped to get prior warning of any attempts by prisoners to plan escapes or to make arrangements for items such as drugs to be smuggled in. In reality, most prisoners do not spend their time planning escape attempts and the few who do are not likely to commit their plans to writing. It was eventually recognized by the authorities that reading prisoners' correspondence on security grounds was not cost effective and could not be justified. The second reason which staff had for reading letters was a paternalistic one. There was concern that if an incoming letter contained bad news, say, of a death in the family or that a partner intended to end a relationship, then staff should break this news to a prisoner and also needed to be aware of the information in case of any adverse reaction from the prisoner. This approach, which regarded the prisoner as an immature person, unable to cope with bad news or disappointment, did not sit easily with the notion that prisoners were mature adults, who should be treated as such.

New arrangements were therefore introduced which significantly reduced the extent to which staff were to scrutinize prisoners' correspondence. This was to be limited to a check on a random sample of 5 per cent of all letters going in and coming out of a prison. In order to ensure that letters did not contain any extraneous items, such as money or drugs, staff were to open prisoners' incoming letters, but not to read them. It was recommended that, if at all possible, letters should be opened in the prisoner's presence to demonstrate that they were not being read.

Correspondence between prisoners and their legal advisers has been exempt from staff scrutiny since two important court cases in the early 1990s. The first was a judgement by the European Court of Human Rights in the case of a prisoner in Scotland that the routine reading of correspondence between a prison and legal adviser was a breach of Article 8 of the European Convention on Human Rights (Campbell v. United Kingdom 1993). The second was an English High Court ruling that prisoners were entitled to unimpeded access to a solicitor for the purpose of receiving advice and assistance in connection with the possible institution of legal proceedings in a court (R v. Home Secretary ex parte Leech No. 2, 1994 QB 198).

Telephones

In 1988 the Prison Service began to install pay telephones in prisons and to allow prisoners to purchase special phone cards to use them. In 1991 this arrangement was extended to all prisons, except high-security units and in 1994 these were also included. According to Prison Service Order 4400, the policy of the prison service on the use of telephones by prisoners is:

- to encourage prisoners to take responsibility for maintaining close and meaningful ties with their family and friends;
- to respect the privacy of calls made by prisoners so far as is reasonably practicable without compromising the security and good order and discipline of the prison;
- to minimize the risk of unauthorized contact by prisoners with victims of crime.

As a matter of course, telephone calls may be monitored (that is, listened to) and recorded by staff, with the exception of calls to legal advisers. Prisoners may not telephone the victims of their offences nor the media and contact with other persons may also be prohibited. There are additional restrictions on high-security prisoners.

Electronic communications

In 2005 prisoners do not have access to electronic mail. However, given the pace of technology and the improving means of controlling access to specific addresses, it seems reasonable to predict that it is only a matter of time before prisoners can send electronic messages in a restricted manner.

'Constructive activities'

The central feature of imprisonment is the restriction on freedom involved in the deprivation of liberty. By definition this is a negative experience. However, as we discovered in previous chapters, over the last 200 years or so there have been a series of redefinitions of the purpose of imprisonment in an attempt to justify it as a more positive experience. It is now presented, not only as a place of punishment, but also one of potential reform. This principle is enshrined in Prison Rule 3, which states, 'The purpose of the training and treatment of convicted prisoners shall be to encourage and assist them to lead a good and useful life'.

The prison service now takes the view that in implementing Rule 3 it should concentrate its efforts on a whole range of activities which have the potential to help prisoners to live within the law after they have been released. This used to be described as rehabilitation. It is now described, in a more negative term, as reducing re-offending. These activities are often described as 'purposeful' or 'constructive' and many prisons have well-developed education and work programmes, as well a variety of skills training courses.

Work

We have already learned that the concept of work has played an important part in the world of prison, at least since the time of the convict prisons. Initially the principle was that prisoners should be required to work, rather than do nothing. In more recent times the aim of the prison service has been to provide all convicted prisoners with work that is meaningful and satisfying but this ambition has been difficult to realize.

A stream of commentators on social and penal issues, including Rusche and Kirchheimer (1939), Foucault (1975), Ignatieff (1978), Melossi and Pavarini (1981), Garland (1990) and van Zyl Smit and Dünkel (2001), have described from a series of different perspectives the importance of work in the prison setting. Throughout the second half of the nineteenth and most of the twentieth century industrial work in one form or another constituted the main activity in most prisons in the United Kingdom. If the work could be of benefit, as with the public works which had been undertaken by convict prisoners, that was all to the good. If not, then it was sufficient to teach prisoners the discipline, as had been the case with the crank and the treadmill. The principle was that work was a good thing in itself, even though in many cases it did not produce much. As the Chairman of the Scottish Prison Commission noted in his evidence to the Elgin Committee in 1899, 'There is no unproductive labour [in prisons], but there is a lot of it not very productive' (*Report of the Departmental Committee on Scottish Prisons* 1900: para 104).

Throughout the twentieth century much of the work done by prisoners involved producing goods for internal prison consumption. For example, uniforms for prisoners and for staff were all made in prison workshops until such time as the staff complained about the quality of the finished goods. There were also attempts at providing goods for other public departments. The most obvious of these were mailbags for the General Post Office, which for many years symbolized in the mind of the public the reality of prison work. This contract ended when the Post Office moved from using canvas mailbags to bags made of artificial material. In some countries government departments are still required to give first refusal to prison industries when they require material such as office furniture or equipment. For example, in some states in America to this day all car licence plates are manufactured in prisons.

For the most part, prisoners were trained 'on the job' for each work party. With the growth of institutions for juvenile offenders in the early twentieth century came the notion that prisoners might also be trained in particular work skills in the hope that this might make it more likely that they could find work on release. The introduction, in Borstal and other institutions, of vocational training courses, with the possibility of City & Guilds qualifications, mirrored developments in education elsewhere. Progressively through the second half of the twentieth century this concept was introduced to adult prisons, culminating with the introduction of what were called 'training prisons'. There were a number of experiments at introducing 'real work' into prisons, the most notable of which was in Coldingley prison, when it opened in 1969.

Coldingley was designated as an 'industrial prison'. A higher level of wages was paid to the prisoners involved and they were expected to work for 40 hours each week, with the opportunity for overtime at evenings and weekends. The majority of jobs available did not require a high level of skill. There was also discussion about the extent to which this attempt at 'normalization' of industrial life should be extended to other aspects of prison life. The intention was to test the hypothesis that training prisoners in the habit of work in conditions which came as close as possible to the outside environment would of itself reduce re-offending. The experiment was not a success for a variety of reasons. In terms of vested interests, the Directorate of Industries and Stores in prison service headquarters was unhappy with the degree of autonomy granted to Coldingley and was determined to pull this back. Some of the prison service trade unions saw this development as a threat to traditional staff working practices and also created difficulties. Overcrowding levels in prisons in the south-east of England meant that there were powerful voices in prison service headquarters which objected to the protection of specialist prisons such as Coldingley. At a more fundamental level it also became clear that prisoners could not be regarded merely as another group of industrial workers. For example, the concept of restricting all other activities such as visits with families and lawyers, education and contact with probation staff to evenings and weekends was not practical.

In the late 1970s and early 1980s the Directorate of Industries and Farms began to take a much more aggressive approach to prison workshops which were not meeting their targets. Shops which failed to meet the productivity targets set for them or which lost production hours because of staff shortages were closed with little consultation with the prison governor. Central management adopted a 'commercial viability' approach to decisions about whether existing workshops should continue to operate or should be built in new prisons. Older inner city prisons have always had limited provision for work. In prisons built in the 1980s, such as The Mount, planned workshops were no more than shells and later designs, such as those for Bullingdon prison, were intentionally built without workshops, leaving governors to occupy prisoners as best they could.

In more recent times the prison service has given a high priority to attempts to 're-settle' prisoners back into their communities. This focus has been based on the premise, as we shall discuss in chapter eight, that persons released from prison will be less likely to offend again if they can return to society with accommodation, work and a support system. As a means of taking this principle on board, the prison service now concentrates on attempting to provide prisoners with the resources to enable them to 're-settle'. For that reason, the department in prison service headquarters which oversees all the activities that go on inside prisons changed its name a few years ago from the Directorate of Regimes to the Directorate of Resettlement. (This department has now transferred to the National Offender Management Service.) In principle the work which prisoners are required to do is aimed at giving them skills which will help them to find employment on release. This has led to a number of new initiatives, such as 'custody to work'. Wherever possible, prisoners are encouraged to gain National Vocational Qualifications, involving those whose work is to keep sections of the prison clean in industrial cleaning qualifications and those who work in prison kitchens in catering qualifications. All of these are worthy initiatives. However, they involve a relatively small proportion of those who are currently in prison.

Remand prisoners generally have no possibility of working. The reality also remains that a high proportion of adult prisoners held in local prisons do not have access to any form of meaningful daily work, as a succession of independent reports has made clear (for example, European Committee for the Prevention of Torture 2005 and HM Chief Inspector of Prisons 2004b). The prison service's annual report for 2003/04 records that on average prisoners spend 3.3 hours a day on some kind of purposeful activity. That means that for 20.7 hours a day there is no purposeful activity.

Education

Until 1991 prison education was delivered by Local Education Authority adult education services and Further Education colleges under contract to the prison service. An important feature of this way of working was that there was a link between local facilities and, if the prisoner came from the locality, there was the possibility of continuing to access this provision after release. In 1991 the system was changed to allow different education contractors to bid for five-year contracts. A number of providers bid successfully for multiple contracts, in some cases geographically dispersed around the country, and many local links were broken. There was very little flexibility in the contract at local level and contracts were based on the number of teaching hours to be delivered, rather than on the content of the teaching.

In 2001, responsibility for prison education was transferred to the Department for Education and Skills. The intention of this change was to create stronger links between prison and mainstream education. In 2005 the House of Commons Education and Skills Committee for the first time undertook an inquiry into prison education. Its report (2005) contained some telling statements:

> It is essential that we are clear about the purpose of prison education. The purpose of prison education should be understood as part of a wider approach to reduce recidivism through the rehabilitation of prisoners. Although contributing to the reduction of recidivism is of key importance, prison education is about more than just this. It is important also because to provide prison education is the right thing to do and this is an important point to bear in mind when making policy decisions.
>
> (para 8)

> We must keep in mind the fact that a prison is a prison and not a secure learning centre. Nevertheless, the Government should be aiming to develop a culture in prisons in which education is a priority.
>
> (para 16)

Until the late 1990s the content of the education programme in each prison was decided locally. This meant that the syllabus in many prisons was developed in an inconsistent and sometimes idiosyncratic manner, depending on the interests of the prison governor or of the education officer. In some instances it depended on the skills of whoever could be recruited to work as a teacher; in other cases a prisoner might press for a class on a subject which was of particular personal interest.

In recent years much of the focus of prison education has been on providing the basic skills of reading, writing and counting in the hope that these will enable prisoners to apply for jobs after they have been released. The prison service annual report for 2003/04 records that a total of 34,482 basic skills awards at entry level or level one or two were achieved, although it is not clear how many prisoners were involved, since some would have achieved more than one award. There has also been criticism that the authorities frequently require prisoners who already have relatively high educational levels to undertake basic skills qualifications so that the prison can meet the targets that have been set.

The House of Commons Education and Skills Committee (2005) was sceptical of this concentration on basic skills.

> It is widely accepted that basic skills are not sufficient to enable a prisoner to improve their employability in isolation of broader learning including soft skills, and that such a concentrated focus has narrowed the curriculum to the detriment of the learners.
>
> (para 11)

The Committee was critical that education in prisons was being driven in an unhelpful manner by key performance targets and it recommended that more research should be carried out into the type of education which should be delivered in prisons in order to help prisoners to enter secure employment on release.

Individualization

We have already discussed how the notion grew in the nineteenth century that criminality was in some way to be explained by the criminals' social, mental or emotional deformity. This idea has never quite gone away. It was the basis for the introduction in the early twentieth century of various forms of indeterminate sentencing and conditional release, some of which were based, in part, on how the prisoner responded to 'treatment' in prison. The latest manifestation of this belief in England and Wales was the introduction in the 1990s of a series of courses known generically as 'offending behaviour programmes'. These were based on the principle of assessing prisoners in order to identify the key features of their character which precipitated their 'offending behaviour'. For some it might be the fact that they were given to irrational outbursts of anger or violence, for others it might be a dependence on alcohol or drugs, for some it might be that they lacked sufficient powers of reasoning, for others it was an inability to control sexual urges. Having identified the key weaknesses in an individual, the prison authorities then set about trying to rectify these personal failings.

The notion of developing sets of behavioural programmes for prisoners came initially from a group of individuals in Canada, a number of whom had links with the prison systems in that country. These programmes were tested in Canada and some of them were copyrighted by their authors. In the early and mid-1990s a number of persons associated with the prison service in England and Wales, several of whom had a psychological background, went to Canada and were impressed by what they saw. They persuaded the prison service to purchase some of these programmes and to begin using them in this country.

As described elsewhere in this text, the mid-1990s was a period when the prison service concentrated on security matters, almost to the exclusion of all other considerations. A few years later there was increasing political interest in developing activities in prison which might reduce the possibility that prisoners would return to a life of crime after release. At a time when the prison service wished to convince the government to increase its budget, these behavioural programmes were a useful tool to secure this funding. It was suggested that there was sufficient evidence from the use of such programmes in North America to show that they had the potential to reduce the likelihood of prisoners returning to crime after release. This evidence, however thin, was sufficient to ensure a significant increase in funding of 'offending behaviour programmes accredited as being effective in reducing re-offending' and one of the key performance targets for the prison service became the delivery of a certain number of these programmes each year. In 1998 the target was 3000 programmes (HM Prison Service 1999) and by 2003 this had been increased to 8444 (HM Prison Service 2004).

From the outset it was accepted that the real test of these programmes would be whether the prisoners who undertook them did, in fact, have a lower rate of re-offending than those who did not. Such hard evidence has been difficult to come by. A report by the Research and Statistics Department in the Home Office in 2002 suggested that two-year reconviction rates for prisoners who undertook cognitive behavioural treatment programmes were up to 14 percentage points lower than a matched group of prisoners who were not on the programme. However, two subsequent studies by the same unit found no differences in the two-year reconviction rates for prisoners who had participated in the programmes and matched groups who had not (Home Office 2003a and 2003b).

Every so often people working in and around prisons decide that in a particular new approach, programme or course they have found the Holy Grail to reducing re-offending. In the 1990s behavioural programmes were thought by some of those involved to be such a panacea. What has since become clear is that, as with so many other courses, they can achieve some change if they are well-thought through, well-focused and well-delivered to individuals who might actually benefit from them. This was the case with many of the earlier behavioural programmes. Once the target became to increase the number of programmes, rather than to focus on individuals who needed them, it soon became clear that the panacea had not yet been found. The latest Home Office research report (Home Office 2003b) concluded that the great expansion of the programmes may have compromised the quality of delivery.

The prison service has taken this on board and in its Business Plan for 2005–2006 it announced a target of delivering 6590 'accredited offending behaviour programme completions', a significant reduction on previous targets. It has balanced this by increasing the target for prisoners undertaking a drug treatment programme to 5250. The target for those undertaking a programme for sex offenders remained stable at 1160 (included within the offending behaviour total).

Health care

As a group, prisoners have significantly greater health problems than the general population (Social Exclusion Unit 2002). For example, a study carried out by the Office for National Statistics (1998) found that 78 per cent of male remand prisoners, 64 per cent of male sentenced prisoners and 50 per cent of female prisoners had a personality disorder. Around two-thirds of prisoners used illegal drugs in the year before imprisonment and around three-fifths of male prisoners and two-fifths of female prisoners admitted to drinking to a hazardous degree (Social Exclusion Unit 2002). Given the previously disorganized lifestyles of many prisoners, these figures are disturbing but not entirely surprising.

In addition to the morbidity of individual prisoners, the prison environment does not lend itself to good health. Many prison buildings are old and even in those which are modern, prisoners are likely to be spending long periods of each day locked in small cells, sometimes with another person. They get comparatively little exercise or fresh air and their diet is institutional.

Providing proper health care for prisoners has always been a daunting task. The Prison Act 1952 requires that each prison should have a medical officer. This obligation can be traced back to legislation of 1774 'for preserving the health of prisoners in gaol', leading one author to describe the prison medical service as 'the oldest civilian medical service' (Smith 1984). Throughout the late nineteenth and most of the twentieth century the prison medical officer was an important person within the prison hierarchy. The status of a member of prison staff could be identified by the number of one's set of keys. The prison governor had set no. 1. Set no. 2 was usually allocated to the prison doctor. The historical basis for this arrangement lies in the notion of the prison as a 'total institution' which provided separately for all the needs of prisoners, rather than made use of the facilities available in the community.

The National Health Act of 1948, which led to the establishment of the National Health Service, did not exclude prisoners from the health care which was to be made available for all. Despite this, the prison service continued with its own medical service, recruiting doctors, many of whom made a career of working in prisons. Larger prisons had several full-time doctors, who were in effect general practitioners. Specialist doctors, such as psychiatrists, were often employed on a contract basis. Each prison had a health bay and larger prisons had hospital style wards. Some, such as Parkhurst on the Isle of Wight, even had fully equipped surgeries. Other health care specialists, such as dentists, were employed on a sessional basis.

For many years generalist prison officers were able to take some basic training in first aid and related issues and then were appointed as 'health care officers'. They were in charge of the health units, provided support for doctors, looked after prisoners with simple illnesses and issued medicines which had been prescribed by the doctor. Over the years these arrangements came in for a great deal of justifiable criticism (Smith 1984; Sim 1990). The first signs of change in prison health came with the introduction of trained nurses. Some were prison officers who were trained as generalist or mental nurses, while others were civilian nurses.

In the course of the 1990s criticism began to focus on the structural arrangements for delivering prison health care and in particular on the need for more integration of prison health with public health services. The Chief Inspector of Prisons published a review of health care provision in prison (HMCIP 1996) which highlighted the need for a new strategy. In April 2000 the prison service entered into a formal partnership with the Department of Health for the gradual transfer of the management and delivery of health care to prisoners to the National Health Service. Over the succeeding two years assessments of prisoners' health needs were undertaken by each prison and the local health authority. These subsequently formed the basis of what were called local prison health delivery plans. The key priorities identified for improvement were primary care, substance misuse, mental health, oral health, health promotion and the development of staff skills. A national work programme was drawn up to reflect these priorities.

In April 2003 the Department of Health assumed financial responsibility for all prison health services, taking on the duties previously discharged by the Home Office. The process of transferring delivery of health care in each prison to the Primary Care Trusts, which commission local health services, began in April 2004, to be completed by April 2006.

As long as the health profile of those who are sent to prison is as poor as it is, the need to improve the standard of care provided to prisoners will remain constant. Significant improvements have been made in recent years and the strategy of bringing prison health from its previous isolation into the mainstream of the health service is a sound one. On the ground, much remains to be done, as the Chief Inspector of Prisons noted in her report for 2003–2004 (HM Chief Inspector of Prisons 2005: 7):

> Prison healthcare has shown considerable improvement. It has moved from a shamingly inadequate service to one that increasingly bears comparison with practice outside ... But here too healthcare staff struggle with the scale of the task. Mental health in-reach teams in some prisons can do little but skim the surface of the severity and breadth of mental illness contained in prisons.

Drug abuse

When it published its new drug strategy in 2005 the National Offender Management Service (NOMS) reported that 'There are an estimated 250,000–280,000 problematic drug users in the United Kingdom. At any one time about a third are serving custodial or community sentences' (National Offender Management Service 2005: 1).

These figures are stark. The Home Office (2003a) reported that around 73 per cent of recently sentenced prisoners had used illegal drugs in the

12 months before imprisonment. Over half of these reported that they had committed offences connected to their drug taking, usually because they needed money to buy drugs. The prison service estimates that between 40 and 50 per cent of men and 60 per cent of women received into prison have a chronic substance misuse problem and that up to 80 per cent of people admitted to some local prisons test positive for opiates on admission (Spurr 2004: 5).

Given these figures, it is no surprise that the prison service has expended considerable effort in recent years in developing a strategy to deal with the problem of prisoners who abuse drugs. The primary aims of the strategy are:

- to deal with the individual needs of problematic drug users;
- to reduce the harm that drug users cause to themselves and others; and
- to reduce the supply of illicit drugs in prison.

In order to deliver the strategy there are a wide variety of drug interventions, which include detoxification programmes, drug rehabilitation programmes, supply reduction measures, including mandatory drug testing, and health education programmes. Over 50,000 prisoners enter clinical detoxification programmes on admission to prison and there are over 600 specialist drug workers.

The prison service reports that, despite the increase in chronic drug dependency among new prison admissions, the rate of drug abuse inside prison fell from 24.4 per cent in 1996/97 to 12.5 per cent in 2003/04, with a significant switch away from Class A drugs (Spurr 2004: 6). It links this fall to the introduction of a programme of mandatory drug testing. This involves obligatory testing of all prisoners on a random basis coupled with targeted testing of suspected drug abusers. This reported success contrasts with the experience in the Scottish prison service which was reported in April 2005 to have decided, with the support of the Scottish Executive, to abolish mandatory drug testing, on the grounds that it was exacerbating the problem of drug abuse in prisons, and to divert the money previously allocated to that to additional drug treatment and counselling (*The Scotsman* 22 April 2005).

The prison service has identified three main priorities in its determination to deal with the problem of drug abuse. The first is to develop a more targeted approach to the individuals most in need of care and support. The second is to develop the number of drug treatment programmes, to make them more generally available and to increase their effectiveness. The third is to generate much better coordination between the support provided in prisons with that available in the community after people are released.

Suicide

In recent years there has been increasing concern about the number of prisoners who have committed suicide or who have deliberately harmed themselves. This matter was first subjected to rigorous independent study by Alison Liebling (1992), who identified this as an issue which required close scrutiny and analysis. Her work was published shortly after a review had been undertaken by the Chief Inspector of Prisons into the matter (HMCIP 1990). Over the 12 years since Liebling's work was published there were 906 self-inflicted deaths in prison custody, including 94 in 2004 (Inquest 2004). Of this latter number, 83 hanged themselves, 10 died from a ligature and two from cuts to their throats or wrists. Thirteen of the 94 were women.

There has been concern in recent years at the growing number of women in prison who have killed themselves and an understanding that a much greater proportion deliberately injure themselves, some very seriously.

On 13 July 1990 there was shock when a 15-year-old boy called Philip Knight hanged himself in Swansea prison. There was a debate in parliament about the tragic event. On 21 January 2005 16-year-old Gareth Price hanged himself in Lancaster Farms Young Offender Institution. This death did not attract much public notice. It was as though the public, politicians and the media had come to accept that, from time to time, unfortunately children would kill themselves in prison service custody.

The prison service itself does not accept that it is inevitable that any of its charges, young or otherwise, should kill themselves. In the years since 1990 the service has developed a set of policies on how to prevent prisoners from either harming or killing themselves. In its annual report for 2003–2004 the prison service listed the impressive number of initiatives which it had launched. These included pilot prisons with 'safer built environments', an increase in the number of suicide prevention coordinators, improved training for staff, an evaluation of previous initiatives, an improvement in the suicide/self-harm warning form and a review of child protection and safeguards. Since the early 1990s the prison service has had an agreement with the Samaritans to train selected prisoners as 'Listeners' to be available for prisoners who need personal help. Yet despite all of this, the service failed to meet the target which it had set itself for limiting the number of suicides.

The annual report included one reference (page 22) which gave a pointer to why the level of suicides remained high:

> Prison population rises have increased the throughput and movements of prisoners with an impact on their distress and vulnerability.

In other words, it is not sufficient to produce excellent policies for preventing suicides if the overall conditions in prisons make it more likely that prisoners will feel depressed and helpless. In his 1999 review of suicides, the Chief Inspector of Prisons noted as much. He commented that the vast majority of suicides occur in local prisons; that these prisons are massively overcrowded with a large throughput; that many of the prisoners spend the bulk of the day locked in their cells (page 4). In 2004 the Parliamentary Joint Committee on Human Rights carried out an inquiry into deaths in custody. Its report (JCHR 2004: para 3) included a concise summary of the issues at the root of the problem:

> As this report shows the majority of people entering custody are extremely vulnerable individuals. Many of those who die in custody are young. Most of those who die are vulnerable or sick, with histories of mental illness and drug and alcohol problems. It must be recognised that by taking people into custody the state takes upon itself a particular duty of care, because of their vulnerability, and a special responsibility to ensure their protection and to uphold their human rights.

Requests and complaints

Prisons are highly regulated with little space left for prisoners to use their initiative or exercise personal choice. Because of this, minor issues of daily routine can take on a significance which those of us who have relative freedom of choice in our daily lives might find hard to understand. An important example of a potential area of stress in prison might be the arrangements for family members to visit prisoners. Convicted prisoners are usually entitled to about two visits a month, each lasting roughly an hour, from their families. These visits are important to all prisoners and to their families. Immediately before the visit the prisoner is likely to become tense, anticipating the short period that there will be to exchange family news with a partner or children. Then for some unknown reason, the visit is delayed. The reason may be that there is a security alert, or that there has been a problem with earlier visits, or that there are not enough staff to supervise visits on that day. Whatever the reason, the prisoner will feel let down and annoyed. The importance of this may not be immediately obvious to many of us, although anyone who has been a patient in hospital, waiting for the daily visiting period may have some understanding of the emotion involved.

Prisoners may also be concerned about delays in correspondence or lost property. Another example, which might not be immediately obvious to someone who has not been in prison, might be the cost of an item, say, toothpaste or hair shampoo which prisoners have to purchase in the prison shop out of their earnings or savings. In normal life we can shop around to find the cheapest brand or the brand which suits us best. Prison shops will stock one or two brands which prisoners must buy. If without warning the brand is changed or the price goes up by a few pence upsetting the prisoners' careful weekly budgeting of their small finances, many will feel aggrieved. The normal person hearing of this might conclude that this is an example of prisoners being small minded and unreasonable. For the prisoner, these can be major issues.

Prisoners may have other questions to do with internal prison matters, such as which work party they are allocated to, whether they can have access to a particular education class, whether they can have an extra shower or change of clothing. All of these are relatively minor matters in themselves but take on considerable significance in the highly regulated life of the prison.

In England and Wales there is a well-developed system for prisoners to make requests and complaints. In the first instance prisoners are encouraged to raise any issue which concerns them with the staff who are their immediate supervisors. An experienced member of staff will know which matters he or she can deal with directly and which will have to be referred to a more senior level. In most prisons staff who directly supervise prisoners have the authority to deal with many personal matters, such as agreeing that a prisoner may have an extra visit with his or her family. In any event, the officer should be able to have a sensible discussion with the prisoner and often to resolve the matter straight away.

Sometimes it will not be possible to resolve a request or complaint in this manner, so there is also a formal procedure for dealing with matters which cannot be resolved informally. This procedure is paper-based, ensuring that there is a record which can be referred to in the event of a future dispute. The prisoner asks for a request and complaint form. When this has been completed, it is passed to the appropriate department for a decision. This is recorded on the form, which is then returned to the prisoner. Prisoners who are unhappy with the reply which they receive can ask that the request be considered at the next level, ultimately reaching a member of senior management who has been given responsibility by the prison governor for overseeing all requests and complaints in the prison.

In parallel with this open system there is a process for what is known as 'confidential access'. In this process prisoners put their written request or complaint in an envelope which they personally seal and address directly to the prison governor. Prisoners may use the confidential access route for a variety of reasons. It may be that they feel junior staff have not taken their complaint seriously or have given an ill-informed response, or it may be that they wish to make a complaint about the treatment they have received from the staff who supervise them. The governor will personally open and read all of these complaints. If he or she concludes that the issue in hand is within the competence of junior staff who have not been given the opportunity to deal with it, he may well then pass it back to them to deal with. In this case, he will inform the prisoner that this has been done. If the matter is one on which only the governor can make a decision, then the governor will make a personal written response to the prisoner. This will invariably be the case where there is a complaint from a prisoner of ill-treatment or verbal or physical abuse. In these cases the governor is likely to appoint a senior member of staff to carry out an investigation and to report back to allow the governor to reply to the prisoner, indicating any action which is to be taken.

The degree to which requests and complaints submitted directly to the governor are genuinely confidential is a matter for frequent discussion and debate in the prison world. If, for example, the complaint is that a member of staff has ill-treated a prisoner in any way, then that member of staff will invariably be asked to explain his or her position and so will become aware that a particular prisoner has made a complaint against him/her. The same will apply to most other requests touching on decisions which have been made earlier by other members of staff. The important principle is that the request must reach the governor in a confidential manner so that he or she is aware of the issue at stake.

On occasion the prisoner's complaint may be against the governor personally in the first instance or against a decision which she or he has made. In that case, the prisoner has the further right of making a confidential written complaint to the area manager, who is the immediate superior of the governor of the prison. As with the previous process, the confidentiality lies in the fact that the complaint goes directly to the area manager, without being read by anyone in the prison. Thereafter, in investigating the matter the area manager is likely to refer the issue back to the prison for explanation and comment. At the end of the inquiry the area manager will send a written reply to the prisoner.

Independent avenues of complaint

However well the prison system is managed, it remains a relatively closed organization. In chapter three we learned about the various external mechanisms which exist to ensure that it operates in a just and humane manner. Most of these deal either exclusively or generally with the way the system itself operates. In the interests of natural justice it is important that prisoners should be able to take personal complaints outside the system. There are several avenues for doing so in England and Wales.

The Independent Monitoring Boards described in chapter three have a direct interest in matters affecting individual prisoners. In each prison members will hold regular surgeries to which prisoners can come to raise matters of concern. Prisoners can also use the 'confidential access' process to put matters directly in writing to the Board. They also have the right to be given a hearing by the full Board at its monthly meeting. Boards may deal with complaints in an open manner, acting as a mediator between the prisoner and the member of staff concerned. In other cases it may take a more formal approach by raising the issue either in writing or orally with the prison governor or another senior member of staff. If the Board is not satisfied with the management response it may raise the matter with the area manager. Once it has investigated the matter to its satisfaction, the Board is required to give an answer to the prisoner. This should be done in the same way that the complaint was lodged, either orally or in writing. While the Independent Monitoring Boards bring an important element of independence, they have no executive authority and cannot instruct prison management to amend a decision or to change the way a prisoner is treated. The ultimate route they can take is to write formally to the Home Secretary to draw to his attention any concerns that they have. They rarely exercise this right in respect of the treatment of an individual prisoner.

The terms of reference of the Chief Inspector do not allow her to investigate complaints about matters affecting individual prisoners. The Woolf Report (1991) identified this as an omission and recommended that there should be a further independent appointment to deal with complaints by prisoners. The role of Prisons Ombudsman was created in 1994. Working independently of the prison service, his task is to investigate complaints made by prisoners about their treatment by prison staff. Following the establishment of a national probation service in 2001 he became the Prisons and Probation Ombudsman. In 2004 the terms of reference were extended to include investigations into all deaths in prisons and deaths of residents of probation hostels and immigration removal and detention centres.

The first holder of this post was a person who had for many years directed one of the leading independent prison reform bodies in the United Kingdom. The initial broad terms of reference of the Ombudsman were to consider grievances from prisoners, including those about disciplinary offences, once all internal procedures had been exhausted. The specific terms of reference were not laid out and in his first annual report the Ombudsman reported that much of this attention had been devoted to resolving differences of interpretation about his terms of reference (Prisons Ombudsman 1996: 5). In 2001 the Ombudsman's remit was extended to cover complaints from persons on probation and in 2003 it was further extended to include investigation of all deaths in prisons, probation accommodation and immigration detention.

In common with the Independent Monitoring Boards, the Prisons Ombudsman has no executive authority and cannot insist that his findings be acted on. This is in contrast to the power of many other Ombudspersons. The British and Irish Ombudsman Association has refused to allow the Prisons and Probation Ombudsman to become one of its members because he is appointed by and accountable to the Home Secretary and subject to the overall authority of the Parliamentary Ombudsman.

In the year 2003–04 the Ombudsman received 3527 complaints from prisoners, an increase of 11 per cent from the previous year. Of these only 46 per cent met the 'eligibility criteria', usually because internal avenues of complaint had not been exhausted. The greatest number of complaints, 18 per cent, were to do with prisoners' property, while 8 per cent were about disciplinary hearings (Prisons and Probation Ombudsman 2004). The Ombudsman reported that whenever possible he attempted to reach 'more local, more restorative' resolutions to complaints. As a result, he resolved 420 complaints locally. Of 114 recommendations made to the prison service, 97 were accepted and one rejected, with the remainder still under consideration.

Before the establishment of the Prisons Ombudsman the main external channel of complaint for prisoners was the Parliamentary Commissioner of Administration, now the Parliamentary and Health Service Ombudsman. Everyone in the United Kingdom is entitled to approach this Ombudsman if they consider that they have legitimate complaint about any decision made by a public body which affects them. For most citizens the approach has to be made through a constituency Member of Parliament. Prisoners, however, have the right to raise an issue directly with the Ombudsman. This is not a complaint procedure which is commonly used by prisoners.

Legal process

As with other citizens, prisoners have the right of access to the court to make complaints or seek judicial review. This was confirmed in a famous judgement by the Law Lords in 1983, which concluded:

> Under English law a convicted prisoner retains all civil rights which are not taken away expressly or by necessary implication.
>
> (Raymond v. Honey 1983, 1 AC 1)

All United Kingdom citizens have had the right to make application to the European Court of Human Rights in Strasbourg in matters affecting themselves. If the Court admits the application, it will then consider the evidence and will make a legally binding finding in the case. Prisoners were among the first in the United Kingdom to make use of the European Court. Early cases in which the Court made decisions in favour of prisoners were to do with interference with correspondence to lawyers (Golder v. UK [1975] 1 EHRR 524, Series A No. 18 and Silver v. UK [1983] 5 EHRR 347, Series A No. 61) and loss of remission (Campbell and Fell v. UK [1985] 15 EHRR 137, Series A No. 80).

In more recent years the European Court has issued a series of judgements in connection with prisons in England and Wales. These include the following:

- In 2001, the Court found that the United Kingdom had violated Article 3 of the Convention, which prohibits torture and inhuman or degrading treatment or punishment, in the case of a prisoner named Mark Keenan in Exeter prison. The finding was in respect of the lack of medical notes, lack of psychiatric monitoring and segregation incompatible with the proper treatment of a mentally ill person (Keenan v. United Kingdom Application 27229/95).

- In 2002 the UK was again found to have violated Article 2 (right to life) in the case of Christopher Edwards, a pre-trial prisoner kicked to death by his cell-mate in Chelmsford prison (Paul and Audrey Edwards v. the United Kingdom Application 46477/99).
- In the same year the UK was found to have violated Article 3 when it held in New Hall prison for seven days Adele Price, a thalidomide victim with no arms or legs, in conditions not adapted in any way to her disabilities. The judgement in this case was particularly damning and deserves close scrutiny (Price v. United Kingdom Application 33394/96).
- Article 6 of the European Convention sets out the right to a fair trial. In 2002 the UK was found to be in violation in a case which is described in more detail in chapter seven (Ezeh and Connors v. the United Kingdom Applications 39665/98 and 40086/98).
- In 2003 the Court found the UK in breach of Article 2 of the Convention in respect of the death of Judith McGlinchey, again in New Hall prison (McGlinchey a.o. v. United Kingdom Application 50390/99).

One of the practical problems of pursuing a case in Strasbourg is the length of time it takes to be resolved, typically stretching over several years. This meant that it was not a practical way of resolving an immediate problem. Rather, it was a method of establishing a precedent which might benefit others at a later date. This was the situation, particularly with some of the early prison cases which resulted directly in changes to prison regulations. In 1998 the UK parliament enacted the Human Rights Act, which incorporated the European Convention on Human Rights (ECHR) into domestic legislation. An immediate consequence of this Act was that, instead of taking action via Strasbourg, United Kingdom citizens can now take up cases under the ECHR in domestic courts. At the time of writing the best known case taken by a prisoner under this legislation is that of Robert Napier v. the Scottish Ministers (Napier 2004), described earlier in this chapter.

Voting

There has been an increasing understanding in some jurisdictions in recent years of the concept of the prisoner as a citizen, a person who, as described in the Raymond v. Honey judgement, retains all civil rights, apart from those which are removed by the fact of imprisonment. An issue which is now being discussed in the United Kingdom in relation to this concept is whether prisoners should have the right to vote in elections. Under current domestic legislation remand prisoners, people imprisoned for contempt of court and fine defaulters held in prison do not lose the right to vote. However, under the Representation of the People Act 1983, amended by the

Representation of the People Acts 1985 and 2000 sentenced prisoners are prohibited from voting. Before the 2005 general election the government announced that the 40 or so prisoners sentenced to intermittent custody, that is who were in prison on a part-time basis, were not subject to this prohibition provided they were not in prison on the day of the election.

The United Kingdom is in a minority among European countries in having this total prohibition for sentenced prisoners. Eighteen European countries, including Ireland, the Netherlands and Spain have no ban, some other countries have a partial ban. In France and Germany, courts have the power to impose loss of voting rights as an additional punishment. The only other European countries which automatically disenfranchise all sentenced prisoners are Armenia, Bulgaria, Czech Republic, Estonia, Hungary, Luxembourg and Romania.

As with the right to family life, the issue of prisoners' voting is one which arouses emotion on both sides of the debate. Some politicians and others have suggested that, as a consequence of their conviction, prisoners have forfeited the moral right to take part in elections which decide how the country is to be governed. The link between morality and the right to vote is not immediately clear in legal terms. If that were to become a condition of eligibility to vote, the prohibition might extend well beyond prisoners. Supporters of prisoners' right to vote claim that this is an inalienable human right enshrined in Article 3 of the Protocol to the European Convention on Human Rights (ECHR) and Article 25 of the International Covenant on Civil and Political Rights. In practical terms, they suggest that the ban is not an effective deterrent and does not protect public safety but that it is an unjust additional punishment. Giving prisoners the vote, they argue, would encourage them to become responsible, law-abiding citizens.

In March 2004 in a case brought by an English life-sentenced prisoner the European Court of Human Rights ruled that the indiscriminate ban on sentenced prisoners voting did indeed violate Article 3 of the Protocol to the ECHR (Hirst (2) v. United Kingdom (2) Application 74025/01).

The decency agenda

In 2000 the prison service launched what it called the 'decency' agenda. Speaking at that year's annual conference the then Director General made it clear that the prison service expected prisoners to be treated 'with dignity' (speech by Director General, Martin Narey, to the prison service conference, 2000. Nottingham, Tuesday, 1 February 2000). When the next Director General was appointed in 2003, he committed himself to 'leading a prison service that treats all prisoners ... with decency and fairness' (prison service website, www.hmprisonservice.gov.uk, home page, June 2003). Since then the prison service has continued to emphasize this issue.

The prison service business plan 2005–2006 defines what the service understands decency to involve:

- Treatment within the law.
- Promised standards to be delivered.
- Clean, properly equipped and properly maintained facilities.
- Prisoners given prompt attention to their proper concerns.
- Prisoners to be protected from harm.
- Prisoners to be provided with a regime that gives them enough variety and choice to make imprisonment bearable.
- Prisoners to be treated fairly and equally.

The business plan concludes (2005: 17): 'And the overall test remains, Would I be content for my son or daughter to be locked up and treated in the way that prisoners are treated in this prison?'

Further reading

Committee for the Prevention of Torture (1991) Report to the Government of the United Kingdom CPT/Inf (1991) 15. Strasbourg.

Committee for the Prevention of Torture (2005) Report to the Government of the United Kingdom CPT/Inf (2005) 1. Strasbourg.

Dunbar, I. (1985) *A Sense of Direction*. London: Home Office.

Maguire, J. (ed.) (1996) *What Works: Reducing Re-Offending*. Chichester: John Wiley.

Player, E. and Jenkins, M. (eds) (1994) *Prisons After Woolf: Reform Through Riot*. London: Routledge.

Woolf Report (1991) *Report of an Inquiry into Prison Disturbances April 1990*. Cmnd 1456. London: HMSO.

Order and control

Finding the right balance

By now we have learned that the prison is a complicated and multi-layered institution with many contrasting and, at times, competing pressures. In the previous chapter we considered what goes on in prison on a daily basis and the attempts that are made to get as much benefit as possible out of the experience of imprisonment. However, there is no hiding the fact that prison is a coercive environment where men and women are held against their will. Although one of the classic prison texts describes prison as a 'Society of Captives' (Sykes 1958), it cannot be regarded as a society in the commonly understood sense of that word. In addition to being kept there forcibly, the residents of each prison are all of the same gender, in most instances young adult males, and for long periods of each day their movement is severely restricted, as is the communication they can have with other people. All of this adds up to a volatile cocktail, where there is an ever present potential for violence and disorder. Yet the reality is that most prisons are safe and non-violent for most of the time.

One of the most important findings of the report produced by Lord Justice Woolf after a number of very serious riots in English prisons in 1990 was that the key feature in an effectively managed prison is the maintenance of a balance between the three important elements of what he called security, control and justice.

> (T)here are three requirements which must be met if the prison system is to be stable: they are security, control and justice.
> For present purposes, 'security' refers to the obligation of the Prison Service to prevent prisoners escaping. 'Control' deals with the obligation of the Prison Service to prevent prisoners being disruptive. 'Justice' refers to the obligation of the Prison Service to treat prisoners with humanity and fairness and to prepare them for their return to the community in a way which makes it less likely that they will reoffend.
> (Woolf 1991, paras 9.19 and 9.20)

This chapter will examine how this balance is achieved and will analyze what is involved in the concepts of security and control.

In identifying the need for balance, Woolf is pointing out that these three key features of prison management are complementary and are not in competition with each other. It is quite wrong to suggest that treating prisoners with 'humanity and fairness' will lead to a reduction in security or control. On the contrary, the objective of preventing escapes and disruption can best be achieved within a well-ordered and positive environment

- which is safe for prisoners and staff,
- in which all members of the prison community perceive they are being treated with fairness and justice,
- in which prisoners have the opportunity to participate in constructive activities and to prepare themselves for release.

In prisons in some countries the balance between these three elements is missing. This may happen because the prison authorities place undue emphasis on security and control at the expense of justice. This can result in oppressive security measures which exclude rehabilitative programmes, brutal methods of control, lack of justice in disciplinary hearings and unlawful punishments (Human Rights Watch 1997). In some other countries the balance has swung to the opposite extreme. Those managing prisons have lost control of their institutions and have allowed powerful groups of prisoners to exert an illegal system of control over both other prisoners and staff (Coyle 2002a: 35). Each of these situations is likely to lead to a breakdown in good order, leading to the possibility of violent and abusive behaviour by either prisoners or staff, the likelihood of disorder, the possibility of escapes and an absence of constructive activities for prisoners. For the majority of prisoners a breakdown in good order is a terrifying and corrupting experience.

In England and Wales the prison service has developed sets of sophisticated procedures to maintain the necessary balance.

Security

The first obligation of any prison system is to keep in custody those whom the courts have decided should lose their liberty. No ordinary person likes being in prison but the majority of prisoners reluctantly accept the reality of their situation. Since they have been sent to prison by a court of law they are prepared to serve their sentences quietly, cooperating with the staff and avoiding trouble. Some would not attempt to escape under any circumstances and require only minimal security and supervision. The majority, if subject to appropriate security measures and fair treatment, will not try to escape or seriously disrupt the normal routine of the prison. In most prison systems there may also be a small number of prisoners who will do everything in their power to try to escape. Some of them may well have committed very serious crimes and, were they to escape, they would be a danger to the public. All of these factors mean that the prison authorities have to make judgements about the level of security needed to hold each prisoner.

Security categories

In England and Wales each convicted prisoner is allocated to one of four levels of security, which are labelled 'A' to 'D' in descending order. This system was introduced following a recommendation by Lord Mountbatten in the report which he produced after the escape of a high profile prisoner from Wormwood Scrubs Prison in 1966 (Mountbatten Report 1966). Mountbatten's definition of each category was as follows:

> Category A: Those whose escape would be highly dangerous to the public or the police or to the security of the State.
>
> (para 15)

> Category B: Those for whom the very highest conditions of security are not necessary, but for whom escape must be made very difficult, and who ought to be kept in very secure conditions.
>
> (paras 15 and 217)

> Category C: Those who cannot be trusted in open conditions, but who do not have the ability or resources to make a determined escape attempt. For them there should be prisons with sufficient defences to make escape difficult.
>
> (paras 15 and 217)

> Category D: Those who can reasonably be entrusted to serve their sentences in open conditions.
>
> (para 217)

Although security was and is the main responsibility of the prison service, Mountbatten saw the need for proportionality in its application and one of the main reasons for his classification system was to focus attention on those who presented the greatest threat of escape.

> There will, no doubt, continue to be escapes, or abscondings as they are better called, from open prisons. These represent a social nuisance and are an additional burden on the police, and everything possible should be done to reduce them. They should not, however, represent a threat to the life and safety of the population if chosen with care, and in regard to these prisoners I would not think it unreasonable for the authorities to take certain risks, always provided that the allocations are made with care and that no absconding is treated as trivial matter.
>
> (para 217)

He also made it clear that security categorization was not to be a tablet of stone, decided at the outset of a sentence and never thereafter to be changed.

> The allocation of prisoners to the categories I have described needs to be kept under continuous review and subjected to careful research to ensure that allocations are being made correctly.
>
> (para 218)

He envisaged that as prisoners progressed through their sentences, the security threat that they presented might reduce and their security category could, therefore, be reduced. On occasion, the reverse might happen and the security category of an individual might have to be increased.

This system of security identification remains largely in force today, although there have been some calibrations. A subdivision of category C prisoners was introduced some years ago to deal particularly with problematic young offenders who had a history of gang membership. The main alteration has been in respect of category A prisoners. Mountbatten envisaged that only a very small number of prisoners would qualify for category A security status and the fact that there were so few of them would mean that all staff would be alert as to their whereabouts at all times. This indeed was what happened when the Mountbatten security categorizations were introduced. A named prison officer had responsibility for the direct supervision of each category A prisoner at all times. The officer carried a book, detailing where the prisoner had been at each moment. When another officer took over responsibility for the prisoner, the book was also handed over. The location of every prisoner in security category A was recorded at all times and the record had to be in the personal possession of a named prison officer.

Over the years, however, the number of prisoners being allocated to security category A increased significantly. There are a number of possible reasons as to why this happened. One was that the proportion of prisoners who presented the threat to security originally envisaged by Mountbatten increased as crime and criminals became more sophisticated. Another possibility was that those who were making decisions about allocating security categories were applying different criteria. This was certainly an influencing factor as the A to D categorization, which was originally only a security tool, was expanded to take account of the threat that a prisoner might present to good order within a prison, as we shall discuss in the next section.

Whatever the reason, the fact that the numbers increased significantly meant that the rarity value of the category A prisoner diminished. Whereas initially every category A prisoner was known individually to staff in his prison, the situation changed to the extent that in some high-security prisons they were almost taken for granted. In 1987 two category A prisoners escaped by helicopter from Gartree prison (King and McDermott 1995: 59). Following this there was a review of the Mountbatten security categories and three subdivisions of category A were introduced. The majority of category A prisoners were defined as 'standard risk'. Those who required additional supervision were known as 'high risk'. A small number were defined as 'exceptional risk' and were allocated to special secure units within the dispersal prisons which are described later in this chapter (Bryans and Jones 2001: 103).

In parallel with security categorization prisons also maintain what is called an 'escape list', which is a list of those prisoners who have escaped or who have been discovered making a real attempt to escape. Although they may be in security category B, prisoners on this list are subject to personal supervision and are required to wear distinctive uniforms. No one on the escape list will be in less than security category B.

The security level of the prison

In some prison systems each prison is allocated a level of security and every prisoner within it is supervised in a manner relevant to that level. In respect of the individual prisoner, the decision to allocate him or her to a specific prison replaces the need for individual categorization. In the Federal Bureau of Prisons in the United States of America, for example, there are five different security levels for prisons. These levels are based on such features as the presence of external patrols, towers, security barriers, or detection devices; the type of housing within the prison; internal security features; and the staff-to-prisoner ratios. The levels are minimum, low, medium, high, or administrative. Administrative facilities are defined as 'institutions with special missions, such as the detention of pre-trial offenders; the treatment of inmates with serious or chronic medical problems; or the containment of extremely dangerous, violent, or escape-prone inmates' (http://www.bop.gov/locations/institutions/index.jsp).

The security levels of prison in England and Wales are something of a hybrid. Generally, prisons are defined according to their level of physical security and this in turn determines the highest category of prisoner they can hold. Physical security includes that surrounding the perimeter. For example, whether this consists of a single barrier of a wall or a fence or a double barrier, and how it is patrolled. It also includes internal security arrangements, such as the extent to which the movement of prisoners is supervised. For example, whether they are supervised by staff at all times, even when in their own living units and workplace, or whether they are allowed a degree of freedom in moving from one part of the prison to another.

Open prisons have no perimeter fence or wall and security will be limited to doors, many of which are locked only at night. All those in open prisons will be in security category D and will be free to go about the prison without being personally supervised by staff. A number of them may also leave the prison each day to work in the community. Typically there will be roll calls or number counts at the beginning and end of each day. Kirklevington Grange prison in Cleveland and Askham Grange prison near York are examples of open prisons.

The next security category of prison will have a secure fence around the perimeter. Almost all of the prisoners in this type of prison will be in security category C, although there may also be some category D prisoners. The latter will be there for a personal reason, such as the completion of a course of education or training, or to work or to attend a course outside the prison. The prisoners will all be convicted. Generally speaking, they will be allowed to move from one part of the prison to another without being escorted by staff, although they will have to obtain permission to go outside their own area. In addition, there may be locked gates at various points, for example, between the various accommodation units or between the living units and the workshops. Dartmoor in Devon and Risley in Lancashire are examples of category C prisons.

Prisons in the next highest security category are capable of holding prisoners in security category B, but may also hold some category C and D prisoners. These prisons will usually have a double fence or a wall and a fence. The perimeter is likely to be covered by closed-circuit television. Internal security arrangements will also be of a high level, with each area securely locked and prisoners escorted by staff when moving from one area to another. Gartree prison in Leicestershire is an example of a category B prison. Also in this group are the majority of the large inner city local prisons. In addition to convicted prisoners they hold remand prisoners and any others who are not convicted. Wandsworth prison in London, Leeds prison and Birmingham prison are examples of this type.

Finally, there are the high-security prisons, which will be referred to shortly. There are only five of them in all and their security is, by definition, of the highest level. They are the only prisons which hold prisoners in the various levels of security category A, as well as some category B prisoners. They are Frankland, Full Sutton, Long Lartin, Wakefield and Whitemoor prisons. In addition, a small number of local prisons have a high enough level of security to hold category A remand prisoners. They are Belmarsh, Manchester and Woodhill.

Dynamic security

There is much more to security in a prison than walls and fences, doors and locks, bars and bolts. We have already discussed the fact that one of the defining features of a prison is the relationship between first-line staff and prisoners. This relationship is also an important factor in respect of security. A closed-circuit television monitor will alert staff to the fact that a group of prisoners are climbing over the wall but it will not let them know in advance that they are planning to do so. This is where the human factor, which is often referred to as dynamic security, comes in (Dunbar 1985). In the United States this is sometimes referred to as direct supervision. It is the opposite of the arrangement whereby staff observe prisoners at a distance, often via television monitors, and rarely come into physical contact with them.

In the dynamic security model staff will mix with prisoners. They will move among them, talk to them and listen to them; there will be the normal dynamics of human interaction. Yet it will not be the same, because all the time staff will be alert to sense the atmosphere among the prisoners, to be conscious of the presence of any tension which will invariably precede the occurrence of an untoward incident. This is not merely a matter of staff seeking to pick up security intelligence from prisoners. It has a much more positive connotation since normal interaction between staff and prisoners is likely to reduce the coercive nature of the environment.

Good order

If the first obligation of a prison system is to ensure security, a close second is the need to ensure that they are places where good order prevails (Sykes 1958). On entering a prison for the first time, whether as prisoner, member of staff or visitor, the reaction of most people, is 'Will I be safe?'. Prison is an unknown environment at first sight and it is by no means clear that the normal rules of civil society will operate there (Sparks, Bottoms and Hay 1996).

The vast majority of prisoners are young males, all of them charged with or convicted of criminal offences. Many of them have volatile or disturbed personalities. Groups and individuals who would not normally mix with each other are thrown into close proximity. Even among families or close friends life in such a hot house would be liable to provoke tensions and to lead to occasional verbal or even physical violence. In a prison setting one also has to factor in the possibility of clashes between different ethnic, racial or criminal groupings. Taking all of these features into account one is entitled to be surprised, not that disorder occurs in prisons from time to time, but that it occurs so infrequently. The fact that prisons in England and Wales are, generally speaking, well-ordered places does not occur by accident. There is a constant awareness among staff that prevention is always better than cure, that stopping violence from taking place is always better that dealing with it when it does.

Violence and unrest is not in the interests of the vast majority of prisoners. In the short term, they are the ones who are likely to be intimidated or assaulted. In the longer term, they will suffer from the inevitable tightening of discipline which comes in the aftermath of unrest. If the general approach of staff to prisoners is fair and consistent it will be more difficult for prisoners who wish to create trouble to secure the support of other prisoners.

In the prison environment, as in many other large institutions where individuals may feel vulnerable, the greatest threat to stability is uncertainty. People like to know where they stand. They like to know what the rules are; what they may do, what they should not do and what the consequences are if they break the rules. In general terms prisoners can cope with a prison where there is a strict regime just as well as with one where there is more flexibility. What they find very difficult to cope with is an inconsistent model of control, where the rules vary or where they are applied differently depending on which staff are on duty. There is evidence that a real threat to good order occurs when a prison is not being consistently managed and when levels of control are not clearly understood. The worst example in recent years of how inconsistent messages can lead to a breakdown of order was the riot at Strangeways prison in Manchester in April 1990, which was described in chapter two.

The role of high-security prisons

In this chapter we are considering two important tasks of the prison service, security and good order. These are closely allied tasks but they are not the same. A small number of prisoners are a real threat to security, that is they will attempt to escape whenever the opportunity presents itself, and are also a real threat to good order, that is they will refuse to obey legitimate prison regulations and will attempt to disrupt the smooth running of the prison in a variety of ways. But some prisoners who are a real security risk are no threat to good order. They live quietly in the prison and have no interest in stirring up unrest among other prisoners for its own sake. To all appearances they are model prisoners except that, at the first opportunity, they will escape. There are other prisoners who have little interest in escaping or capacity to do so, yet who will do everything in their power to disrupt the daily routine of the prison. They may be a real threat to the physical safety of staff and of other prisoners. Good prison management needs to make a distinction between these two groups of prisoners. In England and Wales it has not always done so.

Having been set up in the wake of the audacious escape of the notorious spy George Blake, the Mountbatten Report was concerned primarily with prisoners who were a security risk and the categories A to D which the report advocated were security categories. Since he was not directly concerned with matters of good order, Mountbatten also recommended that the prison service should hold prisoners in the highest security category, the new 'Category As', in one super-secure prison. However, this was not acceptable to the Home Office which wished to consider the wider issue of how to manage all long-term prisoners who needed to be held in maximum security conditions. In other words, it wanted to deal jointly with those who were a threat to security and also with those who were a threat to good order. The Home Office then resorted to the standard ploy of government when an inquiry comes up with a solution which is not quite what it wants: it set up another inquiry. This second one, under the chairmanship of an eminent criminologist, in due course came up with the solution which was wanted (Radzinowicz Report 1968). Mountbatten had produced what was known as the 'concentration' solution to the problem; that is, to put all the prisoners in one prison. The Radzinowicz Report came up with what became known as the 'dispersal' solution; that is, to disperse the prisoners around a small number of high-security prisons. This recommendation was accepted by the government and in the course of the five years after the report was published Gartree, Hull, Parkhurst, Albany and Long Lartin prisons were designated as dispersal prisons.

The resolution of the argument about the relative merits of concentration and dispersal in favour of the latter created the seeds of two sets of problems which were to bedevil the prison service for the following twenty years. In the first place it threw together two groups of prisoners who presented management with different sets of problems and who together became a volatile mix. The dispersal prisons accommodated the group of prisoners who were considered to be 'dangerous' and who were, therefore, placed in security category A, but their perceived dangerousness took two different forms. Those who were escape risks, but not necessarily control problems, were located alongside those who were control problems, but not necessarily escape risks. Different skills were needed to manage each of these groups and this became impossible when they were held together.

The second set of problems resulted from the fact that five prisons were identified to hold 'dangerous' prisoners. One of the reasons for this was that it provided the facility to move prisoners from one prison to another, either for their own good or when the level of risk they presented at one prison became too great. However, the total number of places in the dispersal prisons was far in excess of what was needed for the relatively small number of category A prisoners. The additional places had to be used and so long-term category B prisoners were also held there and in most instances outnumbered the category A prisoners. The result was that all the prisoners were subject to the maximum security and control needed for the smaller group. This meant that the category B prisoners in the dispersal prisons came to be regarded by virtue of association as *de facto* category As. This in turn resulted in what one might describe as 'security creep', with the inexorable rise in the number of category A prisoners as described in the previous section.

The rule of law

Given the fact that prisoners are human, it is axiomatic that from time to time some of them will break the rules and regulations of the prison in a variety of ways. A breach of the rules can take many forms. It may be a refusal to follow the daily routine, disobedience of a legitimate order or an attempt to smuggle into the prison items which are not allowed. It might be a physical attack on another prisoner or a member of staff or theft of something which belongs to someone else. There has to be a clear set of procedures for dealing with such incidents.

In the first place, there has to be a clear understanding that justice does not end at the prison gate (Woolf Report 1991: 14.19). Everyone within a prison, whether prisoner, prison officer or visitor, is entitled to the protection of the law. Prisons are legally public places and if the law is broken inside them the police are entitled, indeed have an obligation, to undertake criminal investigations just as they would anywhere else. For example, any person who is seriously assaulted in prison is just as entitled to the protection of the criminal law as is someone who is similarly attacked in a public place. It should be normal practice in any prison that when a serious criminal act has or is thought to have taken place that a system of investigation similar to that which is used in civil society should operate.

At the same time, it may be that an incident which is serious in the prison context will not be regarded as worthy of further action by the criminal investigating authorities. An example might be when a prisoner is found to be in possession of a small quantity of cannabis for personal use or when there has been a fight in which both parties were equally at fault and no one is seriously injured. However, in both cases the good order of the prison will require that some action should be taken.

In England and Wales there will often be an agreement, formal or otherwise, between the prison governor and the local police chief about which incidents within the prison should be referred to the police for investigation and which should be dealt with through internal prison procedures. For example, in terms of personal assault, it is likely that one in which a weapon is used or in which a bone or limb is broken would be notified to the police for investigation, whereas minor assaults would be dealt with by the prison.

Discipline and punishment

It follows from the above that the prison disciplinary process should deal primarily with breaches of rules and regulations which are administrative in nature rather than criminal. As in all matters of administrative justice it is important that the principles of natural justice should be respected. The first of these is that all prisoners should be informed about the rules and regulations of the prison. These regulations should include a detailed list of the acts or omissions which constitute a breach of prison discipline and which are liable to lead to formal disciplinary action. Similarly, there should be a published list of the punishments which can be imposed for breaches of discipline.

In England and Wales these details are contained in the Prison Rules. These are contained in a Statutory Instrument, approved by Parliament (*The Prison Rules 1999*). The offences against discipline, as amended in 2000, are listed as follows:

Rule 51
A prisoner is guilty of an offence against discipline if he –
(1) commits any assault;
(1A) commits any racially aggravated assault;
(2) detains any person against his will;
(3) denies access to any part of the prison to any officer or any person (other than a prisoner) who is at the prison for the purpose of working there;
(4) fights with any person;
(5) intentionally endangers the health or personal safety of others or, by his conduct, is reckless whether such health or personal safety is endangered;
(6) intentionally obstructs an officer in the execution of his duty, or any person (other than a prisoner) who is at the prison for the purpose of working there, in the performance of his work;
(7) escapes or absconds from prison or from legal custody;
(8) fails to comply with any condition upon which he is temporarily released under rule 9;
(9) administers a controlled drug to himself or fails to prevent the administration of a controlled drug to him by another person (but subject to rule 52);
(10) is intoxicated as a consequence of knowingly consuming any alcoholic beverage;
(11) knowingly consumes any alcoholic beverage other than that provided to him pursuant to a written order under rule 25(1);
(12) has in his possession –
(a) any unauthorised article, or
(b) a greater quantity of any article than he is authorised to have;

(13) sells or delivers to any person any unauthorised article;

(14) sells or, without permission, delivers to any person any article which he is allowed to have only for his own use;

(15) takes improperly any article belonging to another person or to a prison;

(16) intentionally or recklessly sets fire to any part of a prison or any other property, whether or not his own;

(17) destroys or damages any part of a prison or any other property, other than his own;

(17A) causes racially aggravated damage to, or destruction of, any part of a prison or any other property, other than his own;

(18) absents himself from any place he is required to be or is present at any place where he is not authorised to be;

(19) is disrespectful to any officer, or any person (other than a prisoner) who is at the prison for the purpose of working there, or any person visiting a prison;

(20) uses threatening, abusive or insulting words or behaviour;

(20A) uses threatening, abusive or insulting racial words or behaviour;

(21) intentionally fails to work properly or, being required to work, refuses to do so;

(22) disobeys any lawful order;

(23) disobeys or fails to comply with any rule or regulation applying to him;

(24) receives any controlled drug, or, without the consent of an officer, any other article, during the course of a visit (not being an interview such as is mentioned in rule 38);

(24A) displays, attaches or draws on any part of a prison, or on any other property, threatening, abusive or insulting racist words, drawings, symbols or other materials;

(25)

(a) attempts to commit,

(b) incites another prisoner to commit, or

(c) assists another prisoner to commit or to attempt to commit, any of the foregoing offences.

The procedures for dealing with any alleged breach of discipline are laid down in detail. If an officer or other member of staff decides that a prisoner appears to have committed a breach of discipline in terms of Prison Rule 51, a formal charge should be laid in writing against the prisoner. This must be done within 48 hours of the offence being discovered (rule 53). The charge must be prepared on a special form, with the charge or charges specifically defined, together with a brief summary of the allegation and the names of any witnesses who are to be called to give supporting evidence, and signed by the charging officer. The subsequent hearing of the charge by the governor must begin the next working day.

The prisoner must be provided with written details of the charge and the name of the officer making the accusation. These details must be given to the accused person sufficiently in advance of the hearing to allow him to prepare his or her defence to the accusations. The prisoner must be allowed to call witnesses in defence; they may be other prisoners, members of staff or anyone else who witnessed what was alleged to have happened.

At a set time each day, other than Sundays and public holidays, the prison governor or his nominated deputy will hear all cases of alleged breach of discipline. The hearing takes place in a formal environment. Until a number of years ago the experience for the prisoner was made deliberately intimidating. The governor would sit in a quasi-judicial position, flanked by senior staff. The accused person would be marched into the room, escorted by two officers. He would stand facing the governor, with the two officers standing close on either side of him at right angles, which meant that they were looking directly at either side of his face. The accused person was at a distinct disadvantage. The system operated on the broad assumption that staff would not have charged a person unless they were sure he was guilty. Other prisoners who were called as witnesses were also marched in and were treated almost as if they were also defending themselves. As a result, prisoners were very reluctant to give evidence on behalf of other prisoners. The atmosphere suggested that the onus was on the prisoner to prove his innocence and this rarely happened.

Although the environment of the hearings remains quite formal, real efforts have been made in recent years to reduce their intimidating atmosphere. Accused prisoners are allowed to sit and writing materials are provided so that they can make notes. Escorting staff sit on either side, facing the same way as the accused person. The governor hears evidence from all parties and then makes a decision, either finding guilt or dismissing the case. If the prisoner is found guilty, the governor can impose a range of possible punishments, which are:

Rule 55
(1) If he finds a prisoner guilty of an offence against discipline the governor may, subject to paragraph (2) and to rule 57, impose one or more of the following punishments:
(a) caution;
(b) forfeiture for a period not exceeding 42 days of any of the privileges under rule 8;
(c) exclusion from associated work for a period not exceeding 21 days;
(d) stoppage of or deduction from earnings for a period not exceeding 84 days;
(e) cellular confinement for a period not exceeding 21 days;
(g) in the case of a prisoner otherwise entitled to them, forfeiture for any period of the right, under rule 43(1), to have the articles there mentioned;

(h) removal from his wing or living unit for a period of 28 days.

(2) A caution shall not be combined with any other punishment for the same charge.

(3) If a prisoner is found guilty of more than one charge arising out of an incident, punishments under this rule may be ordered to run consecutively but, in the case of a punishment of cellular confinement, the total period shall not exceed 21 days.

(4) In imposing a punishment under this rule, the governor shall take into account any guidelines that the Secretary of State may from time to time issue as to the level of punishment that should normally be imposed for a particular offence against discipline.

The historical position regarding remission of sentence was described in chapter four. The 1952 Prison Rules gave the governor power to reduce the period of remission by up to 14 days for any one finding of guilt at adjudication. At that time the Board of Visitors, the predecessor of the Independent Monitoring Board, had the power to take disciplinary hearings of the more serious breaches of discipline and had unlimited power to reduce periods of remission. This power of the Boards of Visitors first came under scrutiny following a number of cases in the mid-1970s when Boards reduced remission in individual cases by several months. In one case a Board of Visitors reduced a prisoner's remission by 570 days and in another case by 720 days, which in practice increased the length of time the person was to spend in prison by two years. These led to important judgements in domestic courts (R v. Board of Visitors of Hull Prison, ex p St Germain. 1979. QB 425) and in the European Court of Human Rights (Campbell v. UK. 1993. 15 EHRR 137, Series A No. 233-A). These judgements made it clear that reductions of this size were disproportionate and against natural justice. Following the judgements there were important procedural changes in the way Boards carried out hearings and in the right of prisoners to legal representation.

In 1983 the power of Boards of Visitors to order unlimited loss of remission was removed but considerable anxiety remained about the propriety of the entire procedure. In 1985 a Committee of Inquiry (Prior Report 1985) recommended that the disciplinary functions of the Boards of Visitors should be removed, a proposal which the government of the day rejected. The Woolf Report (1991: 14.394) agreed with the Prior Report and in 1992 the power of the Boards of Visitors to adjudicate in serious disciplinary cases was removed by the Prison (Amendment) Rules 1992. This decision was based on the principle described above that breaches of prison discipline which were also serious criminal offences, such as escape from a high-security prison or rioting, should be dealt with through the ordinary criminal justice process and eventually the courts. However, at the same time as the disciplinary powers of the Boards of Visitors were removed the length of remission of sentence which the governor could remove was increased from 14 to 42 days. This was to allay the alleged fears of some governors and staff that discipline in the prison would be put at risk if the removal of the powers of the Boards of Visitors was not compensated for in any way.

Also in 1992 the term 'remission' was replaced by 'added days'. This was a clear acknowledgement that remission was not a privilege to be earned but a right, only to be forfeited as a result of a disciplinary process. This was shortly to prove an important change of emphasis.

Over the years there has been a debate about whether prison disciplinary proceedings should be regarded as quasi-judicial or as merely an administrative process. The Home Office and the Prison Service took the latter view but gradually legal opinion moved clearly in the other direction. This was reinforced by concern about the proportionality of some of the punishments which were being imposed and also that, despite improved procedures, there remained a question mark over the way some hearings were conducted. A change was introduced in 1992 when the adjudicating governor was given authority to consider a request for a prisoner to have legal representation at the hearing, although they were not obliged to grant the request.

The whole matter of the status of prison disciplinary hearings came to a head when two English prisoners presented a case to the European Court of Human Rights, arguing that the prison disciplinary process by which days had been added to their sentences was a breach of Article 6 of the ECHR, which guarantees the right to a fair trial. In its judgement in 1998 the Court upheld the prisoners application, finding that the disciplinary proceedings did not constitute a fair hearing (Case of Ezeh and Connors v. the United Kingdom: Application numbers 39665/98 and 40086/98). As a result of this case the Prison Service introduced changes to the internal disciplinary process (The Prison (Amendment) Rules 2002). Charges considered too serious for the Governor to handle are now referred to an independent adjudicator who is legally qualified. In these cases, the accused prisoner is entitled to have legal representation at the hearing (S. 4.3). In addition to the punishments available under Rule 55, the adjudicator can also 'award additional days not exceeding 42 days'.

It is worthy of note that when the power of governors to reduce remission was increased to 42 days in England and Wales in 1992 the similar powers in Scotland remained at a maximum of 14 days. When the Scottish prison service reviewed its procedures in light of the Human Rights Act 1998 it concluded that it would not be able to defend any challenge under the act to the power of prison governors to reduce remission and it removed that punishment (Scottish Executive Written Answers Friday 4 October 2002). The Ezeh and Connors judgement showed that it had made the correct decision.

The removal of governors' powers to add days to a prisoner's sentence is the latest in a series of reductions which have been made over the years to the punishments which they can 'award' in disciplinary hearings. Over the years, the punishment of reducing the food which a prisoner was given each day, known technically as 'dietary restriction', was removed, as was the power to restrict the number of visits a prisoner could receive. The punishments which remain largely involve loss of what are known as privileges, such as deprival of earnings or reduced access to leisure facilities. The most severe punishment which remains available is that of cellular confinement of up to 14 days. This means that prisoners are removed to the punishment unit of the prison and placed in a cell with no facilities, although the governor may allow access to a radio and to reading materials. They remain in that cell for 23 hours a day, coming out only for one hour in the fresh air on their own.

Incentives and earned privileges

Chapter three included discussion on the emphasis on security following the escapes from Whitemoor and Parkhurst prisons in 1995 and 1996. Consideration was also given at the same time to the need for additional methods of ensuring good order among prisoners. There was a feeling within some parts of the prison service that, in addition to a disciplinary procedure to punish bad behaviour there should also be a system that would provide prisoners with an incentive to behave well. This led to the introduction of what is described as the 'incentives and earned privileges scheme'. Each prison is required to categorize all available activities and privileges into three groups. First, there are those to which all prisoners would be entitled; these include all rights, such as daily exercise, and also limited activities, such as two or three hours recreation during the evening in the wing once or twice a week, access to the prison shop or canteen once a week. This is known as the basic regime. The second group includes additional access to recreation, an additional visit, perhaps the right to wear one's own clothes, to spend a greater amount of one's personal cash in the prison shop. This is known as standard regime. The third group, known as the enhanced regime, gives access to the greatest number of privileges available. It might include better visiting arrangements, television in cell, recreation every evening and access to more personal cash. The arrangements for this scheme are set out in Prison Service Order 4000.

Each week a member of staff who knows the prisoner fills out a report on the prisoner's behaviour during the previous week, giving a numbered marking to items, such as attitude to staff, relationship with other prisoners, time-keeping, cleanliness and tidiness. According to the total number of marks given, prisoners are placed on one of the three levels. There is a general view among prison staff that this scheme has given landing officers considerable additional control over the behaviour of the prisoners for whom they are responsible. Prisoners are keen to get the privileges which go with the higher grades and will make sure they do nothing to slip back to a lower one.

Specific privileges can vary between prisons, according to the facilities that are available. Modern prisons for those serving long sentences are likely to have a greater range of facilities than do Victorian inner city local prisons. One criticism of the scheme is that the facilities available in some prisons are so limited that they do not lend themselves to any gradation. In some local prisons, for example, the basic regime might involve no access to the gymnasium and recreation on only one evening a week. If facilities are restricted, there may be a *de facto* limit on the number of prisoners on standard or enhanced regimes and some prisoners complain that their weekly markings always leave them just one or two below the qualifying standard for the next level. There are also questions, for example, about the propriety of including visits in the scheme, since any restriction affects not only the prisoners but also their families and about whether a prisoner who was on enhanced regime should qualify for the same on transfer to another prison. The prison service now requires that all new prisoners should enter the scheme at the standard level.

When good order breaks down

Chapter two contains a description of the riot at Strangeways prison in April 1990, and the subsequent appointment of Lord Justice Woolf to carry out an inquiry. Woolf decided at an early stage that he would need to expand his terms of reference to include 'the underlying problems (of the prison service) and the remedies which they require' (1991: para 1.12). In doing this, Woolf was making an important point. Violence and riots in prison rarely occur in isolation. They are usually symptomatic of a deeper malaise and there are usually advance warnings that something is about to go wrong.

This is where the benefits of what has previously been described as 'dynamic security' become apparent. On entering an accommodation block or a working area where tension is brewing an alert staff member will immediately be conscious that something is wrong with the atmosphere. They will sense tension in the air. Since they will know all their prisoners, they will be able to identify any who are unsettled or likely to threaten violence and deal with them in a way which prevents the onset of violence. It will also be more difficult for prisoners who wish to create trouble to stir up other prisoners if the general approach of staff has been fair and consistent. However, even where there is good dynamic security there is always the potential for an outburst of individual or collective violence.

Throughout the course of the twentieth century there were a number of infrequent but significant riots in English prisons (Thomas 1972). In 1931 a mutiny at Dartmoor prison was suppressed with the use of firearms by prison officers, assisted by police. This is described in chapter two.

Throughout the 1950s there were a number of acts of 'concerted insubordination' in a number of prisons.

The main developments in the 1960s were the new security arrangements and the creation of the dispersal prisons brought in following the Mountbatten and Radzinowicz reports described above. The 1970s were marked by a series of riots and disturbances mainly in dispersal prisons, as some commentators had anticipated (Thomas 1972: 230). The most violent of these in the early 1970s were in the two Isle of Wight dispersal prisons, Albany and Parkhurst (King and Elliott 1977).

In the early 1980s as the dispersal prisons settled down and staff became more sophisticated in their management of groups of prisoners the nature of prison violence changed and the main problem was with the behaviour of individuals. A number of these were prisoners who simply could not cope with the fact that they were facing long periods in custody; others found the discipline of the regime too hard to cope with; some others were mentally disordered in one way or another and should have been in secure psychiatric hospitals. One worrying feature of the behaviour of this group of individuals was recurring violence against staff or against other prisoners. This often took the form of physical assaults but increasingly there was a new phenomenon of taking hostages.

The response to violence

In prisons, as in all coercive institutions, there is always a danger that violence will be met with violence, that the response to individual assault will be institutional assault. Until the mid-1970s prison staff did not receive specific training in riot control and training in how to subdue a violent prisoner was very limited. When violent incidents occurred in a prison those staff who were available responded and the simple tactic was to overcome force with superior force. This inevitably led in some cases to excessive use of force and in others to the use of force when it was not appropriate, sometimes with tragic conclusions. The death of Barry Prosser in Winson Green prison, Birmingham, in 1981 was one such terrible case in which the subsequent inquest jury returned a verdict of unlawful killing (Scraton, Sim and Skidmore 1991: 133).

From the mid-1970s the prison service set about developing more sophisticated methods of responding to violence from prisoners. One of the first models was the establishment of what were called MUFTI (Minimum Use of Force Tactical Intervention). These were specially formed groups of staff who were called together to respond to any situation where there was concerted violence in a prison. They wore a special uniform similar to that worn by the police in riot situations: helmets, protective pads for the vulnerable parts of their bodies, riot shields and long batons. The training they were given often depended on who was the local trainer and the selection of staff was largely based on who wished to volunteer. As news of the way some of these teams responded to prisoner indiscipline became publicly known, there was increasing concern about their activities. Matters came to a head when the Home Office was eventually forced to admit that 54 prisoners in Wormwood Scrubs prison had been injured when the MUFTI team used excessive force in breaking up a protest demonstration in 1979. It then emerged that similar teams had been used in a number of other prisons (Scraton, Sim and Skidmore 1991: 64).

Control and restraint techniques

The prison service realized that it would have to develop methods of dealing with violent incidents in a manner which reduced the possibility of injury to prisoners and which also provided maximum safety to staff. Throughout the 1980s it developed the techniques of what became known as 'control and restraint', which it still uses today.

The first level of this technique is used when a single prisoner needs to be subdued. The key feature is the application of pressure to vulnerable points of the prisoners' wrists. If the prisoner does not resist, the pressure is reduced. If he does, the officer holding the wrist can apply increasing pressure which eventually becomes excruciating. In order to apply these 'locks', as they are known, a team of four staff overcome the prisoner. One holds his head, two others take an arm each while one holds both legs, with the two holding his hands applying the wrist locks. Staff are trained to subdue the prisoner quickly with minimum possibility of injury to anyone involved, staff or prisoner. When this technique was first introduced it found immediate favour with staff. For the first time they had the possibility of subduing a fighting prisoner with something other than overpowering physical force. Prisoners very quickly understood the principle that if they did not resist the pain would be removed and there is little doubt that the use of this technique contributed to an overall reduction in the amount of physical violence used when staff had to subdue a prisoner. The instructions for the use of control and restraint are contained in Prison Service Order 1600.

However, the technique also carried with it some negative features. One was the danger that staff would continue to apply the restraint techniques even after the prisoner had complied with orders as a means of inflicting pain to teach him a lesson. A second was that staff would apply the techniques in situations where this was not necessary. A further concern was that a few prisoners had such a high pain threshhold that they would continue to struggle and so staff would continue to increase pressure. On a number of occasions this led to the prisoners' wrist being broken.

The first level of control and restraint techniques was for use against one prisoner in a confined space. The second level was also for use against one prisoner, but this time in an open space, where he had room to move about. In this case the technique involved a larger group of staff using large shields to protect themselves against the prisoner as they moved in to subdue him. A third and final level was for use against a number of prisoners and involved several teams of staff being involved at the same time. All staff are trained in the first level of control and restraint techniques. Staff have to volunteer to be trained in the next two levels. Those trained to the third level can also be required to go to assist staff in other prisons if there is a riot or other major incident.

There has been another indirect consequence of the introduction of these techniques and the importance attached to them. Most staff enjoy the physical nature of the training in these techniques and also feel more confident in knowing that they can apply them whenever the occasion demands it. The techniques are taught during the initial training of new staff and have to be reinforced on a regular basis. When training is offered to staff in prisons, the one course which can be sure of a full complement is that in these techniques. As other staff training has been reduced, this form of training has been safeguarded. As explained in chapter five, the training of new prison staff has now been reduced to a minimum, but that minimum always includes control and restraint training. It now represents a significant proportion of the training given to staff.

Incident control teams

One other development in terms of control which should be mentioned is the training of special groups of staff to deal with riots and other serious incidents in a prison. These were initially based on the police model of incident control and were then highly developed in the Scottish prison service as a response to the major riots which occurred there in the late 1980s (Coyle 2002b). The full incident control team includes a team of trained negotiators and a team of level three control and restraint staff, with the latter to intervene only when it became clear that negotiations had broken down. More recently the control and restraint teams have been deployed on their own, with groups, known as Tornado teams, sent from several prisons into a prison where there is a disturbance. As their name implies, their primary task is intervention rather than negotiation. They have also controversially been used in non-violent situations. One such incident was their use in Blantyre House, an open prison in Kent, in May 2000. This was the subject of a highly critical debate in the House of Lords in January 2001 (House of Lords Hansard 17 January 2001 on HMP Blantyre House, cols 1166–93).

Special units

In any prison system there may well be a small number of prisoners who simply refuse to conform to the normal regime in any prison and who present a physical risk to staff and other prisoners. The way a prison system deals with these prisoners is a measure of its professionalism and one of the greatest challenges to penal policy makers (Ward and Breed 1985).

There are two main models for dealing with these prisoners: to hold them on their own in isolation or to hold them in small units separate from the rest of prisoners. The prison service of England and Wales uses both of these models. The authority to hold a prisoner in isolation is contained in Prison Rule 45:

Rule 45
(1) Where it appears desirable, for the maintenance of good order or discipline or in his own interests, that a prisoner should not associate with other prisoners, either generally or for particular purposes, the governor may arrange for the prisoner's removal from association accordingly.
(2) A prisoner shall not be removed under this rule for a period of more than 3 days without the authority of a member of the board of visitors or of the Secretary of State. An authority given under this paragraph shall be for a period not exceeding one month, but may be renewed from month to month except that, in the case of a person aged less than 21 years who is detained in prison such an authority shall be for a period not exceeding 14 days, but may be renewed from time to time for a like period.
(3) The governor may arrange at his discretion for such a prisoner as aforesaid to resume association with other prisoners, and shall do so if in any case the medical officer or a medical practitioner such as is mentioned in rule 20(3) so advises on medical grounds.
(4) This rule shall not apply to a prisoner the subject of a direction given under rule 46(1).

This rule is envisaged as a short-term solution to an urgent problem and that either at the end of the period or before then the prisoner will be returned to normal prison routine. For a few prisoners this is not a safe option and the prison service has always wrestled with how to manage them in a decent and humane manner. The history of doing so over the last 30 years has not been a happy one. For some, there was a pragmatic but highly unsatisfactory solution of simply moving them at 28-day intervals from the punishment unit of one prison to that of another, a process known colloquially as 'the carousel', 'the magic roundabout' or 'the ghost train'. The latter description came from the habit of transferring prisoners first thing in the morning without warning and without letting anyone know where they were being taken. This system remains although its use has significantly reduced in recent years.

In 1974 a 'control unit' was set up in Wakefield prison. The repressive regime in the unit was quickly discredited and in 1975 it was closed. In 1983 the Home Office Control Review Committee recommended that a new system of small special units should be set up (Home Office 1984). The principle of these units was that there should be tight security on the perimeter allied to a relatively free regime inside the unit. The concept of the units was based largely on the experience of the Barlinnie Special Unit in Scotland (Coyle 1987). Units along this model were opened in Parkhurst (1985), Lincoln (1987), Hull (1988) and Woodhill (1993, to replace Lincoln). The escapes from Parkhurst and Whitemoor prisons, which are referred to in chapter three, resulted in a security clamp down which affected these units. In 1995 the prison service undertook a further review of the management of these prisoners and in 1998 a system of 'close supervision centres' was introduced, with two being set up in Woodhill and Durham prisons respectively, although the latter was subsequently closed. Their existence is covered by Prison Rule 46:

Rule 46
(1) Where it appears desirable, for the maintenance of good order or discipline or to ensure the safety of officers, prisoners or any other person, that a prisoner should not associate with other prisoners, either generally or for particular purposes, the Secretary of State may direct the prisoner's removal from association accordingly and his placement in a close supervision centre of a prison.
(2) A direction given under paragraph (1) shall be for a period not exceeding one month, but may be renewed from time to time for a like period.
(3) The Secretary of State may direct that such a prisoner as aforesaid shall resume association with other prisoners, either within a close supervision centre or elsewhere.
(4) In exercising any discretion under this rule, the Secretary of State shall take account of any relevant medical considerations which are known to him.

Current arrangements are that if, after a period of being held under Rule 45 conditions, it is decided that a prisoner cannot safely be returned to normal conditions, he may be held under Rule 46 conditions. In 1999 HM Chief Inspector of Prisons for England and Wales carried out an inspection of close supervision centres and his report was published in 2000 (HM Chief Inspector of Prisons 2000). The report acknowledged the need for these units but included several criticisms of the way they were run and of the fact that the national committee which oversaw the management of these centres was not sufficiently vigorous and was too close to the operational line in the prison service. In response, the Home Office set up a CSC Advisory Group, chaired by an independent person and including a number of academics, psychiatrists, psychologists and others. This group currently meets quarterly and, among other matters, considers the monthly reviews that must be held of every prisoner's case. At the time of the Chief Inspector's inquiry into close supervision centres 41 male prisoners were held in these units.

Conclusion

It is appropriate that public criticisms of a prison system will often focus on matters of security and control. These will be heard when there is a breakdown of security. The most severe criticism will come when a high security prisoner, who is a threat to public safety, escapes; this was what happened after the escapes from Whitemoor in 1994 and Parkhurst in 1995. Criticisms of control tend to come when it breaks down, either when it is excessive, as in Wormwood Scrubs in 1979, or when it is thought to be too lax. The prison service in England and Wales has a comparatively positive record in its overall attitude to these two key aspects of its performance. However, it remains far from perfect.

The management of the small number of prisoners who are determined to be violent and destructive will always be problematic. There is a difficult management balance between ensuring that the risk which these prisoners present to other prisoners, to staff and to themselves should be minimized, while at the same time ensuring that a person who is likely to be held for a very long time in extremely restricted conditions is treated decently and humanely. It is by no means clear that the prison service always gets this balance right. What it has managed to do is to keep the numbers of prisoners who fall into this category to a minimum and to acknowledge that its management of them needs to be open to scrutiny.

The prison service has improved its level of order and control in recent years. The number of escapes from prison has fallen dramatically and no prisoner in security category A has escaped since 1995. The possibility of violence is always present in a prison and from time to time it occurs. However, the level of concerted violence appears to have reduced in recent years and, when it does happen, the response by staff is much better organized than it was previously.

Further reading

Bottoms, A. and Light, R. (1987) *Problems of Long Term Imprisonment*. Aldershot: Gower.

Cohen, S. and Taylor, L. (1972) *Psychological Survival*. Middlesex: Penguin.

King, R. and Elliott, K. (1977) *Albany: Birth of a Prison – End of an Era*. London: Routledge & Kegan Paul.

Scraton, P., Sim, J. and Skidmore, P. (1991) *Prisons under Protest*. Milton Keynes: Open University Press.

Sparks, R., Bottoms, A. and Hay, W. (1996) *Prisons and the Problem of Order*. Oxford: Clarendon Press.

chapter eight

Beyond the prison walls

Preparing for return from exile

We have learned in this book that the genesis of the modern prison was as a place in which offenders were exiled from their communities as a punishment for some legal wrong that they had done. In the early years of the nineteenth century there were attempts to make that exile complete by denying prisoners any contact with the outside world or even with each other, by implementation of either the 'silent' or the 'separate' system of prison management. The total application of both of these systems was abandoned, both because of the harm caused to the mental health of prisoners and also because it proved impossible to enforce them. However, remnants of them remained until well into the twentieth century, with prisoners not being allowed to talk to each other in workshops and with prison officers being discouraged from having any conversation with prisoners, other than when necessary.

Throughout the course of the twentieth century the concept of the separation of the prisoner from external influences gradually became less in tune with the times. When the Borstal system was introduced, ideas about the treatment of the young people were much more oriented to their future rehabilitation and these ideas were picked up with the development of training prisons for long-term prisoners. Prison chaplains played a key role in breaking down the impermeability of the prison wall. Before any formal educational or welfare structures were introduced to prisons, the chaplains had responsibility for arranging all provision on these matters (Atherton 1987: 35). They began gradually to involve local church members in voluntary activities in prisons, providing friendship and personal support to individual prisoners and arranging cultural and other activities. The expansion of formal provision for education and other courses for prisoners has already been described in chapter six.

The concept of the prison as a place of total isolation from external influence was also undermined by a realization that if one of the objectives of prison was to encourage and assist prisoners to lead 'a good and useful life' after they were released, many of them needed help to prepare for what would face them on release. As early as 1838 the governor of Glasgow prison recorded his concern about the negative influences which faced young people immediately on leaving prison. They 'not only found no opening to earn their bread by honest industry, but were watched on the day of their liberation by the profligate and the criminal, and drawn back, alike by the absence of every virtuous, and the presence of every vicious influence, to the course they had resolved to abandon' (quoted in Coyle 1991: 34).

The provision of help to people leaving prison has been recognized as a worthy and important charitable activity for two centuries. In 1813, the Quaker Elizabeth Fry visited the women imprisoned in Newgate prison in London. She was horrified by the 'filth' and the 'abandoned wickedness' she saw. In 1817 with a group of other women she founded the Ladies Association for the Improvement of Female Prisoners in Newgate (Bryans, Walker and Martin 2002). The association was to provide work and education for the women which, it was hoped, would 'render them docile and peaceable whilst in prison, and respectable when they leave it' (quoted in Dobash, Dobash and Gutteridge 1986: 43–4).

Following her example and as part of the wider movement for social reform, other local organizations to help prisoners were created. In 1862 the Discharged Prisoners' Aid Act was passed which permitted the organizations to be attached to local prisons (Bryans, Walker and Martin 2002). The emphasis of these organizations was on helping prisoners when they were released. In their 'prison gate work', as it was called, the societies linked practical help with injunctions towards moral reform. For example, in Liverpool in 1870 'prison gate work' was established and released prisoners were offered a free breakfast and encouragement to sign the pledge and become teetotallers (Maguire, Raynor, Vanstone and Kynch 2000). When Londoner Arthur Harding was discharged from Wormwood Scrubs prison in 1903 he was met by a lady at the prison gate. She gave him a ticket for a free breakfast and a religious tract (Samuel 1981). Help was sometimes given at the prison gate to those released ex-prisoners who felt a new start was their way to salvation and wanted to emigrate to the colonies.

The after-care organizations worked independently and were usually linked to their local prison. By 1897, 56 of the societies were employing staff called 'agents' who gave advice to released prisoners and put in applications for funds for them to the Society (Bryans, Walker and Martin 2002). In 1937 these local organizations came together to form the National Association of Discharged Prisoners Aid Societies (Davies 1974). Until 1965 welfare of prisoners in prison and the care of prisoners when discharged was in the hands of these voluntary organizations. In 1953 a Home Office report, the Maxwell Report, suggested the time had come to professionalize after-care work and this conclusion was reinforced in 1963 by a report by the Advisory Council on the Treatment of Offenders (ACTO), The Organization of After-Care. In 1967 professionalization took over when the Probation Service was renamed the Probation and After-Care Service. The newly-named service assumed the responsibility for the after-care of released prisoners as well as welfare services in prisons. Probation officers were seconded from the local probation service and employed in prisons in their area to provide social work services. The National Association of Discharged Prisoners Aid Societies was dissolved and its assets given to the newly created National Association for the Care and Resettlement of Offenders (NACRO). The main role for NACRO was seen, at that time, to be to keep alive the involvement of volunteers in prisons and the after-care of prisoners.

After-care: an overview

Arrangements for after-care, resettlement or social re-integration, as it is variously called, are a feature of the prison systems of all developed countries. It is universally accepted that, whatever may be the good done by imprisonment in keeping prisoners exiled from society and teaching them a lesson, incarceration is very damaging to the individuals subject to it. Damage is done to prisoners' social functioning and their ties to the lawful community, making them vulnerable to a rapid return to crime when they leave. Sir Godfrey Lushington was Permanent Secretary at the Home Office in England for the decade 1885 to 1895. Giving evidence to the Gladstone Committee in 1895 (para 25) he said,

> I regard as unfavourable to reformation the status of a prisoner throughout his whole career; the crushing of self-respect, the starving of all moral instinct he may possess, the absence of all opportunity to do or receive a kindness, the continual association with none but criminal . . . I believe the true mode of reforming a man or restoring him to society is exactly in the opposite direction of all these; but, of course, this is a mere idea. It is quite impracticable in a prison. In fact the unfavourable features I have mentioned are inseparable from prison life.

The literature on the effects of imprisonment (Cavadino and Dignan 2001: 114) suggests a large number of damaging effects that make ex-prisoners less able to survive beyond the walls. Imprisonment can affect the mental health and functioning of individuals. It also ruptures their social ties. Prisoners can become institutionalized and unable to function without the rigid framework of the carceral environment. They can become dependent on others to make decisions for them and lose their own decision-making capacity. Prison can also be an experience that humiliates and crushes. Self-confidence and self-esteem can be seriously harmed. A woman teacher imprisoned in 1985 said of her experience, '. . . I understood the fragility of the hold that a civilized being has on civilization, and how much easier it is to relapse. And I understood how people can give up washing' (Peckham 1985: 112). The stigma of a prison record lasts for many years if not for life. Discrimination by employers against ex-prisoners is well documented.

We have already seen in chapter four that prisoners are not a representative group of society but come grossly disproportionately from the most socially disadvantaged whose interactions with public services have not been particularly satisfactory. Many are not registered with a doctor. They often live in public housing. Many come from fractured home backgrounds and have been in the care of local authorities as children. Their education has been spasmodic and often truncated. The experience of imprisonment reduces the stability of these already damaged people even more. It has been estimated that a third of prisoners lose their housing whilst in prison. Two-thirds lose their employment. More than 20 per cent face increased money problems and more than 40 per cent lose contact with their families (Social Exclusion Unit 2002). Taken together, these factors constitute important elements of what has been described as 'the pain of imprisonment' (Christie 2000).

After-care services provided by a government body have therefore been accepted as necessary since the 1965 adoption of the recommendations of the ACTO Report and the creation of the Probation and After-Care Service. Helping those leaving prison to find a place to live, some work to do and some basis for a social network are all tasks for an after-care service. However, the Probation and After-Care Service had another important function also, that of supervising prisoners released on parole, on life licence or subject to some form of statutory supervision. The main responsibility in these cases was to ensure that the released prisoner stayed out of trouble, kept the conditions of the parole or licence, saw the probation officer as required and carried out the probation officer's instructions. The experience of the years after 1965 showed that this statutory supervision was the priority for the probation service. Voluntary after-care, the title given to helping those ex-prisoners who were not subject to statutory orders but just needed help with somewhere to live, finding work, or dealing with loneliness, depression and difficulties in getting health care, came very low down the list of priorities (Home Office Research Findings No. 73). Voluntary organizations became the main deliverers of services to these ex-prisoners. Hostels for homeless ex-offenders were provided by voluntary organizations such as NACRO and the Stonham Housing Association. Employment training and work experience for ex-prisoners were organized and delivered by a wide range of voluntary organizations. Projects for befriending and mitigating social isolation also came under the aegis of the voluntary sector. This provision was, however, subject to funding fluctuations, frequent changes in government priorities and chronic instability.

The end result of these arrangements was deeply unsatisfactory. A study of after-care provision carried out jointly by the Chief Inspectors of Prison and Probation in 2001 concluded that the resettlement needs of many prisoners were being 'severely neglected', particularly those of the large number of prisoners serving less than twelve months. The Inspectors estimated that more than 80 per cent of people sentenced would serve a year or less in prison (HM Inspectorates of Prisons and Probation 2001). The probation service, the Inspectors said, needed to re-order its priorities. The need for change had already been recognized by the setting up of the National Probation Service in April 2001 to oversee the work of the existing probation services and in June 2004 the National Offender Management Service was established. This service 'covers a number of organisations, including prisons and probation, to ensure that a range of services are available to adult offenders and those on remand throughout England and Wales' (NOMS 2005: 4).

The role of the prison in resettlement

The probation service became responsible when prisoners left prison. Before they left, the arrangements for what would become of them were in the hands of the prison service. How far has resettlement been a priority for the work of prisons? Helping prisoners to find their place in the community and re-establish themselves was not in the minds of the early managers of the prison system. When the East End gangster Arthur Harding first went to Wormwood Scrubs prison in London to serve a three-month sentence in 1902 he slept on a plank of wood. He spent the first month picking oakum which made the fingers sore, the second sewing coalbags and the third making mailbags. He was then released. His situation before he entered prison and his prospects when he left were quite irrelevant to the authorities (Samuel 1981).

Certainly the stated focus of imprisonment has moved steadily over the years away from such simple containment and correction through hard labour. The prison service's Statement of Purpose adopted in 1988 defines its duty to help prisoners to 'lead law-abiding and useful lives ... after release'. In principle the prison service gives a high priority to preparing prisoners for release back into the community. This preparation begins during the course of the sentence, often expressed in a 'sentence plan' drawn up in consultation with the prisoner, and, for those who are serving long sentences, may also involve a phased release, either by means of a period of temporary or conditional release or by maintaining some form of supervision immediately after release, as described in chapter four.

The prison service considers that many of the activities which go on inside prison should help prisoners to prepare for release, as described in chapter six. More specific planning is also undertaken on an individual basis. A large number of outside bodies and voluntary organizations visit prisons to offer programmes such as job preparation and job finding. Work is done to help prisoners find somewhere to live on release. Help is given to enable those prisoners interested in furthering their education or training to continue it when they leave. Debt and general money problems are very common especially amongst the short-term prisoners and advice is made available on dealing with debt and benefit entitlements. Money is a problem for many released prisoners who leave with a small amount (a discharge grant) which has to last them until the authorities on the outside sort out their entitlements. Temporary release is allowed for prisoners who have passed a risk assessment so that they can attend interviews for jobs, housing or education or make other preparations for their release. Prisoners serving less than four years who have not been convicted of a violent or sexual offence are eligible to be released early provided that they agree to wear an electronic monitoring device, which is monitored by a private contractor, and stay at home or in their hostel between certain hours, usually 7.00 pm to 7.00 am. If accommodation arrangements break down or their family no longer wants them at home, then they have to return to prison.

For those who have served long sentences a graduated approach is taken. Such prisoners move through the system of security categorization towards lower security prisons and may spend the last year or so of their sentence in a special resettlement prison, which will concentrate on preparing prisoners within a carefully monitored environment for living in the outside world. Some of the prisoners leave the prison each day to work and return at night. Initially they undertake community work or work in workshops in the prison and move on to normal paid employment in the locality if it can be found.

The structure and design of resettlement prisons are specifically targeted at preparing prisoners for life outside prison. Unfortunately in most prisons activities aimed at helping prisoners to resettle after release are largely added on to the internal structure of the prison system and cannot really be said to constitute a serious attempt to change the nature and culture of imprisonment with a view to reducing its damaging aspects and reformulating its purpose towards social reintegration. Practical problems abound. Efforts to put prisoners in touch with services in the area where they intend to live on release are hampered by pressure on space and the resultant need to move prisoners around the country. Education and training courses can be cut short and planned examinations not taken because prisoners are transferred. Drug treatment programmes have been criticized because of the poor follow-up when prisoners leave prison only to find that the best they can hope for is that their names are added to the long waiting lists for community drug services.

When key performance indicators, by which the prison service was to measure its efficiency in delivering its objectives, were first introduced in the early 1990s, they made no mention of resettlement activities. The current list of key performance indicators (HM Prison Service 2005) includes a commitment 'To ensure that 34,890 prisoners have a job, training or education outcome on release'. The lay reader might assume that this involved a commitment to ensure that this number of released prisoners obtained a job or a place in training or education. In fact, as the House of Commons Education and Skills Committee (2005: para 188) discovered, the commitment is merely to an 'outcome' and there was uncertainty about what this meant. The Prison Reform Trust suggested to the Committee that the figure was based on a survey of the personal expectation of prisoners who were about to be released, together with a smaller number who had the promise of a job interview. The Prison Reform Trust's own research found that prisoners' expectations of finding employment or training post-release were low, and concluded that 'the achievements that the prison service would claim on resettlement are not reflective of the general practice on the ground in establishments across the country'.

Families and other personal relationships

The resettlement programmes described above are carried out as part of a relationship between the prison and the individual prisoner. They rarely involve other significant people in the prisoner's life, such as family, friends, a teacher or social worker from outside. Yet, when people are sent to prison they leave behind families, friends and many links from their previous life and the 'pains of imprisonment' are felt by all of them as much as by the prisoner. For many the family will be the main source of support in the prisoner's resettlement and ensuring that links with families are kept alive and strong might bring great benefits. Yet maintaining family links has traditionally been seen as of small importance in prison policy in England and Wales. In chapter six we described the arrangements for visits to prisoners by family and friends. These arrangements meet the needs of the prison system rather than of the prisoners and their families. They are generally structured in such a way as to minimize any risk to security and are scheduled at times that suit the administration. One of the key considerations for personnel involved is to ensure that no drugs or other illegal items are smuggled in and to ensure an orderly rotation of visits so that everyone gets their minimal entitlement. With a few notable exceptions, little consideration is given to arranging visits in ways that are likely to reinforce links between partners, children, parents or siblings.

Prisoners' families are the group outside the prison most directly affected by imprisonment and government policies for implementing it. Civil society groups involving and representing prisoners' families have been active over many years in a dual role. They have provided social support on the outside for individual families with a member in prison and they have campaigned to improve visiting arrangements. It was in the past a sad sight to see visitors, mostly women and children, standing in a long line in the street outside a prison in the full view of all passers-by waiting to enter. A campaign took place in the early 1990s to establish visitors' centres at London prisons which would provide a place for shelter, a hot drink, baby-changing facilities, advice and support for those visiting prisons. This scheme was gradually introduced across the country. Prisoners' families groups also campaigned to improve the treatment of visitors by prison staff, for financial support for low-income families to visit their family member in prison and for better information to families about their family member's whereabouts in order to prevent the situation where family members arrived at a prison for a visit only to find that the person they intended to visit had just been transferred to another prison many miles away.

The prison and desistance from crime – models of change

The community prison

When considering the role of the prison in encouraging desistance from future crime, there are a number of fundamental questions to be asked. The first is whether the experience of imprisonment has to be as damaging as it is at present. Another is whether it might be possible to organize the prison in a different manner so that it could prepare prisoners for release, rather than making them less fit to survive outside.

In answering these questions, there are two main factors to be considered. One is the relationship of the prison to the locality, the structural place of prison in relation to the other public services. The other is the relationship of the prisoner to society. The relationship of the prison to the other structures of society is a strange one. Other public services, such as health, education and social services, are administered locally. Prisons are different in that they have no direct local organizational links. Although the system tries to keep prisoners in their home area, the prison service is nationally controlled and organized and the prisoners it contains can be moved anywhere in England and Wales. Decisions about where a prisoner will go will be a balance between the prisoner's home address, the availability of space and the security category of the prisoner. Thousands of prisoners are routinely held more than a hundred miles from their home. With such a dysfunction at its organizational heart, resettling prisoners in their home communities will always be a task the prison service can carry out only with great difficulty and with little chance of success.

This dysfunction is one of many that were identified in the Woolf Report (1991) and which led the report to call for the establishment of 'community prisons'. These prisons would be in the locality that most prisoners came from, mainly the large urban areas, and prisoners would be sent to their local prison. To accommodate different security categories and special needs, the community prisons would have different sections offering different levels of security. In the early 1990s the Home Office carried out some studies of the feasibility of introducing community prisons but before any structural change could be introduced, attention was diverted from implementation by other events and a changing penal climate, as described in chapter three. A policy that prisoners should be held near home and that the prison should be local as are schools and hospitals would require a very profound change.

What is to be said of the relationship between prisons and the locality where they are situated? We have seen that when prisons first came into common use they were a local responsibility, mainly locally funded and managed. In 1878 funding and control of prisons was taken over by central government. From then on there were no structural local links apart from a requirement, now dropped, that some of the members of the local Board of Visitors (now Independent Monitoring Board) should be appointed from amongst the local magistracy. In the absence of any structural or statutory link, relationships between prisons and the communities where they are located are patchy. Some local communities have little knowledge of the prison in their town. Some prisons make no effort to establish a relationship. In some instances, the link between the prison and its local community is deliberately hidden by giving the prison an anonymous name, rather than that of the town in which it is situated. Other prisons work hard to establish good relationships with the area where they are located. Open days have been held where the public are invited to visit parts of the prison and meet selected prisoners. Prisoners have been involved in a range of activities to benefit local communities. A voluntary organization, the Inside Out Trust, was set up in 1994 to create projects for prisoners to work for the benefit of the community. As part of these projects workshops in prisons produce, for example, toys for children with special needs or transcribe books into Braille. Elsewhere children with disabilities have been able to use prison facilities with help from prisoners. In other instances prisoners who present a low security risk have been allowed out on day release to work as helpers in charitable settings.

Most people spend relatively short periods in prison (Home Office 2003a) and then return to the communities from which they came. It makes sense for everyone that, when offenders have completed their sentences, they should leave prison with a sense of purpose and ready to contribute positively to society, rather than with a sense of bitterness and alienation which will make it likely that they will commit further offences.

This sense of commitment to society will be strengthened if prisoners are given an appreciation of their worth as persons and of what they can contribute to society. As we have seen there are many ways in which this can be developed, even behind the walls of the prison.

The former prisoner as outcast

The relationship between the individual prisoner and society is ambiguous. On the one hand it is officially accepted that those leaving prison should be helped and encouraged, found somewhere to live, trained for work, be given access to employment advisers and debt counsellors. On the other hand the stigma of the prison record is not to be forgotten. A theme running through this book has been the prison as a place of exile and the prisoner as an outcast. How far does this 'cancellation of citizenship' as David Garland (Browne and Wilkie 2002: v) has called it extend? In relation to one of the central aspects of social reintegration, that is work, it extends very deeply. Criminal records are to be consulted before employment can be considered in a wide range of occupations. The legal basis for declaring a prison record and criminal convictions generally is the Rehabilitation of Offenders Act 1974, which requires those whose sentence was six months or less to declare their conviction for the next seven years (if they were over 18 at the time of conviction) and for three-and-a-half years if they were under 18. If the sentence was between six months and two-and-a-half years the time before the conviction is spent is 10 years for those over 18 at the time of conviction and five years for under 18s. Convictions resulting in a prison sentence of more than two-and-a-half years are never spent and must always be declared. Anyone applying for a licence to drive a taxi, a heavy goods vehicle or a passenger vehicle must always declare unspent convictions. In July 2002 a new provision was enacted allowing employers access to information about any unspent criminal conviction. For certain types of work, such as any job involving contact with persons under 18 or other vulnerable people, convictions are never spent and must always be declared.

Desistance from crime

Reconviction rates of those leaving prison have not shown much variation over the years, hovering around 60 per cent. The aim of the resettlement effort is to reduce these rates by taking action that changes prisoners' lives or reduces those aspects of their lives that make them commit crimes. So it is worth asking what is known about resettlement and what will help ex-prisoners change their lifestyles. For many years the commonsense approach to resettling offenders was based on the view that what was needed was a stable personal relationship and a good job. A stable personal relationship was often outside the bounds of official intervention so probation officers concentrated on cultivating employers and persuading them to give work to ex-prisoners. As described in chapter six, in the 1990s an attempt was made to introduce more psychologically-based approaches to individual behaviour. These signalled a move away from a focus on outside influences and social situations towards identifying the need for change in the prisoners themselves and the way they thought and reacted to the world around them. The new century saw some disappointment with the results of approaches based on individual pathology and more research interest in what was called 'desistance theory' and an analysis of the complex process of former prisoners changing their lives and stopping criminal activities (Sampson and Laub 1995). According to Sampson and Laub, the stable personal relationship and job theory had good evidence to back it. They argue though that neither of these will be successful on its own. It is the quality of these institutions that makes the difference. The personal relationship must involve 'strong attachment' that creates 'a social bond of interdependence between two individuals' (1995: 140). The work must involve relationships 'characterised by an extensive set of obligations, expectations, and interdependent social networks' (1995: 141). It must have some stability.

Other theorists on desistance, such as Maruna (2001), have emphasized the importance of focusing on what ex-prisoners themselves say about how they see their future, whether they want to change (most do) and whether they can imagine themselves living a different kind of life. Having listened, the role of those working to resettle ex-prisoners is to build around them a support system that is based on emphasizing positive qualities rather than trying to reduce negative ones. Maruna's study of 50 similar offenders showed a difference between those who carried on with their criminal activities and those who did not. Those who desisted from crime gave their reason for knowing they could achieve it as the influence of someone who 'believed in them' and in their ability to succeed. 'Social capital', meaning a network of relationships, a sense of belonging, obligations and reciprocities is seen as one of the most important bases of successful resettlement (McNeill 2004).

As we come to the end of our attempt to understand the place which we call the prison, we are drawn to a number of conclusions. We have looked at the role of the prison as a place of punishment, a place of deterrence and of public protection. We have also considered the extent to which it can be a place of personal reform. The modern, utilitarian description of this concept is reducing recidivism. The question is, how best to break the cycle of crime which brings the same people back, year in, year out, to repeated terms of imprisonment. If we wish to achieve this, it will not be sufficient to tinker with current organizational structures. We need to have a more radical review of what we mean by 'the prison' and the extent to which the nineteenth-century structure which we still use is relevant today. We need to consider a different structure and a different set of relationships with the communities which prisons are intended to serve. These issues lead us into our final chapter.

Further reading

Braithwaite, J. (1989) *Crime, Shame and Reintegration*. Cambridge: Cambridge University Press.

Bryans, S., Walker, R. and Martin, C. (2002) *Prisons and the Voluntary Sector: A Bridge into the Community*. Winchester: Waterside Press.

Maruna, S. (2001) *Making Good: How ex-convicts reform and rebuild their lives*. Washington DC: American Psychological Press.

Zehr, H. (1990) *Changing Lenses: A New Focus for Crime and Justice*. Scottsdale, PA: Herald Press.

chapter nine

The future of the prison

In this text we have considered the history of the prison and have discovered that in its present format it is a relatively modern invention. However, unlike most modern institutions, the prison has not changed significantly since it was created. In recent years the central organizational structure that governs prisons has expanded considerably. In hand with this growth in bureaucracy has come an increasingly sophisticated set of arguments to justify why the prison must continue in its present form. Much of this justification is based on the symbolism which the prison carries. In chapter one we considered the importance of the 'clang of the prison door' in the minds of many people and extent to which the prison satisfies a public need to see criminals punished and a need for politicians to be seen to be doing something about what is described as the problem of crime. Successive governments have presented the prison as an essential tool in the 'war against crime', despite the fact that no research has shown any direct correlation between levels of imprisonment and levels of crime.

So, at the end of this volume, what is to be written about the future of the prison? As the twenty-first century unfolds, will societies continue to lock up large numbers of men, women and children in confined spaces behind high walls, cut off for all practical purposes from their families and contact with the normal world? Will the numbers of people in prison continue to rise as they have in recent years? Or will the thoughts of a former Minister of State for Internal Affairs in Uganda be realized?

Speaking about prisons at a conference in Kampala in 1995, William Omaria said:

> One day in the distant future, people will probably look back on what happens in most countries today and will wonder how we could do that to our fellow human beings in the name of justice.
>
> (Omaria 1997: 89)

Very few human institutions last forever. Many of the methods of judicial punishment which existed when prisons first came into use have long since ceased to be acceptable. They include the stocks, corporal punishment, transportation to another country and capital punishment. As things stand at present, it seems inconceivable in the foreseeable future that prisons should go the way of the stocks, branding and whipping and cease to exist. However, despite the current enthusiasm for imprisonment and the growth in its use in many countries, it may be that the time has come for a radical review of the use of imprisonment as a sentence of the court, for a discussion about the extent to which it benefits society, satisfies victims and is the best way of dealing with those who break the criminal law.

Current attitudes to imprisonment

Before looking to the future, it may be useful to stand back and consider how imprisonment is used in different countries and cultures around the world. We have seen in this volume that, to some extent at least, the United Kingdom has led the way in the development of the use of prison since the eighteenth century. Along with the United States of America, Britain has been at the fore in regarding the prison as much more than a place of detention and in envisaging it as a place of personal reform for those who are sent there. Although only a relatively small proportion of all offenders are sent to prison, the institution has been given a central place in the criminal justice process in the United Kingdom. This is not the case in all countries.

In respect of their use of imprisonment, it is possible to divide the countries of the world into five main groupings. The first group includes a significant number of developing countries, most of them formerly dominated by colonial powers. Prisons were introduced to these countries by the formal imperial powers. Even today one can visit towns in sub-Saharan Africa or South Asia and come across a large building in a prominent position which is clearly a model of an English Victorian prison. The layout of many prisons in East Africa, the Caribbean, India and in some parts of the Middle East is exactly the same. One goes through the main gate into an inner vehicle area; the orderly room is to the right, the visiting room to the left, upstairs are the administrative offices; beyond the inner gate is the inner compound with accommodation units to one side and workshops to the other. Somewhere in the Public Record Office in Kew there must be a set of plans which was used as the template for all of these prisons.

To the indigenous culture of these countries, the concept of taking a large number of able bodied young men, who should be contributing to the upkeep of their families, and depriving them of their liberty in private places, where they become a burden on society and give little or no satisfaction to the victims of crime, is seen as very odd. In many of these countries, short as they are of human and economic resources, prisons are a terrible drain on the shallow public purse. In many instances prison conditions are appalling and governments do not have the resources to make them decent and humane places.

A prisoner in Nigeria has described what this means in practice:

> We have three batches in my cell, and I am in Number Two. Other cells have four, even five, when there are many prisoners. When it is time to sleep, we all make space for the first batch. We stand at one end of the cell, or sit. Some of us sleep while standing, but you do not lie down. Only the first batch lies down. After four hours, they get up, and we lie down to sleep. After four hours, we get up, and the third batch will sleep.
>
> (Civil Liberties Organisation 1996: 32)

The other side of this coin is that in some of these countries there is a real possibility of change for the very reason that the only historical resonance which imprisonment carries is a negative one and the suggestion of finding other ways of dealing with crime and the harm it does to society is culturally attractive. In a number of these countries one can find some of the most innovative ideas for developing other, more inclusive forms of justice. The work that has been done in developing community service as an alternative to prison in some parts of East Africa is a good example of this (Stern 1998).

In the second group of countries the main characteristic in many of the prisons is a complete breakdown in good order. This is the case in a number of countries in Latin America. The staff are paramilitary and their main task is to guard the perimeter of the prison to ensure that no one escapes. They have little direct contact with prisoners other than when absolutely necessary and they only go inside the prison compounds in large numbers and fully armed. The prison accommodation is divided into patios. A different gang is allocated to each one and the leaders control all that goes on inside the prisons. No one who is not an affiliated gang member can survive within the group. For the majority of those held there, prisons are very dangerous places. Every aspect of the daily lives of prisoners is determined by the gang leaders. Prisoners often have to pay for the most basic necessities of life, including a place on the floor to sleep.

Venezuela jail riot leaves 11 dead

At least 11 prisoners have been killed in gang-related violence in one of Venezuela's largest jails, officials say. The dead men were hacked and shot to death by prisoners armed with pistols, knives and shotguns at the Yare 2 prison in the central state of Miranda, about 40 kilometres (25 miles) south of the capital, Caracas, they said. At least two inmates were reported to have been decapitated. A further 40 prisoners were injured.

Prison authorities quelled the riot after calling in national guard troops and police to restore order to the jail complex. It is not clear how the disturbance started. The police say they intervened to stop a violent clash between two rival gangs of prisoners, but some of the inmates' relatives said it was the police who started the riot.

The Yare 2 prison complex, which holds about 1200 prisoners, once held current Venezuelan President Hugo Chavez after he led a failed coup in 1992. Last month, inmates at the prison went on hunger strike to protest conditions at the complex and continual delays in trial processing, French news agency AFP reports.

Correspondents say violence is common-place in Venezuela's over-crowded and poorly-regulated prisons, with a series of major riots taking place in the last few years. More than 200 prisoners were killed and more than 1200 injured in violence within the Venezuelan prison system between October 2001 and September 2002, according to statistics from the Venezuelan ministry of interior and justice.

(Story from BBC NEWS 19 April 2003: http://news.bbc.co.uk/
go/pr/fr/-/1/hi/world/americas/2959851.stm)

Much of the violence in the prisons mirrors the violence in the communities from which the prisoners come and is an extension of it. Enmities between gangs on the street spill over into the prisons and tensions in the prisons carry over into wider society. In these environments the possibility for reform of prison systems can only be limited until the wider community issues are dealt with.

The third group of countries includes many from the former Soviet Union in Eastern Europe and Central Asia. In these countries there are terrible problems in the prisons, with high levels of imprisonment leading to overcrowding, which in the worst situations means three prisoners having to sleep in turns in one bed, ill-health, with 10 per cent of all prisoners suffering from active tuberculosis, and of shortage of resources. However, in a number of countries in this group there have been significant changes over the last five or ten years. There has been a determination to reduce the level of imprisonment, with governments regarding excessive use of imprisonment as a negative reflection of the democratic values of society. The greatest change is occurring in the largest country in the region. In Russia there has been a recognition that reform of the prison system cannot be achieved in isolation from the rest of the criminal justice system. It can only be achieved if there is political will, if there is legislative change, if the other major elements in the criminal justice process, especially the judiciary and the prosecution service, are involved in the process and if the public and the media are re-assured that these changes will not threaten public safety.

> When the socialist system collapsed, many of the ideological and economic conditions, which had provided the basis of the old penal system, became irrelevant and as a result the foundations of the penal system began to collapse as well. For many progressively inclined people it became obvious that the system simply could not continue to exist in its previous form. It had to be changed fundamentally and to undergo reform . . .
> (The) penal system cannot change on its own, separately from society as a whole. Its reform is possible only as part of a wider range of measures aimed at creating a democratic state and at the introduction of legal and judicial reforms.
>
> (Kalinin 2002: 5)

As a direct consequence of this strategic approach, the level of imprisonment in Russia has fallen by 25 per cent over a period of six years. In real terms this has meant a reduction from 1,010,000 prisoners in 1998 to 763,000 at the beginning of 2005 (ICPS 2005).

The fourth group includes those countries which have historically regarded prison as a place of last resort, to be used only for those who have committed the most serious crimes or who pose a major threat to public safety. This group has traditionally included most of the countries of Western Europe, with imprisonment rates of between 60 and 120 per 100,000. In these countries there has been a recognition that there is little correlation between rates of imprisonment and rates of crime and there has been an historical determination that the criminal justice system should not be used to resolve social problems. For example, Dr Tapio Lappi-Seppälä, Director of the Finnish National Research Institute of Legal Policy has summarized the current Finnish position as follows:

> The ongoing total reform of the Finnish Penal Code has been executed . . . with respect for the principles of due process and legal safeguards. The reform of the penal system has been carried out in the direction of the expansion of community-based measures. Also, the first national crime prevention program, approved by the government in 1999, focuses on situational and local crime prevention. For now, it still is difficult to imagine that the claim that 'prison works' will find its way into Finnish political campaigns.
>
> (Lappi-Seppälä 2002: 33)

In recent years, however, this minimalist consensus has come under political challenge in a number of countries as governments seek solutions to modern problems such as drug abuse and illegal immigration. The

Netherlands is an extreme example of how a change in government policy can affect rates of imprisonment. Throughout the second half of the twentieth century the Netherlands had an international reputation for having a relatively low rate of imprisonment and a progressive prison system. Within a few short years it has lost that reputation. In 1975 the rate of imprisonment was 17 people per 100,000 of the population, by 1995 the rate had risen to 66, by 1998 to 85 and by 2004 it had reached 123 (ICPS 2005). Features which would previously have been unheard of in the Netherlands, such as two people being accommodated in a single cell, have now been written into legislation. Developments such as these, which have also occurred in a less dramatic fashion in a number of other European countries, suggest that some jurisdictions may be in danger of moving from the fourth group of countries to the fifth group.

This final grouping includes those countries which make extensive use of prison as a matter of social policy. The leader of this group is the United States, which has a rate of imprisonment far in excess of any other country in the world. In the first quarter of 2005 its rate of imprisonment was 714 per 100,000 of its total population. Three countries, including Russia, have the joint second highest rate of 532 (ICPS 2005). With just under 5 per cent of the world's population, the United States has 23 per cent of its prisoners. At a conference in New York in December 2003, a senior American judge talked about 'America's love affair with imprisonment' (Lasker 2004). Increasingly in this group of countries prison is being used for reasons not directly linked with crime, nor with the reduction of crime, nor even with the punishment of crime. Instead it is linked to the control of marginalized and impoverished groups in society and among this group there is a gross racial distortion. Changes in legislation have led to punitive sentences, which have lost all sense of proportionality.

> America's bitter legacy of slavery, segregation and Jim Crow lives on in the criminal justice system. The poll tax is no more, but a third of the African-American men in three Southern states are permanently barred from voting because of their criminal records. Not only are our prisons and death rows filled with people of color in gross disproportion to their numbers in the population, but at every stage of the system, from who the police stop and question to who is strapped on the gurney awaiting the executioner's needle, we make it clear that we value the lives of whites more than those of blacks: you are twelve times more likely to be sentenced to death, for example, if your victim was white than if he or she was black.
>
> This very state (Texas) has a criminal justice system that should shame all decent people. There are now 77,000 people imprisoned here for non-violent crimes. African-Americans are incarcerated in Texas at a rate seven times that of whites, and nearly one of every three black men in their 20s in this state is under some form of

criminal justice control. The sad fact is that Texas is worse than the other 49 states only in degree.

(LaMarche 2003)

There is now a growing recognition in some sectors in the United States that the relentless growth in the use of prison cannot continue. This understanding of the need for a different approach is coming from different quarters and for different reasons. In California, for example, with one of the biggest prison populations in the country, Governor Arnold Schwarzenegger, who was elected on a ticket of controlling public spending, very quickly turned his attention to the need to do something about the spiralling prison budget (http://www.latimes.com/news/local/la-me-prison7jan07,0,2161596.story?col). At the same time the American Bar Association (2003: 1) produced a report which urged 'states, territories and the federal government to ensure that sentencing systems provide appropriate punishment without over-reliance on incarceration'. The committee which produced the report was set up following criticism of the criminal justice system from Supreme Court Justice Anthony M. Kennedy, who had commented 'The political phrase "tough on crime" should not lead us into moral blindness'.

Imprisonment in England and Wales

Since this text is primarily concerned with imprisonment in England and Wales, the reader is entitled to ask to which of these five groups this country belongs. Until the end of the twentieth century that question would have been relatively easy to answer. England and Wales was clearly in the fourth group of countries, those which regarded prison to be used as a place of last resort. In the words of the Woolf Report, 'only those for whom prison is essential should be there' (para 1.204). In principle, courts were to reserve imprisonment for those convicted of committing very serious crimes. There was a recognition that in practice prison was sometimes used as a sentence on other offenders for whom the courts had no alternative solution: persistent shoplifters, drunkards who regularly caused a breach of the peace and those who were unable or refused to pay fines. But it was acknowledged that for these offenders prison was generally an inappropriate punishment, a sentence which the court imposed out of frustration rather than of necessity. There was an understanding that, other than in a minority of cases, prison could offer little in terms of personal rehabilitation or reform. In the famous words of former Home Secretary David Waddington, when it is used inappropriately prison can be 'an expensive way of making bad people worse' (Home Office 1990b).

Since the mid-1990s the position in England and Wales has been much less clear. The use of imprisonment has risen inexorably since then.

Date	Number	Rate per 100,000
1992	45,817	90
1995	51,047	99
1998	65,298	125
2001	66,301	127
Aug 2005	77,025	145

This rise has not been fuelled by an increase in the overall crime rate, nor in police detection rates. There have been two main causes: courts have been committing more offenders to prison, including those convicted for the first time, and they have been imposing longer sentences. As a result of these factors the rate of imprisonment is now one of the highest in Western Europe and places the country just above the world average. With a rate of over 140 per 100,000, England and Wales is well behind the United States figure of 714 but the trend certainly takes this country further west into the Atlantic than it has been in the past. This is not a development which the prison service has welcomed. Speaking at the prison service annual conference in 2002, the Director General said:

> As I have told the Home Secretary, no one, including me, thinks that locking more and more people up is a sensible way of spending public money. Many of the people we are locking up will not benefit in any way from their sentence. Many of them will lose jobs, accommodation and family support and will become more criminal. Meanwhile, the very significant numbers in prison who we can change, whose lives can be given a new direction, get too little of our attention as we struggle to cope with the insanity of a prison population that may hit 70,000 this summer.
>
> (Narey 2002a)

The Home Office produces a regular set of statistics predicting future rates of imprisonment. In 2002 the Home Office predicted that, based on a number of different scenarios, the prison population would be between 91,400 and 109,600 by June 2009 (Home Office 2002a). These predictions are an inexact science, dependant on a raft of variables, some of which, such as historic and predicted crime rates, can be subjected to scientific analysis and others which cannot. Among the latter will be any new pieces of legislation which the government may pass and which will increase the number of offences for which one can be sent to prison. Another will be whether courts will continue their recent trend of imposing more and longer prison sentences for crimes which would not previously have attracted a prison sentence. In November 2004 the chief executive of the National Offender Management Service told *The Guardian* newspaper that in the previous year the courts had imprisoned 3000 people 'for thefts such as shoplifting or stealing a bicycle, even though they did not have any previous convictions' (Travis 2004).

Until recently the Home Office took the view that, while it is ultimately responsible for providing prison places, it could do nothing to influence the number of people who were sent to prison since that was a matter to be decided solely by the courts. However, in the face of ever-increasing prison numbers the Home Office now takes a rather different view. In January 2004 it announced that it intended to restrict the number of prison places available to 80,000 in 2009 (Blunkett 2004: 17). This was a tacit acknowledgement that levels of imprisonment are affected less by rates of crime and more by political decisions. To put it briefly, prison rates can be talked up or down by politicians and public commentators, including the media. Judges are independent when it comes to passing individual sentences but they do not live in ivory towers and their overall attitude to sentencing is affected by external factors. The Home Office has taken account of this explicitly in the terms of reference it has given to the National Offender Management Service, the first of which is:

> To influence judges and magistrates to slow growth of the prison population and make greater use of community punishments and fines.
>
> (*Prison Service News* December/January 2004 Number 234: 19)

The decision to limit the number of available prison places as a means of limiting the number of people being sent to prison was something which had been advocated over 80 years previously by Alexander Paterson: 'Wherever prisons are built, Courts will make use of them. If no prison is handy, some other way of dealing with the offender will possibly be discovered (Ruck 1951: 26).

The reason for limiting the number of prison places is not so that murderers, rapists and other major criminals may walk free but to ensure that they are not used as places into which we sweep everyone for whom we have no other solution. Paterson again:

> A prison is variously regarded by the casual outsider as a cloakroom for trial prisoners, a dustbin for nuisances, and a limbo for those whom society is reluctant to see again. The word merely connotes a place of confinement, where men have to be kept in custody for many different reasons. As a result the prison is apt to become an *omnium gatherum*, a convenient receptacle into which a puzzled Court may put anyone for whom no alternative method of disposal is very obvious.
>
> (Ruck 1951: 26)

Prison in the future

Setting a cap on prison places, as the government proposes to do, has the potential to be the first step towards restricting the power of courts to send to prison offenders who might better be dealt with in other ways and to raise the possibility that prison might indeed become a place of last resort. If that were to happen then we could begin to map out the place which prison might have in this country in the future. In the first place imprisonment would be used much more sparingly. Convicted persons would be sent to prison only when the serious nature of their crimes meant that no other sentence would be reasonable or because they posed a serious threat to individuals or to society at large. The same criteria would apply to those who are accused of committing a crime. It might be that when deciding to send a person to prison, the court would be required to state which of the reasons for doing so applied in each case. People would no longer be sent to prison on the grounds that there was no alternative option available. In a word, prison would cease to be the default option and other disposals would not in future be referred to as 'alternatives to prison'. Neither would offenders be sent to prison 'for their own good'; that is, to learn a skill, to be educated, to undergo treatment for drug abuse or because they were mentally disordered and needed a place of safety. That is not at all to suggest that prisons would cease to offer skills training, education or drug treatment programmes; but none of these would be a justification in itself for sending someone to prison.

An immediate consequence of these changes would be a significantly reduced prison population in England and Wales. It is difficult to be precise about how big this reduction might be. Simply to bring the rate of imprisonment to the average for Western Europe would mean a prison population of about 57,000. To return it to the 1992 level would mean a prison population of just over 45,000, a reduction of around 29,000 in the number at the beginning of 2005. On the basis of the experience in some other comparable countries there is no reason to fear that such a reduction would result in any increased threat to public safety.

An important outcome of such a reduction in prison numbers would be that the prison service could perform its core objectives more effectively than it does at present. These objectives should include:

- managing prisons in a just, decent and humane manner;
- protecting the public by ensuring that prisoners who pose a threat to the public do not escape;
- maintaining good order in prisons;
- providing prisoners with opportunities to develop their personalities, talents and skills in a positive manner;
- encouraging prisoners to face up to the consequences of their actions in a manner which recognizes the harm which they have done and

which makes it less likely that they will act in a similar way in the future;

• preparing prisoners for integration into society on their release.

At present the prison system delivers the second of these objectives satisfactorily and also, arguably, the third but overall is unable to deliver consistently to appropriate standards on the others. With the pressures which it currently faces on a daily basis removed or at least minimized, it could set about delivering the remainder.

In order that this could happen, the structure within each prison would need to be radically altered. It is not normal for human beings to live together in groups of several hundred, thrown together with large numbers of persons they would not otherwise know and with whom they may have little in common. If the prison of the future is to be more than a warehouse then it should hold its prisoners in groups small enough that they can mix together in a manner that will encourage social interaction without the fear that comes from anonymity. The best prison units already achieve this.

Unfortunately the tendency in many countries now is to build large prisons so that the common services can deliver what are described as economies of scale. In each prison, regardless of the number of prisoners it holds, there has to be an infrastructure which includes a kitchen, a health care centre, visiting facilities and an administration unit. For ten separate prisons each holding 200 prisoners, there will have to be five of each of these facilities. For one prison holding 2000 prisoners there would only have to be one of each. Certainly the facilities will have to be larger, but not ten times as large. The biggest prisons in the world hold up to 10,000 prisoners. The biggest prisons in England and Wales in terms of prisoner numbers are Wandsworth, Birmingham and Liverpool, each holding 1300–1400 in overcrowded conditions. In recent years the government has suggested that in future new prisons might be expected to hold several thousand prisoners. To go down this road might provide an economy of scale in terms of finances; it would not provide a more efficient prison system.

Local links

A major advantage of having a network of smaller prisons around the country would be that they could be more locally based and be more closely identified with their local communities than prisons are at present. The Victorian inner city prisons were all originally identified with their geographical areas: Brixton in London, Armley in Leeds, Walton in Liverpool. In more recent times local authorities have been reluctant to have their communities identified with prisons, so the latter have been given anonymous names: Holme House (Teesside), Dovegate (Uttoxeter) and most recently Bronzefield (Ashford), although the new prison at Peterborough has been an exception to this.

Unlike hospitals and schools which generally have a strong sense of serving their local communities, prisons are organized nationally. Given the pressure to admit all prisoners who are received on a daily basis from courts all over the country, the prison service has had to give a priority to finding beds wherever they may be rather than to allocating offenders to prisons close to the communities from which they have come and to which they will return. An extreme example of what this might entail would be the young man from east London, who is sentenced at a court in central London and is taken first to Feltham Young Offenders Institution in Middlesex. There is no bed for him there, so he is transferred on an eight-hour journey by road to serve his sentence in Castington near the Scottish border. The likelihood of a young woman serving her sentence close to home is even more remote, given the small number of institutions for women prisoners.

The obligation to serve one's sentence far from home has a number of detrimental consequences. It means that maintaining direct contact with other family members, be they a partner, parents, children or siblings, is difficult. Families will have a long way to travel to visit, made more complicated if they depend on public transport. Even the cost of a regular telephone call home may be increased considerably. Being away from one's own community also makes it much more difficult to build up the links which will be necessary for long-term re-integration on release. These will include making provision for somewhere to live, contacting potential employers, arranging future training courses or continuing drug counselling. At present the hard-pressed providers of these local services, whether statutory or voluntary, are unlikely to make provision for the future needs of people who are in prisons hundreds of miles away.

If prisons were to have a stronger identity with their local communities there would also be a greater possibility that they would be able to foster links with local community groups. This could be a two-way process. There is a depth of untapped potential in many prisons which could be realized for the benefit of communities. Prisoners have little incentive when they go each day to a workshop where there is not a great deal in the way of meaningful work and for which they receive very little pay. Experience has shown that their commitment increases significantly when they know that the work they are doing will benefit disadvantaged or needy people or will help their own communities. In 2003 the School of Social Sciences and Law in Teesside University undertook an evaluation of work carried out by prisoners in three prisons in the north-east of England to help Middlesbrough council in renovating a large Victorian park in the middle of the town. The researchers reported (Teesside University 2003: 4) that

There were many positive outcomes perceived by prisoners in working for the Albert Park Project, such as a sense of pride and achievement. Some prisoners thought their families would be proud of them, particularly if they lived in the locality of the park or knew it well. Working for the Project was a source of satisfaction for many of the prisoners, not only because of the quality of work they had produced, which they considered to be of a good/high standard, but also because of who the beneficiaries would be (that is, the public in general and, more specifically for some, their own families and other families).

The researchers also interviewed members of the public who used the park. They reported (page 87) that

All of the respondents agreed that for prisoners it was a way of putting something back into society. Some thought that the project would help them (the prisoners) become more aware that they could fulfil more worthwhile roles as members of the community. Respondents also indicated that such work could instil confidence, responsibility, and self-esteem and that this psychological gain would aid reintegration into society.

There is a long tradition in some prisons of help being given to old persons groups or to charities. The benefit of this becomes even more real to all involved if those helping and those being helped come from the same communities. This can be the beginning of a process through which ordinary members of the community, perhaps educated by reports in the local media, can begin to understand that the people who are in the local prison are from their communities, will return to their communities and that it is in everyone's interest that they should be integrated into those communities when they are released.

A local prison structure

So far we have considered the possibility of a reduced number of people in prison and smaller prisons with much stronger local connections. The third leg of this triangle would be the sort of infrastructure which is required to support such a model. We saw in the previous chapter that the prison system is virtually the only major organization in this country which is totally under central government control. Most other large institutions, such as the education system, the health system and the police are under a mixture of national and local control. In this respect, the prison system is a child of its history. The large inner city prisons are still referred to as local prisons and hold mainly remand and short-term convicted prisoners. Until recently the prisons holding those people serving long sentences were either training or dispersal prisons, many of them located in remote rural areas.

This arrangement is a remnant of the division before 1877 between local and convict prisons.

This division is no longer as watertight as it once was because of the need described above, to fill every available prison bed. This has meant that prisoners serving relatively long sentences cannot be sure that they will remain in one prison where they can pursue an education or work training programme. Even prisoners on remand are liable to be moved long distances while awaiting trial. This has led to the introduction of a new word in the prison vocabulary, the 'churn' (Wheatley 2002b), which conveys the sense of constant movement when large numbers of prisoners are constantly moved around the country.

If prisons are to have stronger links with the communities in which they are located there is a strong argument for making them more locally accountable. One way of achieving this would be by dismembering the current national prison system and replacing it with a series of local administrative structures. As well as strengthening local community links, this new structure would also reinvigorate the relationship between prisons and the courts which they serve. It would also make fiscal arrangements for prisons more transparent. At an annual cost per prisoner of around £30,000, a prison for 500 people costs the taxpayer in the region of £15 million per year. This does not mean much at a local level when the amount is subsumed into a national budget controlled from Whitehall. If, on the other hand, the spend was identified locally, as it is for schools and hospitals, there might be much closer scrutiny of whether the local taxpayer was getting value for money. If prisons were to be organized locally there would be greater awareness that prisoners were local and it should also be possible to recruit staff locally and to manage each prison in a manner which met the needs of the local community.

One of the most fundamental problems which the prison service as currently structured has to grapple with is its sheer complexity. The problem is not only one of size, with about 77,000 prisoners and 40,000 staff. It is also that the 141 prisons differ greatly in so many respects, such as the level of security, their facilities, the different types of prisoner which they hold, their links with other criminal justice agencies and with community bodies. It is neither efficient nor effective to try to manage all of this in detail on a national basis.

There are a variety of possible models as to how local prison systems might be structured but a textbook such as this is not the place to examine them in detail. The National Offender Management Service is unlikely to be a good model, since this will remain a national service, as its name indicates, with more regional management. There are a number of existing local structures, both within the criminal justice system and in other arrangements for local government, which could be considered for application to the prison system. A major difficulty would be that, since many prisons were built as places of exile far from major centres of population, the spread of prisons across the country is very uneven but this would be a logistical problem capable of solution in the longer term.

Re-organization of prisons on a local basis would provide an opportunity to re-define the nature of imprisonment. We have seen how the original concept of imprisonment as a place of exile has not changed a great deal in reality over the last 200 years, despite a number of changes in rhetoric. Offenders who are sent to prison are still taken away from their own communities in the hope that the experience they undergo in the closed world of the prison will somehow change their behaviour and attitude to life, making it more likely that they will become honest citizens. The fact that 56 per cent of them are reconvicted within two years of being released is regarded as a failure of the prison system to engineer change. Perhaps it would be more honest to acknowledge that it is a failure of the concept of imprisonment as a vehicle for personal change. Rather than responding to this problem by doing more of the same and doing it more efficiently, the future may lie in a more rigorous examination of what the model of imprisonment which was conceived in the nineteenth century and flowered in the twentieth century should look like in the twenty-first century.

A network of smaller local prisons underpinned by integrated links to local services and with a series of two-way channels of support between the prison and society would oblige us to re-examine the link between the prisoner and the community. Prison would become an opportunity to analyze where those links were weakest and needed strengthening, where they were non-existent and needed to be created. This is not to advocate soft treatment for criminals. On the contrary, rather than being the place of boredom, monotony and escape from reality that it is so often today, prison would become a place where offenders had the opportunity to refashion their lives and connections, not by identifying and minimizing personal failings, as happens at present, but by identifying their strengths and building on them. Prison would become a much more challenging place than it is at present.

Provision would have to be made for the small number of criminals from whom the public needs to be protected at all costs and for those who refuse to conform to normal prison life. In any country the number who fall into these categories is likely to be very small and good prison management can ensure that it is not artificially increased. Present arrangements tend to inflate the number who fall into this category for reasons that were discussed in chapter seven. There could be a variety of options for dealing with this small group of prisoners. One would be that the national government body which would still be required to ensure consistency of policy in penal matters should manage one maximum security prison. This prison could be used as a model of good management for the other prisons managed on a local basis, as used to be the case in the United States of America when the Federal Bureau of Prisons managed only a small number of prisons.

When he was himself a prisoner, Vaclav Havel, who was to become President of the Czech Republic, wrote to his wife:

I never feel sorry for myself, as one might expect, but only for the other prisoners and altogether, for the fact that prisons must exist and that they are as they are, and that mankind has not so far invented a better way of coming to terms with certain things.

(Havel 1990: 270)

At some point in the future we may indeed invent 'a better way of coming to terms with certain things'. For the foreseeable future there will still be a need for prisons. However, just as we aim for honesty in sentencing so we should aim for honesty in imprisonment and recognize that the prison can never in itself be a place of reform. Prisons are expensive resources where people are sent as punishment for the harm they have done and in the hope that somehow they may benefit from that experience. If we acknowledge this, we can go on to identify the essential features of the prison of the future:

- It will be used as a place of last resort, as an alternative to other disposals which will become the norm.
- It will hold a small number of people.
- Its staff will be recruited locally and trained according to local needs.
- It will have strong links to the community in which it is based.
- Throughout their sentence prisoners will be given access to local resources and facilities which they can continue to use after release.

The vision of William Omaria remains as 'one day in the distant future'. But it is worth remembering that, in their day, no one thought that the public stocks would disappear, that transportation would be abolished or that capital punishment would be removed from the statute books.

Further reading

Cayley, D. (1998) *The Expanding Prison: The Crisis in Crime and Punishment and the Search for Alternatives*. Toronto: Anansi Press.

Denborough, D. (ed.) (1996) *Beyond the Prison*. Adelaide: Dulwich Centre Publications.

Mauer, M. (1999) *The Race to Incarcerate*. New York: The New Press.

Scull, A. (1984) *Decarceration: Community Treatment and the Deviant – A Radical View*. New Jersey: Prentice Hall.

Stern, V. (1998) *A Sin Against the Future: Imprisonment in the World*. Middlesex: Penguin.

Bibliography

American Bar Association (2003) http://www.abanet.org.

Ashworth, A. (ed.) (2000) *Sentencing and Criminal Justice*. London: Butterworth.

Atherton, R. (1987) *Summons to Serve: Ministry to prisoners*. London: Geoffrey Chapman.

Barham, P. (1992) *Closing the Asylum: The Mental Patient in Modern Society*. Harmondsworth: Penguin.

Bennett, J. (2003) Winston Churchill: Prison Reformer? Leyhill: *Prison Service Journal* No. 145.

Blau, P. and Scott, W.R. (1966) *Formal Organisations*. London: Routledge & Kegan Paul.

Blunkett, D. (2004) *Reducing Crime – Changing Lives: The Government's plan for transforming the management of offenders*. London: Home Office.

Boin, A. (1998) *Contrasts in Leadership: An Institutional Study of Two Prison Systems*. Delft: Eburon.

Bottomley, A.K. (1973) *Decisions in the Penal Process*. London: Martin Robertson.

Bottomley, A. and Pease, K. (1986) *Crime and Punishment: Interpreting the Data*. Milton Keynes: Open University Press.

Bottomley, K., James, A., Clare, E. and Liebling, A. (1996) Home Office Research Findings No. 32, *Wolds Remand Prison – An Evaluation*. London: Home Office.

Bottoms, A. and Light, R. (1987) *Problems of Long Term Imprisonment*. Aldershot: Gower.

Bowling, B. (1999) *Violent Racism*. Oxford: Clarendon Press.

Bowling, B. and Phillips, C. (2002) *Racism, Crime and Justice*. London: Longman.

Boyle, J. (1977) *A Sense of Freedom*. London: Pan Books.

Boyle, J. (1984) *The Pain of Confinement: Prison Diaries*. Edinburgh: Canongate.

Braithwaite, J. (1989) *Crime, Shame and Reintegration*. Cambridge: Cambridge University Press.

Brown, D. and Wilkie, M. (eds) (2002) *Prisoners as Citizens: Human Rights in Australian Prisons*. Sydney: Federation Press.

Bryans, S. and Wilson, D. (1998) The Prison Governor: Theory and Practice. Leyhill: *Prison Service Journal*.

Bryans, S. and Jones, R. (2001) *Prisons and the Prisoner: the work of the Prison Service in England and Wales*. London: HMSO.

Bryans, S., Walker, R. and Martin, C. (2002) *Prisons and the Voluntary Sector: A Bridge into the Community*. Winchester: Waterside Press.

Burnside, J. and Baker, N. (eds) (1994) *Relational Justice: Repairing the Breach*. Winchester: Waterside Press.

Cameron, J. (1983) *Prisons and Punishment in Scotland*. Edinburgh: Canongate.

Campbell v. United Kingdom, European Court of Human Rights, 1993, 15 EHRR 137.

Carlen, P. (1983) *Women's Imprisonment*. London: Routledge & Kegan Paul.

Carlen, P. (1998) *Sledgehammer: Women's Imprisonment at the Millennium*. London: Macmillan.

Carlen, P. (ed.) (2002) *Women and Punishment: The struggle for justice*. Cullompton: Willan.

Carlisle Report (1988) *The Parole System in England and Wales, Report of the Review Committee chaired by Lord Carlisle of Bucklow*. Cmnd 532. London: HMSO.

Carter, P. (2004) *Managing Offenders, Reducing Crime: A new approach*. London: The Home Office.

Cavadino, M. and Dignan, J. (2001) *The Penal System: An Introduction*. London: Sage.

Cayley, D. (1998) *The Expanding Prison: The Crisis in Crime and Punishment and the Search for Alternatives*. Toronto: Anansi Press.

Christie, N. (1978) Prisons in Society, or Society as a Prison – A Conceptual Analysis in John Freeman (ed.) (1978) *Prisons Past and Future*. London: Heinemann.

Christie, N. (2000) *Crime Control as Industry: Towards Gulags Western Style*. London: Routledge.

Civil Liberties Organisation (1996) *Behind the Wall: A Report on Prison Conditions in Nigeria*. Lagos: Civil Liberties Organisation.

Clarkson, C. and Morgan, R. (eds) (1995) *The Politics of Sentencing Reform*. Oxford: Oxford University Press.

Clemmer, D. (1965) *The Prison Community*. New York: Holt, Rinehart and Winston.

Cohen, S. (1985) *Visions of Social Control*. Cambridge: Polity Press.

Cohen, S. and Scull, A. (eds) (1983) *Social Control and the State*. Oxford: Blackwell.

Cohen, S. and Taylor, L. (1972) *Psychological Survival*. Middlesex: Penguin.

Coleman, C. and Moynihan, J. (1996) *Understanding Crime Data: Haunted by the Dark Figure*. Buckingham: Open University Press.

Committee for the Prevention of Torture (1991) *Report to the Government of the United Kingdom* CPT/Inf (1991) 15. Strasbourg.

Committee for the Prevention of Torture (2002) *Report to the Government of the United Kingdom* CPT/Inf (2002) 6. Strasbourg.

Committee for the Prevention of Torture (2005) *Report to the Government of the United Kingdom* CPT/Inf (2005) 1. Strasbourg.

Consedine, J. (1999) *Restorative Justice: Healing the Effects of Crime*. Lyttleton, New Zealand: Ploughshares Publications.

Consedine, J. and Bowen, H. (eds) (1999) *Restorative Justice: Contemporary Themes and Practices*. Lyttleton, New Zealand: Ploughshares Publications.

Council of Europe (1987) *European Prison Rules* Rec No. R (87) 3 of the Committee of Ministers to Member States on the European Prison Rules. Strasbourg: Council of Europe.

Council of Europe (2003) SPACE 1 Annual Penal Statistics. Strasbourg: Council of Europe.

Coyle, A. (1987) 'The Scottish experience with small units' in Bottoms, A. and Light, R. (1987) *Problems of Long Term Imprisonment*. Aldershot: Gower.

Coyle, A. (1991) *Inside: Rethinking Scotland's Prisons*. Edinburgh: Scottish Child.

Coyle, A. (1994) *The Prisons We Deserve*. London: Harper Collins.

Coyle, A. (2002a) *Managing prisons in a time of change*. London: International Centre for Prison Studies.

Coyle, A. (2002b) Prison Governor, in *Incident Command: Tales from the Hot Seat*, Flin, R. and Arbuthnot, K. (eds) Ashgate.

Coyle, A. (2002c) *A Human Rights Approach to Prison Management: Handbook for staff*. London: International Centre for Prison Studies.

Coyle, A., Campbell, A. and Neufeld, R. (eds) (2003) *Capitalist Punishment; Prison Privatization and Human Rights*. London: Zed Books.

Coyle, A. (2004) Penal Policy, in *Handbook of Public Policy in Europe: Britain, France and Germany*, edited by H. Compston. Basingstoke: Palgrave Macmillan.

Crawley, E. (2004) *Doing Prison Work: The public and private lives of prison officers*. Cullompton: Willan.

Cressey, D. (ed.) (1961) *The Prison: Studies in Institutional Organisation and Change*. New York: Holt, Rinehart and Winston.

Cross, R. (1971) *Punishment, Prison and the Public*. London: Stevens & Sons.

Davies, M. (1974) *Prisoners of Society: Attitudes and after-care*, International Library of Social Policy. London: Routledge & Kegan Paul.

Denborough, D. (ed.) (1996) *Beyond the Prison*. Adelaide: Dulwich Centre Publications.

Department of Health (1999) *Managing Dangerous People with Severe Personality Disorder: Proposals for policy development*. London: Home Office.

DiIulio, J. (1987) *Governing Prisons: A Comparative Study of Correctional Management*. New York: The Free Press.

Ditchfield, J. (1990) *Control in Prisons: A Review of the Literature*. London: HMSO.

Dobash, R., Dobash, E. and Gutteridge, S. (1986) *The Imprisonment of Women*. Oxford: Blackwell.

Downes, D. (1988) *Contrasts in Tolerance: Post War Penal Policies in the Netherlands and England and Wales*. Oxford: Clarendon Press.

Duff, A. and Garland, D. (1994) *A Reader on Punishment*. Oxford: Oxford University Press.

Dunbar, I. (1985) *A Sense of Direction*. London: Home Office.

Du Parq Report (1932) *Report on the Circumstances Connected with the Recent Disorder at Dartmoor Convict Prison*. Cmnd 4010. London: HMSO.

European Committee for Crime Problems (2002) *Report on the 13th Conference of the Directors of Prison Administrations CDAP* (2002) 28. Council of Europe: Strasbourg.

Evans, P. (1980) *Prison Crisis*. London: George Allen and Unwin.

Faulkner, D. (2000) *Crime, State and Citizen: A Field Full of Folk*. Winchester: Waterside Press.

Fawcett Society (2004) *Women and the Criminal Justice System*. London: Fawcett Society.

Foucault, M. (1979) *Discipline and Punish: The Birth of the Prison*. Middlesex: Peregrine.

Fox, L. (1952) *The English Prison and Borstal Systems*. London: Routledge & Kegan Paul.

Garland, D. (1985) *Punishment and Welfare*. Aldershot: Gower.

Garland, D. (1990) *Punishment and Modern Society*. Oxford: Oxford University Press.

Garland, D. (2001) *The Culture of Control: Crime and Social Order in Contemporary Society*. Oxford: Oxford University Press.

Garland, D. (2002) Of Crimes and Criminals: The Development of Criminology in Britain, in Maguire M., Morgan, R. and Reiner, R. (2002) *The Oxford Handbook of Criminology*, 3rd edition. Oxford: Oxford University Press.

Garland, D. and Young, P. (eds) (1983) *The Power to Punish*. London: Heinemann.

Genders, E. and Player, E. (1989) *Race Relations in Prison*. Oxford: Oxford University Press.

Genders, E. and Player, E. (1993) *Grendon: A Study of a Therapeutic Prison*. Oxford: Oxford University Press.

General Board of Directors of Prisons in Scotland (1840) *Annual Report for 1840*. HMSO, London.

Gladstone Report (1895) *Report from the Departmental Committee on Prisons*. HMSO, London, C.7702.

Grew, B. (1958) *The Prison Governor*. London: Herbert Jenkins.

Hagan, J. (1987) *Modern Criminology*. New York: McGraw Hill.

Halliday, J. (2001) *Making Punishments Work: Report of a Review of the Sentencing Framework for England & Wales*. London: Home Office.

Harding, R. (1997) *Private Prisons and Public Accountability*. New Brunswick, NJ: Transaction Publishing.

Havel, V. (1990) *Letters to Olga*. London: Faber and Faber.

Hawkins, G. (1976) *The Prison: Policy and Practice*. Chicago: University of Chicago.

Hill, F. (1893) *An Autobiography of Fifty Years in Time of Reform* (ed. Constance Hill). London: Richard Bentley.

HM Chief Inspector of Prisons (1990) *Report of a Review of Suicide and Self-harm in Prison Service Establishments in England and Wales*. London: HMSO.

HM Chief Inspector of Prisons (1996) *Patient or Prisoner? A new strategy for health care in prisons*. London: Home Office.

HM Chief Inspector of Prisons (1997) *Women in Prisons: A Thematic Review*. London: Home Office.

HM Chief Inspector of Prisons (1999a) *Suicide is Everyone's Concern*. London: Home Office.

HM Chief Inspector of Prisons (1999b) *Report of an unannounced inspection of HM Prison Wormwood Scrubs, 8–12 March 1999*. London: Home Office.

HM Chief Inspector of Prisons (2000a) *Inspection of Closed Supervision Centres*. London: Home Office.

HM Chief Inspector of Prisons (2000b) *Unjust Desserts: A Thematic Review by HM Chief Inspector of Prisons of the Treatment and Conditions for Unsentenced Prisoners in England and Wales.* London: Home Office.

HM Chief Inspector of Prisons (2001) *Follow up to Women in Prison.* London: Home Office.

HM Chief Inspector of Prisons (2004a) *Report on an announced inspection of HMYOI Portland, 12–16 July 2004.* London: Home Office.

HM Chief Inspector of Prisons (2004b) *Report of an announced inspection of HM Prison Preston, 26–30 July 2004.* London: Home Office.

HM Chief Inspector of Prisons (2005) *Annual Report 2003/2004,* HC 204. London: HMSO.

HM Chief Inspector of Probation (2003) *Annual Report 2002/2003.* London: Home Office.

HM Inspectorates of Prisons and Probation (1999) *Lifers: A Joint Thematic Review.* London: Home Office.

HM Inspectorates of Prisons and Probation (2001) *Through the Prison Gate: A Joint Thematic Review.* London: Home Office.

HM Prison Service (1999) *Annual Report and Accounts April 1998 to March 1999.* London: HMSO.

HM Prison Service (2003) *Corporate Plan 2003–2004 to 2005–2006, Business Plan 2003–2004.* London: HM Prison Service.

HM Prison Service (2004) *Annual Report and Accounts: April 2003–March 2004.* London: HM Prison Service.

HM Prison Service (2005) *Business Plan 2005–2006.* London: HMSO.

Home Office (1965) *The Adult Offender.* Cmnd 2852. London: HMSO.

Home Office (1982) *Report on the Work of the Prison Department 1981.* Cmnd 8543. London: HMSO.

Home Office (1984) *Managing the Long Term Prison System: The Report of the Control Review Committee.* London: HMSO.

Home Office (1984) *Tougher Regimes in Detention Centres: Report of an Evaluation by the Young Offender Psychology Unit.* London: HMSO.

Home Office (1990a), *Report on the Work of the Prison Service April 1989–March 1990.* Cmnd 1302. London: HMSO.

Home Office (1990b) *Crime, Justice & Protecting the Public.* Cmnd 965. London: HMSO.

Home Office (1991) *Custody, Care and Justice: The Way Ahead for the Prison Service in England and Wales.* London: HMSO.

Home Office (1997) *No More Excuses – A New Approach to Tackling Youth Crime in England & Wales.* London: HMSO.

Home Office (1998) Research Findings 73, *Voluntary After-care.* London: Home Office.

Home Office (1999) *Digest 4: Information on the Criminal Justice System in England and Wales.* London: Home Office Research and Statistics Department.

Home Office (2002a) *Projections of Long Term Trends in the Prison Population to 2009.* London: Home Office Research and Statistics Department statistical bulletin 14/02.

Home Office (2002b) Research Findings 161, *An evaluation of cognitive behavioural treatment for prisoners.* London: Home Office.

Home Office (2003a) *Prison Statistics England and Wales 2002.* Cmnd 5996. London: HMSO.

Home Office (2003b) Research Findings 206, *Searching for 'What Works': an evaluation of cognitive skills programmes*. London: Home Office.

Home Office (2003c) Research Findings 226, *Understanding What Works: accredited cognitive skills programmes for adult men and young offenders*. London: Home Office.

Home Office (2004) *Statistics on Women and the Criminal Justice System, Home Office*. London: Home Office.

Home Office (2005a) *National Offender Management Service Corporate Plan 2005–06 to 2007–08*. London: Home Office.

Home Office (2005b) *Population in Custody December 2004 England and Wales*, available at www.homeoffice.gov.uk.rds/pdfs05/prisdec04.pdf.

Home Office (2005c) *Population in Custody March 2005*. London: Home Office Research and Statistics Department.

Hood, R. (1992) *Race and Sentencing*. Oxford: Clarendon Press.

Hood, R. and Shute, S. (2000) *The Parole System at Work: A study of Risk Based Decision-making*, Home Office Research Study No. 202. London: Home Office.

Hoskison, J. (1998) *Inside: One man's Experience of Prison*. London: John Murray.

Hough, M., Jacobson, J. and Millie, A. (2003) *The Decision to Imprison*. London: Prison Reform Trust.

Hough, M. and Mayhew, P. (1985) *Taking Account of Crime: Key findings from the 1984 British Crime Survey*, Home Office Research Study No. 85. London: Home Office.

House of Commons (1826) *Report of the Select Committee on Scottish Prisons*. London: HMSO.

House of Commons Education and Skills Committee (2005) *Prison education: Seventh Report of Session 2004–05*, HC 114-1. London: The Stationery Office.

House of Commons Home Affairs Committee (2005) *Rehabilitation of Prisoners: First Report of Session 2004–05*, HC 193-1. London: The Stationery Office.

Howard, J. (1791) *Prisons and Lazarettos: Vol. 2, An Account of the Principal Lazarettos in Europe*. Reprinted (1973), New Jersey: Paterson Smith.

Howard, J. (1792) *Prisons and Lazarettos: Vol. 1, The State of the Prisons in England and Wales*, reprinted (1973). New Jersey: Paterson Smith.

Howard, M. (1993) Soft Touch Jails Are an Insult to Victims. *Sunday Express*, 29.8.93.

Hudson, B. (1996) *Understanding Justice*. Milton Keynes: Open University Press.

Hughes, R. (1987) *The Fatal Shore*. London: Collins.

Human Rights Watch (1997) *Cold Storage: Super-Maximum Security Confinement in Indiana*. London: Human Rights Watch.

ICPS (2005) World Prison Brief at <www.prisonstudies.org>.

Ignatieff, M. (1978) *A Just Measure of Pain: The Penitentiary in the Industrial Revolution 1750–1850*. London: Macmillan.

Inquest (2004) *Submission to the Joint Committee on Human Rights Inquiry into Deaths in Custody*. London: Inquest.

Jacobs, J. (1977) *Stateville: The Penitentiary in Mass Society*. Chicago: University of Chicago Press.

James, A., Bottomley, K., Liebling, A. *et al.* (1997) *Privatizing Prisons: Rhetoric and Reality*. London: Sage.

Joint Committee on Human Rights (2004) *Third report: Deaths in Custody*. HL 15-1/HC 137-I, etc.

Kalinin, Y. (2002) *The Russian penal system: past, present and future*. London: International Centre for Prison Studies.

Kauffman, K. (1988) *Prison Officers and their World*. Cambridge, Mass: Harvard University Press.

King, R. (1994) Order, Disorder and Regimes in the Prison Services of Scotland and England & Wales, in *Prisons after Woolf – Reform through Riot*, Player, E. and Jenkins, M. London: Routledge.

King, R. (1999) The Rise and Rise of Supermax: An American Solution in Search of a Problem?, in *Punishment & Society*, Vol. 1, No. 2, 163–186. London: Sage.

King, R. and Elliott, K. (1977) *Albany: birth of a prison – end of an era*. London: Routledge & Kegan Paul.

King, R. and Maguire, M. (eds) (1994) *Prisons in Context*. Oxford: Oxford University Press.

King, R. and McDermott, K. (1995) *The State of Our Prisons*. Oxford: Oxford University Press.

LaMarche, G. (2003) Speech by Gara LaMarche, Vice-President, Open Society Institute, accepting the 2003 Paul Ylvisaker Award for Public Policy Engagement to OSI from the Council on Foundations, April 29, 2003. New York: Open Society Institute.

Lappi-Seppälä, T. (2001) Sentencing and Punishment in Finland: The Decline of the Repressive Ideal in *Punishment and Penal Systems in Western Countries*, edited by Tonry, M. and Frase, R. New York: Oxford University Press.

Lappi-Seppälä, T. (2002) *Penal Policy and Incarceration Rates in Finland*. Corrections Today, Baltimore.

Lasker, M. (2004) Prison Reform Revisited: The Unfinished Agenda. *Pace Law Review*: 24-2004.

Learmont Report (1995) *Review of Prison Service Security in England & Wales & the Escape from Parkhurst Prison on Tuesday 3 January 1995*. Cmnd 3020. London: HMSO.

Lewis, D. (1997) *Hidden Agendas: Politics, Law and Disorder*. London: Hamish Hamilton.

Liebling, A. (1992) *Suicides in Prison*. London: Routledge.

Liebling, A. and Price, D. (2001) The Prison Officer. Leyhill: *Prison Service Journal*, No. 135.

Liebling, A. (2004) *Prisons and Their Moral Performance: A Study of Values, Quality and Prison Life*. Oxford: Oxford University Press.

Livingstone, S. and Owen, T. (1999) *Prison Law*, 2nd edn. Oxford: Oxford University Press.

Logan, C. (1990) *Private Prisons: Cons and Pros*. Oxford: Oxford University Press.

Lombardo, L. (1981) *Guards Imprisoned: Correctional Officers at Work*. New York: Elsevier.

Lombroso, C. (1876) *L'Uomo Delinquente*. Turin, Fratelli Bocca.

Lygo, R. (1991) *Management of the Prison Service*. London: Home Office.

McCleery, R. (1957) Policy Change in Prison Management, in Etzioni, A. (ed.) (1969) *A Sociological Reader on Complex Organizations*. New York: Holt, Rinehart and Winston.

McConville, S. (1981) *A History of English Prison Administration, Vol. I*. London: Routledge & Kegan Paul.

McConville, S. (1994) *English Local Prisons 1860–1900*. London: Routledge.

McDonald, D. (1990) *Private Prisons and the Public Interest*. New Brunswick, New Jersey: Rutgers University Press.

McLachlan, N. (1974) Penal Reform and Penal History, in *Progress and Penal Reform*, edited by Blom-Cooper L. Oxford: Oxford University Press.

McMahon, M. (1992) *The Persistent Prison? Rethinking Decarceration and Penal Reform*. Toronto: University of Toronto Press.

McNeill, F. (2004) Desistance, Rehabilitation and Correctionalism: Developments and Prospects in Scotland, *Howard Journal for Penal Reform*, Vol. 43, Issue 4.

Maguire, J. (ed.) (1996) *What Works: Reducing Re-Offending*. Chichester: John Wiley and Sons Ltd.

Maguire, M., Morgan, R. and Reiner, R. (eds) (2002) *The Oxford Handbook of Criminology*, 3rd edn. Oxford: Oxford University Press.

Maguire, M., Vagg, J. and Morgan, R. (eds) (1985) *Accountability and Prisons*. London: Tavistock.

Maguire, M., Raynor, P., Vanstone, M. and Kynch, J. (2000) *Howard Journal of Criminal Justice*, Vol. 39, No. 3, 234.

Martinson, R. (1974) What Works: Questions and Answers about Prison Reform, *The Public Interest*, No. 35.

Martinson, R. (1979) New Findings, New Views: A Note of Caution Regarding Sentencing Reform, *Hofstra Law Review* 7.

Maruna, S. (2001) *Making Good: How ex-convicts reform and rebuild their lives*. Washington DC: American Psychological Association.

Matthews, R. (ed.) (1989) *Privatizing Criminal Justice*. London: Sage.

Matthews, R. (1999) *Doing Time: An Introduction to the Sociology of Imprisonment*. London: Macmillan.

Matthews, R. and Francis, P. (eds) (1996) *Prisons 2000: An International Perspective on the Current State and Future of Imprisonment*. London: Macmillan.

Mauer, M. (1999) *The Race to Incarcerate*. New York: The New Press.

May Report (1979) *Report of the Committee of Inquiry into the United Kingdom Prison Services*. Cmnd 7673. London: HMSO.

Mayhew, P., Elliott, D. and Dowds, L. (1989) *The 1988 British Crime Survey*. Home Office Research Study, No. 111.

Melossi, D. and Pavarini, M. (eds) (1981) *The Prison and the Factory: Origins of the Penitentiary System*. London: Macmillan.

Miller, A. (1976) *Inside Outside: The Story of a Prison Governor*. London: Queensgate Press.

Milton, N. (1973) *John Maclean*. London, Pluto Press.

Mirlees-Black, C., Mayhew, P. and Percy, A. (1996) *The 1996 British Crime Survey: England and Wales*. London: Home Office.

Mirlees-Black, C., Budd, T., Partridge, S. and Mayhew, P. (1998) *The 1998 British Crime Survey: England and Wales*. London: Home Office.

Morgan, R. (2002) Imprisonment: Current Concerns and a Brief History, in Maguire, M., Morgan, R. and Reiner, R. (eds) *The Oxford Handbook of Criminology*, 3rd edn. Oxford: Oxford University Press.

Morgan, R. and Evans, M. (eds) (1999) *Protecting Prisoners: The Standards of the European Committee for the Prevention of Torture in Context*. Oxford: Oxford University Press.

Morris, N. and Rothman, D. (1995) *The Oxford History of the Prison: The Practice of Punishment in Western Society*. Oxford: Oxford University Press.

Morris, T. and Morris, P. (1963) *Pentonville: A Sociological Study of an English Prison*. London: Routledge and Kegan Paul.

Mountbatten Report (1966) *Report of the Inquiry into Prison Escapes and Security*. Cmnd 3175. London: HMSO.

Muncie, J. (1999) *Youth and Crime: A Critical Introduction*. London: Sage.

Napier, R. (2004) Robert Napier against The Scottish Ministers. http://www.scotcourts.gov.uk/opinions/P739_01.html.

Narey, M. (2002a) Director General's opening address to prison service conference, Prison Service.

Narey, M. (2002b) Speech to No. 10 Policy Seminar, 13 May 2002, unpublished.

Nathan, S. (2003) Prison Privatization in the United Kingdom, in Coyle, A., Campbell, A. and Neufeld, R. (eds) (2003) *Capitalist Punishment; Prison Privatization and Human Rights*. London: Zed Books.

National Audit Office (2001) *Managing the Relationship to Secure A Successful Partnership in PFI Projects, Report by the Comptroller & Auditor General*, HC 375, Session 2001–2002: 29 November 2001. London: HMSO.

National Audit Office (2003) *The Operational Performance of PFI Prisons, Report by the Comptroller and Auditor General H C Session 2002–2003*: 18 June 2003. London: HMSO.

National Offender Management Service (2005) Press Release 012/2005, 20 January 2005, *NOMS launches new drug strategy*.

Noblett, W. (1998) *Prayers for People in Prison*. Oxford: Oxford University Press.

Office for National Statistics (1998) *Psychiatric morbidity among prisoners in England and Wales*. London: HMSO.

Office for National Statistics (2001) *Census 2001*. London: HMSO.

Omaria, W. (1997) *Afterword in Prison Conditions in Africa: Report of a Pan-African Seminar, Kampala, Uganda 19–21 September 1996*. London: Penal Reform International.

Omega Report on Justice Policy (1984), Adam Smith Institute (ASI Research).

Peay, J. (2002) Mentally disordered offenders, mental health and crime, in Maguire, M., Morgan, R. and Reiner, R. (eds) *The Oxford Handbook of Criminology*, 3rd edn. Oxford: Oxford University Press.

Peckham, A. (1985) *A Woman in Custody*. London: Fontana Paperbacks.

Phillips, R. and McConnell, C. (1996) *The Effective Corrections Manager*. Gaithersburg, US: Aspen.

Player, E. and Jenkins, M. (eds) (1994) *Prisons After Woolf: Reform Through Riot*. London: Routledge.

Posen, D. (2003) Managing a Correctional Marketplace: Prison Privatization in the United States and the United Kingdom, *Journal of Law and Ethics*, Vol. XIX: 253–284.

Prior Report (1985) *Report of the Committee on the Prison Disciplinary System*. Cmnd 9641. London: HMSO.

Prison Reform Trust (2000) *Justice for Women: The Need for Reform*. London: Prison Reform Trust.

Prison Reform Trust (2004) *Prison Reform Trust Factfile, July 2004*. London: Prison Reform Trust.

The Prison Rules 1999, Statutory Instrument 1999 No. 728. London: HMSO.

Prison Service (2004) *Safer Custody News*, June 2004. Prison Service.

Prisons Ombudsman (1996) *Annual Report 1995*. London: HMSO.

Prisons and Probation Ombudsman (2004) *Annual Report 2003–2004*.

R v. Secretary of State for the Home Department, ex parte Anderson. 2002. UKHL 46.

R v. Secretary of State for the Home Department, ex parte Doody. 1994. 1 AC 531.

R v. Secretary of State for the Home Department ex parte Leech (No. 2) 1994, QB 198.

Radzinowicz Report (1968) *Report of the Advisory Committee on the Penal System on the Regime for Long Term Prisoners in Conditions of Maximum Security*. London: HMSO.

Ramsbotham, D. (2004) *Prisongate*. London: Free Press.

Report of the Departmental Committee on Scottish Prisons (1900). Cmnd 218. London: HMSO.

Report of the General Board of Directors of Prisons in Scotland (1840). London: HMSO.

Report of the Select Committee of the House of Commons on Scottish Prisons (1826). London: HMSO.

Rich, C. (1932) *Recollections of a Prison Governor*. London: Hurst and Blackett.

Rock, P. (1996) *Reconstructing a Women's Prison: The Holloway Redevelopment Project 1968–88*. Oxford: Clarendon Press.

Ruck, S.K. (ed.) (1951) *Paterson on Prisons: Being the Collected Papers of Sir Alexander Paterson*. London: Frederick Muller Ltd.

Ruggles-Brise, E. (1921) *The English Prison System*. London: Macmillan.

Rusche, G. and Kirchheimer, O. (1939) *Punishment and Social Structure*. New York: Russell and Russell.

Rutherford, A. (1993) *Criminal Justice and the Pursuit of Decency*. Oxford: Oxford University Press.

Ryan, M. and Ward, T. (1989) *Privatization and the penal system: The American experience and the debate in Britain*. Milton Keynes: Open University Press.

Ryan, M. and Sim, J. (eds) (1995) *Western European Penal Systems*. London: Sage.

Sampson, R. and Laub, J. (1995) *Crime in the Making: Pathways and Turning Points Through Life*. Cambridge, MA: Harvard University Press.

Samuel, R. (1981) *East end underworld: Chapters in the life of Arthur Harding*. London: Routledge & Kegan Paul.

Scottish Prison Service (2004) *Seventh Prison Survey*, Prisons Research Branch. Edinburgh: Scottish Prison Service.

Scraton, P., Sim, J. and Skidmore, P. (1991) *Prisons under Protest*. Milton Keynes: Open University Press.

Scull, A. (1984) *Decarceration: Community Treatment and the Deviant – A Radical View*. Englewood Cliffs, NJ: Prentice Hall.

Shankardass, R. (ed.) (2000) *Punishment and the Prison: Indian and International Perspectives*. New Delhi: Sage.

Shaw, A.G.L. (1966) *Convicts and the Colonies*. London: Faber and Faber.

Sim, J. (1990) *Medical Power in English Prisons*. Milton Keynes: Open University Press.

Smith, R. (1984) *Prison Health Care*. London: British Medical Association.

Social Exclusion Unit (2002) *Reducing Re-offending by Ex-prisoners*. London: Office of the Deputy Prime Minister.

Solomon, E. (2004) Jail Capital of Western Europe, in *Prison Reform Report No. 63*. London: Prison Reform Trust.

Sparks, R., Bottoms, A. and Hay, W. (1996) *Prisons and the Problem of Order*. Oxford: Clarendon.

Spurr, M. (2004) Is Imprisonment Dealing with Addiction? Leyhill: *Prison Service Journal*, No. 156.

Stanhope Report (1923) *Report of the Committee Appointed to Inquire into the Pay and Conditions of Service at the Prisons and Borstal Institutions in England and Scotland and at Broadmoor Criminal Lunatic Asylum*. Cmnd 1959. London: HMSO.

Steele, J. (2002) *The Bird That Never Flew*. Edinburgh: Mainstream Publishing.

Stern, V. (1989) *Bricks of Shame*. London: Penguin.

Stern, V. (1998) *A Sin Against the Future: Imprisonment in the World*. London: Penguin.

Stern, V. (1999) *Alternatives to prison in developing countries*. London: International Centre for Prison Studies.

Stöver, H. (2002) *Drugs and HIV/AIDS Services in European Prisons*. Oldenburg: Carl von Ossietzky Universität.

Sykes, G. (1958) *The Society of Captives: A Study of a Maximum Security Prison*. Princeton: Princeton University Press.

Teesside University (2003) *The Restorative Prison Project: An evaluative study of the Albert Park Project*. London: International Centre for Prison Studies.

Thomas, J.E. (1972) *The English prison officer since 1850: A study in conflict*. London: Routledge & Kegan Paul.

Tonry, M. and Hatlestad, K. (eds) (1997) *Sentencing Reform in Overcrowded Times*. Oxford: Oxford University Press.

Törnudd, P. (1993) *Fifteen Years of Decreasing Prisoner Rates in Finland*. Helsinki: National Research Institute of Legal Policy. Research Communication 8/1993.

Travis, A. (2004) Blunkett on film sways judges, *The Guardian*, 17 November 2004.

United Nations (1977) *Standard Minimum Rules for the Treatment of Prisoners Adopted by the First United Nations Congress on the Prevention of Crime and the Treatment of Offenders, held at Geneva in 1955, and approved by the Economic and Social Council by its resolution 663 C (XXIV) of 31 July 1957 and 2076 (LXII) of 13 May 1977*.

van Zyl Smit, D. and Dünkel, F. (2001) *Imprisonment Today and Tomorrow*, 2nd edn. Deventer: Kluwer.

Vinson, T. (1982) *Wilful Obstruction*. North Ryde: Methuen.

von Hirsch, A. and Ashworth, A. (1998) *Principled Sentencing: Readings on Theory and Policy*. Oxford: Hart Publishing.

Waddington, P. (1983) *The Training of Prison Governors: Role, Ambiguity and Socialisation*. London: Croom Helm.

Walmsley, R. (2005) *World Prison Population List* (sixth edition). London: International Centre for Prison Studies.

Ward, D. and Breed, A. (1985) *Report on the US Penitentiary Marion, presented to the Committee on the Judiciary of the US House of Representatives*. US Government Printing Office, Washington.

Wheatley, P. (2002a) Running Successful Prisons. Leyhill: *Prison Service Journal*, No. 141.

Wheatley, P. (2002b) Speech at a conference held in Wakefield in September 2002, 'Local Prisons – The Way Forward'. HM Prison Service.

Williams, J. (1994) *Silver Threads: A Life Alone*. London: BBC Books.

Williamson, H. (1990) *The Corrections Profession*. London: Sage.

Wilson, J.Q. (1983) *Thinking about Crime*. New York: Basic Books.

Wilson, D. and Bryans, S. (1998) The Prison Governor: Theory and Practice. Leyhill: *Prison Service Journal*.

Windlesham, D. (1993) *Responses to Crime, Volume 2: Penal Policy in the Making*. Oxford: Clarendon Press.

Woodcock Report (1994) *Report of the Inquiry into the Escape of Six Prisoners from the Special Security Unit at Whitemoor Prison Cambridgeshire on Friday 9th September 1994*. Cmnd 2741. London: HMSO.

Woolf Report (1991) *Report of an Inquiry into Prison Disturbances April 1990*. Cmnd 1456. London: HMSO.

Youth Justice Board (2005) www.youth-justice-board.gov.uk/YouthJusticeBoard.

Zehr, H. (1990) *Changing Lenses: A New Focus for Crime and Justice*. Scottsdale, PA: Herald Press.

'Zeno' (1968) *Life*. London: Macmillan.

Index

UNDERSTANDING DRUGS, ALCOHOL AND CRIME

Trevor Bennett and Katy Holloway
Both at the University of Glamorgan, UK

- What is the connection between drugs, alcohol and crime?
- What works in reducing drug and alcohol-related crime?

The book provides a succinct overview of current theory and research on the links between drugs, alcohol use and crime. It discusses the legal and social context of drug and alcohol use and identifies current levels of consumption. Focusing on the UK context, it also takes into account international research.

- Detailed review of the research literature on the connections between drug use and crime
- Examines the current government anti-drugs policy and assesses the effectiveness of programmes that have been used to reduce drug and alcohol-related crime.

The authors conclude that future government drugs policy should pay particular attention to the lessons learned from research on the connection between drug and alcohol use and crime. Ideal for criminology, criminal justice, social policy and social work students, this book is also a useful source for policy makers, the police, probation workers, social workers, drugs and alcohol counsellors, treatment agencies, sentencers, voluntary agencies, Drug Action Teams, and others with an interest in research on drugs and crime.

Contents
The nature of the problem – Policy context: from defining to reducing harm – Extent of drug misuse – Types of drug misuse – Explaining the drugs-crime connection – The statistical association: just coincidence? – The causal connection: more than coincidence? – The effectiveness of interventions – The nature of the solution.

c.160pp   0 335 21257 3 (Paperback)   0 335 21258 1 (Hardback)